Oil Wealth and the Po

M000030977

How can we make sense of Algeria's post-colonial experience – the tragedy of unfulfilled expectations, the descent into violence, the resurgence of the state? *Oil Wealth and the Poverty of Politics* explains why Algeria's domestic political economy unraveled from the mid-1980s, and how the regime eventually managed to regain power and hegemony. Miriam R. Lowi argues the importance of leadership decisions for political outcomes, and extends the argument to explain the variation in stability in oil-exporting states following economic shocks. Comparing Algeria with Iran, Iraq, Indonesia, and Saudi Arabia, she asks why some states break down and undergo regime change, while others remain stable, or manage to re-stabilize after a period of instability. In contrast with exclusively structuralist accounts of the rentier state, this book demonstrates that political stability is a function of the way in which structure and agency combine.

MIRIAM R. LOWI is Professor of Political Science at The College of New Jersey. Her previous publications include *Water and Power: the Politics of a Scarce Resource in the Jordan River Basin* (Cambridge University Press, 1993) and *Environment and Security: Discourses and Practices* (2000).

Cambridge Middle East Studies 32

Editorial Board

Charles Tripp (general editor)
Julia Clancy-Smith
F. Gregory Gause
Yezid Sayigh
Avi Shlaim
Judith E. Tucker

Cambridge Middle East Studies has been established to publish books on the nineteenth- to twenty-first-century Middle East and North Africa. The aim of the series is to provide new and original interpretations of aspects of Middle Eastern societies and their histories. To achieve disciplinary diversity, books will be solicited from authors writing in a wide range of fields including history, sociology, anthropology, political science, and political economy. The emphasis will be on producing books offering an original approach along theoretical and empirical lines. The series is intended for students and academics, but the more accessible and wide-ranging studies will also appeal to the interested general reader.

A list of books in the series can be found after the index.

Oil Wealth and the Poverty of Politics

Algeria Compared

Miriam R. Lowi

CAMBRIDGE
UNIVERSITY PRESS

CAMBRIDGE UNIVERSITY PRESS
Cambridge, New York, Melbourne, Madrid, Cape Town,
Singapore, São Paulo, Delhi, Tokyo, Mexico City

Cambridge University Press
The Edinburgh Building, Cambridge CB2 8RU, UK

Published in the United States of America by Cambridge University Press, New York

www.cambridge.org
Information on this title: www.cambridge.org/9781107402966

First published 2009
First paperback edition 2011

A catalogue record for this publication is available from the British Library

ISBN 978-0-521-11318-2 Hardback
ISBN 978-1-107-40296-6 Paperback

For Jazia and Ismael, with love

Contents

Tables

Figures

Preface

As this book goes to press, the news from Algeria and developments in the international oil market are especially noteworthy given the arguments I make about the challenge of stability following economic shocks. Throughout the work, I underscore the importance of agency for political outcomes, and I explore the ways in which agency and structure interact. To make sense of the Algerian experience, as well as that of other oil-exporting states, I affirm the need to recognize the autonomy of individual agents in politics. How then do recent events validate this position?

On the one hand, Abdelaziz Bouteflika, currently serving the end of his second term as president, has announced pending changes to the country's constitution. Having hinted, for some time, at wanting to abrogate the two-term limit of the presidency, Bouteflika is paving the way for his third term in office. What explains Bouteflika's bold decision and what does it suggest about the Algerian political economy? On the other hand, the price of oil, that had surged over the course of the past year to a record $140 per barrel in July (2008), has been falling rapidly, reaching less than $50 in recent weeks. What effect will this combination of forces have on political outcomes? Given these developments, in Algeria and in the international economy, what can we expect for the Algerian people in the months ahead?

To be sure, Bouteflika would not have been able to implement change of such consequence without the approval of the powerful military and heads of intelligence services – those often referred to as the real *décideurs* in the country. The president's relationship with the military is indeed striking. It was the military, in fact, who brought Boumedienne's close collaborator back from obscurity in 1999, and put him into power. In recent years, however, Bouteflika has cleverly managed to enhance his powers relative to theirs, and has gently shepherded them back toward the barracks. A brilliant strategy, combined with favorable international structural forces, assisted him in his efforts. In 2005, into his second term, Bouteflika extended a second amnesty to those engaged in the insurgency that had plagued the country since 1992. He included in the amnesty provisions the total exoneration of the military and security forces for their activities during the civil war years. By guaranteeing to the military that their own involvement in the perpetration of violence would not come to light, Bouteflika was assured their backing in his quest for a third term. (How interesting, though, that it was a military general, Liamine Zeroual, who, in his capacity as president [1994–9], decided in 1996 to limit the presidency to two terms, while a civilian president would choose to overturn that ruling twelve years later!)

Who would have thought that even the military – that most powerful institution – could be manipulated and coopted? Furthermore, if indeed the military is part and parcel of the regime, while manipulation and cooptation have been essential tools for regime maintenance, what does it mean about the nature of power and authority when those at the very heart of the power structure are themselves manipulated and coopted? These questions remain to be answered, but I would suggest that developments in the international political economy – and in the hydrocarbon sector, in particular – offer important hints at an explanation.

To be sure, the tables have turned for Bouteflika and for Algeria – but alas, not for the general population. Record hydrocarbon revenues, beginning with the steady increase in the price of the barrel of oil as of 2000 and continuing until the fall of 2008, have filled the coffers of the state. The regime has accumulated more than $100 billion of foreign currency reserves for a population of 34 million. Moreover, its foreign debt is currently only 4 percent of GDP, as opposed to 86 percent in 1988 and just under 50 percent in 1994. How transformed the country's financial situation is today from twenty years ago – the last time that serious political reform was contemplated!

The extended period of high oil prices, coinciding with Bouteflika's tenure, was a great boon to the presidency. Not only did it give the president the wherewithal to step up the fight against what remained of the insurgency, but it also provided him with vast resources with which to drown out demands for reform. Indeed, he has managed in recent years to virtually eliminate any organized opposition of note. Moreover, among the other planned changes to the constitution, introduced by Bouteflika, are provisions to reduce the authority of the prime minister so as to make the political system more overtly presidential. Alas, even the meager parliamentary scrutiny that currently exists will be reduced further, as will government accountability. Stability has certainly returned to Algeria, when compared with the 1990s; however, the political landscape is being leveled out and the (civilian) president is enjoying a freer hand than ever before.

It is interesting to note that Bouteflika has recently back-pedaled in the economic domain as well. Recall that he came to power at a time when the country was slowly emerging from an extended period of negative or low growth rates and virtually all non-hydrocarbon economic sectors were moribund. In response, the president pushed for the diversification of the oil-driven economy and, with the support of key ministers with World Bank credentials, he oversaw the privatization of several state companies. However, during the last two years of remarkably high oil prices, he has slowed down the economic reform process and halted or reversed many policies that smacked of liberalization. For one, the regime's impressive earnings have provided little incentive to accelerate what was, in any case, a sluggish diversification program. As for privatization, the hydrocarbon giants, SONATRACH and SONELGAZ, have been excluded from the process due to their strategic value, while plans to sell off Air Algérie, for example, have stalled. Moreover, key elements of the 2005 hydrocarbons law, which introduced one of the most liberal oil and gas licensing regimes in the Middle East, were overturned in 2006. And liberalization measures that would constrain the lucrative economic activities and assets of prominent members of the military – Bouteflika's supporters – have been deferred as well. Have features of the Boumedienniste system of the mid-1970s come back to roost? *Plus ça change, plus c'est la même chose.*

In Algeria in recent months, as in previous boom periods, the leadership has rebuffed much-needed reforms in the political and economic domains. At the same time, it has distributed rents in ways that fragment social formations and neutralize (potential) threats to its hegemony. Clientelist practices of cooptation and manipulation – even of the seemingly all-powerful yet deeply divided military – figure prominently in regime strategies. As in the past, these strategies are consistently being refined and reinvigorated. And insofar as the general population is concerned, the extension of political incorporation and participation has once again been set aside.

This state of affairs is bound to continue for some time. To wit, Chakib Khalil, Algeria's Minister of Energy and Mines and current chairman of OPEC, has suggested that the Algerian economy is not likely to be negatively affected in the short term by the most recent slumping oil prices and global recession (reported by *El Khabar* newspaper, 7 October 2008). In the medium term, however, the impact will indeed be negative. It may well be that the resurgence of relative scarcity and rising frustrations in an impoverished political environment will encourage, as in the past, the (re-)mobilization of (previously marginalized or silenced) social forces.

In the absence of political will and astute leadership decisions – alas, the scarcest of resources – in the face of the latest structural challenges,

Algeria could plunge back into turmoil. The prospects are chilling. However, as I argue in the pages that follow, leaders can maintain stability at moments of economic constraint and in the absence of economic resources. They can do so precisely by extending political resources and investing in the creation of participatory political structures. In that way, they make possible the assemblage of the productive capacities in society and the circulation of creative solutions to the problems at hand. The challenge, in the first instance, is for leaders to seize.

This book has been a long time in the making. In some ways, it began when I was in high school. On a long weekend visit with my older brother in Boston, Henry insisted that we see the film *The Battle of Algiers*. The Pontecorvo classic – and Henry's mentoring – were among the most important early influences on my political development. Moreover, it was from that time that I became intrigued by Algeria and the FLN – a movement that inspired other nationalist movements, even ones as far afield as my own home of Québec in the 1960s.

As I went on to study the political economy of commodities and natural resources, first at the undergraduate level and then as a doctoral student in Middle East politics, I followed Algeria's post-colonial experience from a distance. Although I was far more engaged, as a young adult, with the unfolding of the Israeli–Arab relationship and the plight of the Palestinian people, I cheered the Algerians' success at forcing out the French and I hailed the newly independent state's socialist development path. (When I gave up cheerleading for exploring, I quickly became far more circumspect about glorifying the Algerian state and the path it had taken.)

Indeed, Algeria was never far from my sights. My personal life eventually took me to North Africa, where I would live for five years and then return to for several months every year from the early 1990s. Little did I know in the initial years of my North African life that my next *terrain* was just next door. Toward the end of the 1990s, my former teacher and dear friend, Richard Falk, suggested in passing that I write an article investigating the likelihood that water would be to the twenty-first century what oil had been to the twentieth. While I knew very little about oil, my curiosity was sufficiently piqued to do some preliminary investigating. Within no time, my research interests shifted from inter-state conflicts over access to scarce water, to the effects of oil on domestic politics; and my original fascination with Algeria evolved into both a research agenda and a passion. I am most grateful to my brother, Henry Lowi, for telling me about Algeria in the first place, to my husband, Abdellah Hammoudi, for taking me to Morocco next door, and to Richard Falk, for gently pushing me to "broaden my resource base."

Over the years that I have been engaged in this research, the book project has been through several iterations. It began as an application of the rentier state framework to the case of Algeria. However, as the statecraft variable emerged at the center of the argument that I was crafting, I was urged by friends and colleagues to undertake a multi-case comparative study. The choice of comparators changed, it seems, every time I discussed the project with someone else. At times the task seemed unwieldy and overwhelming as I struggled to become an expert in the trajectories of four, five, or even six different countries across the developing world, and make a contribution to our understanding of their relative successes and failures. Eventually, I acknowledged that my comparative advantage was in Algeria's experience. I chose to keep Algeria at the very center of my study, and enrich the arguments I was making by suggesting comparisons with four other cases within the Muslim world. I benefitted in the early stages of my research from helpful conversations with Lisa Anderson, Michael Doyle, Atul Kohli, Roger Owen, Michael Ross, John Waterbury, and the late Rémy Leveau. Furthermore, several people read and reacted to project proposals at different stages of elaboration. Among them were Jeff Goodwin, Richard Snyder, and Nicolas van de Walle – whom I had not even met – in addition to John Entelis, Bill Quandt, Mark Tessler, Dirk Vandewalle, and Bob Vitalis. Richard Auty, Elisabeth Picard, and Lucette Valensi offered valuable comments on articles in which I either outlined what would later be the book's research design, or analyzed one aspect of the Algerian experience. Especially generous was Jack Goldstone, who not only has offered lots of constructive suggestions over the years, but always graciously accepted to write far too many letters of recommendation for fellowships and grant applications for this project. I am most grateful to all these people for their support at crucial stages of my work.

As I prepared myself to do fieldwork in Algeria, I met and discussed my research with numerous Algerians living outside the country. I was most fortunate to have enjoyed the trust of three people in particular who have been key players in their country's history: Mohamad Harbi, Hocine Ait-Ahmed, and Kamal Abdallah-Khodja were enormously generous to me; each spent many hours on several occasions, sharing their knowledge and experience. I am truly indebted to them, and I do hope that the analysis presented in this book resonates positively with them. Kamal Abdallah-Khodja and his lovely wife, Claudie, welcomed me into their home and their life. Apart from their warmth and hospitality, they never tired of my constant questions about Algeria during the Boumedienne years.

Also very instructive were the conversations I had with, among others, Nordine Ait-Laoussine, Reda Belkhodja, Sadek Boussena, Hélène Cuénat, Sid-Ahmed Ghozali, Smaïl Goumeziène, Ali Haroun, Ghazi Hidouci,

Ali El-Kenz, Ahmed Moussaoui, André Prenant, Rachid Sekak, and Mohamad Sahnoun. Ali El-Kenz, Josée Garçon, Agnès Levallois, and Raymond Ben-Haïm put me in contact with key figures, and Idriss Jazairy, then Algerian Ambassador in Washington, DC, facilitated my research trips to Algeria.

In Algeria, numerous people extended themselves to me. Those I interviewed were most helpful: whether they were or had been in government, were part of the official or 'unofficial' opposition, were scholars, attorneys, journalists, industrialists, technocrats, or military personalities, many met with me several times. Everyone was attentive to my security, especially during my first two research trips – in spring 2001 and winter 2002 – when violent confrontations just outside Algiers were regular occurrences. As many people requested that I protect their identities, I will not name my interlocutors. They know who they are, and I hereby thank them wholeheartedly for sharing with me and helping me understand. Three individuals deserve special mention, and have given me permission to name them. Daho Djerbal was in no small measure responsible for the success of my research in Algeria. In advance of my first visit, he organized meetings and guest lectures for me. When I arrived in Algiers in spring 2001, he took me around, introduced me to many people, and answered an endless stream of questions. He made sure, at all times, that I was safe and at ease. I am most grateful to him for all that he did for me. Farid Chaoui, a physician who had been in Mouloud Hamrouche's government, put me in touch with key personalities and discussed my research with me at length. Moreover, he and his wife, Anisa, welcomed me into their home. Hocine Zahouane always made himself available when I was in Algiers. He not only shared with me his long experience with and keen understanding of the vagaries of Algerian politics, but also encouraged me to try out my arguments on him and happily engaged in heated debate.

In the final stages of writing, several people most graciously read all or parts of the book and offered essential feedback. I wish to thank Eva Bellin, Chris Boucek, Mark Gasiorowski, Ellis Goldberg, Steffen Hertog, Tim Mitchell, Tom Naylor, Michael Ross, Ben Smith, and Charles Tripp. Bill Liddle, Indonesia scholar and master comparativist, was enormously helpful to me. Not only did he read meticulously and check everything I wrote about Indonesia, but he also discussed the leadership variable with me at great length and introduced me to important literature. He encouraged me not to shy away from the variable just because it was difficult to operationalize. I am most grateful to him – and to Ben Smith who had suggested I contact Bill in the first place. (I have yet another debt of gratitude to Ben: when he told me, at our first exchange, that a presentation I had made about my Algeria research four years earlier had provided some of the foundation for the argument he was making in his own book manuscript, I was jarred into realizing that I had to get moving on my project and circulate my ideas more effectively.) Isabelle Werenfels, whom I met in Algiers on my first visit and quickly became a dear friend and close collaborator, has read just about every word I have written about Algeria. I consider myself most fortunate to share with her friendship, scholarship, and a fascination for the same place – indeed, a rarity in the world of academia. Last but not least, an anonymous reader for Cambridge University Press pushed me on certain analytical issues, forcing me to clarify my thinking and work toward greater precision. I know that his/her suggestions for revision have contributed to making this a better book. Thank you, whoever you are! Needless to say, as helpful as all these people have been, the work, and all the errors therein, are my very own. I accept complete responsibility for them.

In the course of working on this research, I was very fortunate to have been invited to join two multi-case collaborative projects: the Yale University/World Bank project, entitled "The Economics of Civil Wars, Crime, and Violence" (2000–2) and the UCLA project, "Rebuilding War-Torn Economies in the Middle East" (2003–5). While I had feared initially that they would distract me from my book project, my participation in these collaborations – both of which culminated in noteworthy edited volumes (Collier and Sambanis 2005; Binder 2007) – allowed me to deepen my knowledge of Algeria by giving me the occasion to explore other domains of its experience. Moreover, the interaction with other scholars working on the same themes in different settings was invaluable for broadening my comparative perspective. I wish to thank Paul Collier and Nicolas Sambanis, and Lenny Binder for including me in their projects, and the other participants for sharing with me these enriching experiences.

At different stages of my research and writing, I was invited to present my work to various colloquia, speakers' series, and research institutes. The opportunity to share my research and get feedback from diverse audiences has been most helpful for clarifying my ideas and sharpening the arguments I was trying to make. Among the various institutions I wish to thank are: the (former) Center of International Studies (CIS), the Department of Near Eastern Studies and the Transregional Institute at Princeton University, the Browne Center for International Politics at the University of Pennsylvania, the Woodrow Wilson Center in Washington, DC, the Middle East Institute of the School for International and Public Affairs at Columbia University, the Centre de Recherche en Anthropologie Sociale et Culturelle in Oran (Algeria), the Ecole Nationale de l'Administration in Algiers (Algeria), the Politics Forum at The College of New Jersey (TCNJ), the Association of Geography Graduate Students at Rutgers University, the summer institute of the University of the Middle East in Toledo, Spain, and the School of Forestry at Yale University.

Over the course of the years that I have been working on this project, several institutions have supported my research through grants, fellowships, and affiliations. A very generous grant from the United States Institute of Peace (USIP), Unsolicited Grants Program allowed me to conduct interviews in Europe and in Algeria in 2001, and supported a leave from my teaching position at The College of New Jersey. I am most grateful to the USIP and Steve Riskin, the Senior Program Officer, for having provided critical assistance early on in the project. The second research trip was funded by the Yale University/World Bank project, noted above, and supplemented by a mini-grant from The College of New Jersey. To Nick Sambanis and Paul Collier, as well as to Susan Albertine, former Dean of the School of Culture and Society at TCNJ, I extend my gratitude. I was able to squeeze in a third set of interviews in Algeria, in conjunction with my (completely unexpected but most appreciated) invitation from the Algerian government to attend the International Symposium on Terrorism and the Algerian Precedent, in Algiers in October 2002.

Princeton University provided a scholarly home away from home for me as I worked on this project. I was a Visiting Fellow at the (former) Center of International Studies in 2000–1, when my ideas were in their early gestation period. Michael Doyle, then Director of the CIS, was forthcoming with feedback and opportunities to present my work. I was invited back to Princeton University in spring 2007 and then again in 2007–8 as Visiting Research Scholar, first at the Transregional Institute (TRI) and then at the Environmental Institute (PEI), within the multi-year program on Oil in the Middle East. It was at the TRI that I finished the first draft of the book manuscript; the final revisions were completed the following year, at PEI. I am most grateful to Greg Bell, Michael Cook, Bernard Haykel, and Rob Socolow for hosting me and providing generous research assistance.

My home institution, The College of New Jersey, has supported me in innumerable ways. In addition to two sabbaticals, I was accorded 'leave' from the college when in the course of working on this book, I received an external grant and then a fellowship to pursue the research. Moreover, I have been awarded a reduced teaching load on a yearly basis, and mini-grants have routinely assisted me in the conduct of my research. I am most grateful to the college-wide Committee for the Support of Scholarly Activity (SOSA), Angela Sgroi and the Office for Grants and Sponsored Research, and (former Dean) Susan Albertine of the School of Culture and Society for finding value in my work and providing critical support. My colleagues in the Department of Political Science have been collegial and encouraging, and our chair, Bill Ball, has been supportive at all times. Catherine Allen has provided all sorts of logistical help with this project and with my responsibilities at TCNJ more generally, and always with good cheer. Daniel Wilkens, a former student, and Katherine Hespe were my research assistants as I was finishing up the book. Both worked diligently, amiably, and with great care. Over the years, my students at TCNJ have been far more than a captive audience: they have been interested and insightful, and have, unwittingly, pushed me to work even harder and demand more of myself. I am very grateful to them.

Several other people deserve special mention. My writer-friend, Carolyn Slaughter, has been a constant source of support; with her I could always talk about writing and she would offer her thoughts on how to ease the task. My cousin-friend, Suzanne Flom, has cheered me on while providing a superlative model of professionalism, motherhood, and the art of multi-tasking. Marigold Acland, my editor at Cambridge, waited patiently as I finished up. With good sense and always a striking hair color, she has advised me well and as before, produced a handsome volume.

The sudden death of Umm Hassan in the spring of 2006 was a terrible blow. It was with her and partly because of her that I began my long journey in the Arab–Muslim world. Her grace, supreme warmth, gentle determination, and commitment to home inspired me. It was those qualities of hers that I have found, again and again, in the people and culture that I became so drawn to, and eventually, so much a part of. It was largely through Umm Hassan that I found my self in the other, and the other in my self. She included me in her beautiful family and enriched my world. My debt to her is enormous.

My parents, Beno Lowi and Naomi Paltiel Lowi, have been, unbeknownst to them, deeply implicated in this book in more ways than the obvious one: my father survived Krakow-Plaszow KZ; my mother was one of 9 women with 91 men in her medical school class of 1947. From them I learned a lot about agency. Abdellah Hammoudi has been with me throughout; he has read, discussed, and encouraged endlessly. Jazia and Ismael have helped me most of all: they have filled my life with joy.

Princeton, NJ
November 2008

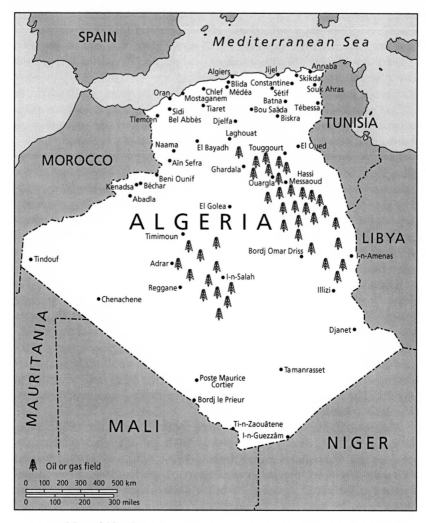

Map of Algeria

Part I

Introduction

1   Oil shocks and the challenge to states

In the mid-1970s, after the first oil shock, Algeria had the highest growth rate (8.5 percent) of all oil-exporting late developing countries (LDC). It was touted as one of the most successful experiments in economic development and one of the most politically stable oil exporters. Algeria was hailed as a model revolutionary, post-colonial state: having brought to an end 130 years of French settler colonialism after a seven-year long war of national liberation, and faced with mass exodus of the European population with their expertise and capital, the leadership of the newly independent state embarked upon broad programs of reconstruction and development. In the first decades, and especially under President Houari Boumedienne, social and economic policies suggested a commitment to development with social justice. With burgeoning oil revenues, enormous efforts were made at rapid industrialization, building up infrastructure, and educating the population – roughly 80 percent of whom were illiterate at independence.

By 1982, however, world demand for oil was declining. Demand for OPEC oil was declining even more as increased output from Mexico and the North Sea cut into OPEC's share of a shrinking market. Oil prices fell from their peak of close to $40/barrel in 1980. Then in 1986, and largely in response to the increase in Saudi production to keep up with the market force of new producers, the price of oil collapsed – to less than $10/barrel. During this same period, the value of the dollar, the currency in which hydrocarbons are traded, declined as well.

The effect of the oil price shock on Algeria's external revenues was striking: they declined by 55 percent in value in a single year. Similarly, the role of hydrocarbon revenues in total government revenues fell from 44 percent to 24 percent. From 1986 until the mid-1990s, the Algerian economy's growth rate remained consistently negative (Aissaoui 2001: 10; Amuzegar 1999: 235).

In reaction to the severe socioeconomic dislocations precipitated by the price shock – among them, inflation, high unemployment, shortages of essential goods – and the failure of the regime to address them effectively, anti-government riots wracked the country for days in October 1988, bringing together those who felt socially and economically marginalized by the system. President Chadli Benjedid responded to the growing unrest with political liberalization. In 1989, after seventeen years of single-party rule, he initiated a transition to multi-party politics and called the first competitive elections for December 1991. At the same time, he installed a reformist government, led by Mouloud Hamrouche, to assist in the transition. In those heady days, political parties mushroomed across the country; over the next two years, they campaigned vigorously.

In the first round of multi-party legislative elections in December 1991, an Islamist party – the Front Islamique du Salut (FIS – Islamic Salvation Front) – won 47 percent of the popular vote. In response, the military, which had dominated the political arena behind the façade of the FLN (Front de Libération Nationale) single party, annulled the election results and called off the transition. It staged a symbolic coup d'état in January 1992, deposed Chadli Benjedid, outlawed the FIS, and declared a state of emergency.

The fallout from the coup was protracted political violence. From 1992 through 2002, the institutions of the state were pitted against an array of Islamist groups – that had emerged initially out of the banned FIS party and its supporters – in a bloody civil war. For several years, the regime's political authority was severely weakened as it battled growing numbers of insurgents, divided among several different groups and benefitting from logistical support from the population. The regime appeared at times to be on the verge of collapse: it could neither contain the insurgency, nor dominate the terrain, while the death toll rose rapidly and there was a heightened sense of insecurity throughout the country. Moreover, the leadership's choice of tactics in the early years of the violence undermined support for itself from both the domestic and international environments, and fed the ranks, and radicalization, of the insurgency (Lowi 2005).

From the mid-1990s, however, the military-backed regime was actively engaged in restoring its grip on power. Through a combination of strategies that included co-optation and manipulation, and assisted eventually by changes to international structural forces, it would take the regime several long years to bring the insurgency to heel. By the beginning of the new millennium, the violence had wound down considerably; the civil war took on the form of a low-intensity conflict. Insurgent forces were depleted, and the regime was back in control.

How can we explain Algeria's post-independence trajectory? Why did the domestic political economy unravel from the mid-1980s, and the regime become acutely unstable, despite impressive natural resource wealth and what appeared, from the outside, as auspicious beginnings? What, if anything, has oil got to do with it? Furthermore, how did the regime eventually manage to recapture power and neutralize its opposition? What factors were decisive in its ability to re-equilibrate: to reassert its power and hegemony "after a crisis that had seriously threatened the continuity and stability of ... the basic political mechanisms" (Linz and Stepan 1978b)?[1] And what does the Algerian experience teach us, more generally, about the durability of patrimonial systems, the contingency of oil, and the determinants of political outcomes in oil-exporting states following economic shocks?[2] These are the main questions this book seeks to answer.

To be sure, Algeria was not alone among oil-exporting states to be deeply shaken by the shock of 1986. As the price of oil fell by 75 percent over a period of several months, government revenues plummeted (Table 1.1). From the highest per capita income oil exporter (United Arab Emirates) to the lowest (Nigeria), independent states had to drastically adjust their spending patterns and development programs overnight, find ways to ensure macroeconomic stability, and address the severe social effects created by fiscal crisis. Across the developing world and within the community of oil-exporting states, the capacity of states to manage the shock diverged considerably, as did political outcomes.[3]

---

[1] For their discussion of how democracies can "re-equilibrate" following regime breakdown, see Linz and Stepan (1978b: 88–91).

[2] Patrimonialism derives from Max Weber's concept of "patrimonial authority" as distinct from "rational-legal authority." It includes the following features: power is personalized – based on the personal preferences of the ruler, who dominates the state apparatus and stands above its laws. The ruler, considering the country his patrimony, appropriates public resources for his own private use. Whatever rights or privileges "subjects" enjoy are granted to them by the ruler who considers them, as well, a part of his estate. Moreover, functionaries of the state benefit from their proximity to power; their loyalty is acknowledged largely through material and professional rewards. In fact, it is via the distribution of favors and material rewards to loyal subjects ("clients") that political stability is maintained. For an excellent discussion of the characteristics of patrimonial systems see Bratton and van de Walle (1997: 61–96). Note that the term "neopatrimonial" has been used to refer to "those hybrid political systems in which the customs and patterns of patrimonialism co-exist with, and suffuse, rational-legal institutions" (62). (See, as well, Murphy 2001.) Since patrimonial features can be found in many regimes, while the singularly "modern" features of rule tend to be de-emphasized, the relative merits of the term "neopatrimonial" versus "modern authoritarian" may be subject to debate. For further elaboration see below, chapter 8, fn.8.

[3] Smith (2006: 58) writes that of twenty-one oil exporters, eleven experienced political crisis during the bust period of either 1977 or 1986 (or both), and four of the eleven regimes collapsed.

Table 1.1 *Sample of oil-exporting states: changes to per capita GDP following price shock*

GDP per capita (constant 2000 US$); [GDP per capita, purchasing power parity (constant 2000 international $)]; (percentage change from last date)

Country	1984		1986			1988		
Algeria	1956	[5894]	1918	[5751]	(−1.92)	1785	[5417]	(−6.95)
Congo Brazz.	1389	[1065]	1199	[852]	(−13.7)	1146	[960]	(−4.42)
Ecuador	1277	[3278]	1299	[3415]	(1.76)	1312	[3544]	(0.96)
Gabon	4791	[6937]	4353	[6367]	(−9.15)	3813	[5577]	(−12.41)
Indonesia	467	[1752]	494	[1839]	(5.73)	534	[1978]	(8.10)
Iran	1468	[5378]	1260	[4620]	(−14.21)	1133	[4157]	(−10.05)
Kuwait	13,901	[12,766]	13,355	[10,619]	(−3.92)	11,883	[10,060]	(−11.02)
Libya	2814		2183		(−22.44)			
Malaysia	2161	[4820]	2051	[4572]	(−5.07)	2257	[4973]	(10.05)
Mexico	5016	[7904]	4754	[7496]	(−5.24)	4712	[7288]	(−0.86)
Nigeria	298	[679]	317	[754]	(6.35)	327	[739]	(3.0)
Oman	6527	[10,071]	6958	[10,576]	(6.61)	6605	[10,330]	(−5.07)
Saudi Arabia	10,453	[13,616]	9403	[11,853]	(−10.04)	8817	[11,231]	(−6.23)
UAE	34,846	[33,352]	23,643	[22,540]	(−32.15)	21,923	[20,749]	(−7.28)

Source: World Development Indicators Online

When we narrow our focus to a subset of oil-exporting states that shares political cultural attributes – among them the Islamic religion and ("modern") authoritarianism[4] – and evaluate the states' performance following not just one but three discrete economic shocks, we find significant variation: some states failed and experienced regime change, others handled crisis fairly successfully and remained stable, still others – like Algeria – underwent tremendous upheaval, yet eventually managed to restabilize.

What accounts for political instability in high-growth, development-oriented oil-exporting countries? Is oil a causal variable? Does acute instability derive from the ways in which oil distorts economic activities and political relations, as rentier state theorists suggest (Mahdavy 1970; Luciani 1987)? Alternatively, are (exogenous) economic shocks necessary or sufficient causes?[5] If so, how could we

---

[4] On authoritarianism as a political cultural variable in the Middle East and North Africa (MENA), see Hammoudi (2001); Sharabi (1988). On patrimonialism as "culturally familiar" in the MENA, see Murphy (2001: 9).

[5] Exogenous shocks include such things as (externally generated) environmental catastrophe, fiscal crisis, or a sudden, drastic change in export prices. Note that crude oil prices

explain that several oil exporters in the Muslim world – among them, Libya, Malaysia, Saudi Arabia – did not become highly unstable, even though they too were subjected to price shocks with severe growth effects? What allows states to forestall their weakening and the onset of civil violence in the face of economic crisis? Do such things as regime type or political culture, for example, make a difference? In other words, if we consider a sample of oil-exporting states that share certain commonalities, how can we explain that in some, contentious politics on the heels of economic crisis provoked regime collapse, while in others it did not, and in still others, states on the brink of collapse managed to re-stabilize?

In addressing this puzzle, the book provides an in-depth study of Algeria's trajectory – the tragedy of unfulfilled expectations, the descent into violence, and the resurgence of the state. Then, to both enrich and contextualize the argument about the vagaries of regime stability in Algeria, I consider, toward the end of the book, a sample of four other oil-exporting states in the Muslim world. Like Algeria, the four states are/were "late developers" with authoritarian-modernizing regimes and patrimonial structures; together, they reflect the variation in political outcomes, noted above. I offer some preliminary comparisons among them and Algeria in order to shed light on the variation in stability following economic shocks.

Like Algeria, pre-Gulf War Iraq underwent regime crisis and considerable political upheaval after 1986, yet it managed in the 1990s to avert breakdown.[6] In contrast, Iran in 1979 and Indonesia in 1998, on the heels of economic shock, experienced political instability, regime breakdown (and system change) – although Indonesia had weathered the oil price downturn of 1986 remarkably well. Moreover, Saudi Arabia, despite the devastating effects to gross domestic product (GDP) from the 1986 shock, has enjoyed regime continuity without a major crisis. In terms of outcomes, therefore, pre-revolutionary Iran and Indonesia can be thought of as "positive" cases – of instability and breakdown – while Saudi Arabia is a "negative" case, and Algeria and pre-Gulf War Iraq are "in between" cases – of acute instability

---

increased more than fifteen times between 1973 and 1980, and fell by close to 80 percent between 1981 and 1986. Prices increased more than 400 percent between 1987 and 1990, and fell around 50 percent between 1991 and 1994 (Amuzegar 1999).

[6] Indeed, it would take foreign intervention in 2003 – a quintessential exogenous shock – for the Iraqi regime to implode.

followed by re-equilibration.[7] (Interestingly, Indonesia until the early 1990s would have been considered a "negative" case, like Saudi Arabia.)

Addressing this variation – occurrence, non-occurrence, and something in between – is noteworthy given that authoritarian regimes with patrimonial structures, which tend to thrive on the distribution of favors, are especially challenged at moments of economic crisis. The combination of "shrinking economic opportunities and exclusionary rewards" encourages social protest (Bratton and van de Walle 1997: 83; Chehabi and Linz 1998).[8] How, then, can we explain the variation in the ability of such regimes to manage shocks and retain power?

Explaining instability

Political instability, in the form of the weakening of the state – its diminishing capacity to exercise a monopoly of power and control within and across the country – and the onset of civil violence, must be understood within the framework of the creation of the modern state in post-colonial environments. For the most part, newly independent states inherited from their European colonizers modern administrations, but not modern states built on social inclusion, the rule of law, values of responsibility and progress through work and merit, and the exclusion of violence as a mechanism of social regulation.

---

[7] Instability in the form of either a temporary or a persistent "breakdown of order," in which the state no longer exercises sole, or decisive, control over the political landscape, may assume different forms: protracted or even random acts of violence (Iraq), revolutionary mobilization (Iran), civil war (Algeria), secessionist struggle (Indonesia). As with recent work in the field of "contentious politics," I believe that the different forms share similar components and causal mechanisms. For this reason, weakened, failed, and failing states – those that collapse and those that re-equilibrate – constitute coherent objects of study (Aminzade *et al.* 2001; Goldstone 1998: 125–45; McAdam *et al.* 2001; Tarrow 1998; Tilly 2008). They differ in how the components assemble and how they function in the context of different regimes, historical legacies, and the mobilizational capacities of social forces. See, as well, Esty, *et al.* (1998); Rotberg (2004).

[8] Geddes (1999) notes that of the three different types of authoritarian regime: (1) personalistic (patrimonial, neo-patrimonial, clientelistic, sultanistic), (2) single-party, (3) military – the first (personalistic) is most likely to end in popular uprising, invasion, revolution, or assassination. Given that all five cases in my study fall within the first type – even though the Algerian and Indonesian regimes were intertwined with the military, as were, to a lesser degree, the Iraqi and Iranian regimes – all five, according to Geddes, would be prone to unstable, or destabilizing, outcomes. With regard to the categorization of regimes, however, it is important to heed Larry Diamond's reminder that "most regimes are 'mixed' to one degree or another" (2002: 33).

The modern nation-state was to be built from scratch, and for many hybrid post-colonial states today, that challenge remains (Young 1988).[9]

As for newly independent states endowed with oil, the availability of substantial rents early on in the state-building process and their concentration in the hands of political leaders at the center presented the latter with the means to perhaps create institutions and consolidate the nation/state differently from their capital-constrained counterparts.[10] Hence, to make sense of political instability in post-colonial, oil-exporting states, it is necessary to explore not only the sectoral particularities of oil-based development and their effects, but also the relationship among oil-based development, the choice of political institutions, and the distribution of resources.[11]

I concur with Rodrik (1999) that in environments where societal cleavages remain deep, while institutions are brittle, narrow, and poorly equipped to manage the social conflicts that derive from the deep divisions, states – whether oil- or non-oil-exporting – are prone to become unstable in the aftermath of a shock that triggers a "crisis of distribution." During such crises, social conflicts come to the fore, yet institutional mechanisms for addressing them and the capacity of leadership to reform may be lacking. Social forces re-align to destabilize, capture, or transform the state.

Furthermore, the presence of substantial oil rents in LDCs with authoritarian regimes and patrimonial structures encourages a perception of well-being, which, in turn, discourages political reform. Hence, in most settings, the availability of rents tends to consolidate what is already in place: typically, weak institutions remain weak, and smug elites, "attuned above all to rent-seeking," eschew reform (Luciani 1995).[12]

---

[9] More often than not, the strategy for nation-building has focussed, almost exclusively, on economic development and has ignored – except in a few cases, most notably, China under Mao and India under Gandhi – political and cultural matters. With respect to the imperative domestication of violence in the creation of the modern (nation-)state, see Bates (2001).

[10] See, in this regard, Moore (2004: 297–319) for a lucid discussion of differences in the context of state formation in LDCs compared with that in countries of Western Europe, with a focus on the source of state revenues.

[11] Regimes assume control over a variety of resources that they both retain for themselves and selectively distribute: among them are economic goods and services, status, authority, information, and coercion (Ilchman and Uphoff 1969: 32–3).

[12] An exception to this can be found among the Arab Gulf states, including Saudi Arabia. There, as we will see below (chapter 7), political elites have initiated piecemeal reform to appease social forces; at the same time, they continue to strengthen their instruments

Deep social cleavages, combined with relatively narrow state institutions, are common features of post-colonial states, and especially those with authoritarian regimes and patrimonial leadership structures. They are characteristic of Algeria and the four comparators as well. I suggest that two conditions related to the above features, plus a third, favor political instability in oil-exporting countries following an economic shock.

The first condition concerns the inception of oil-based development: when the state, through an explicit program of policies and investments, promotes economic, social, and infrastructural development, and deploys important revenues from the sale of oil to that end.[13] Instability is more likely to ensue when oil-based development is initiated in a context in which the state is weakly institutionalized.[14] This is because predictable patterns of (accountable) behavior were not in place at the time of the first massive inflow of oil wealth, nor were they established over time. Politically motivated distribution has been the norm, while rent-seeking behavior has been encouraged. Moreover, the norm tends to become exaggerated at times of economic

of rule. The Kuwaiti regime, for one, has maintained a semblance of democracy (Henry and Springborg 2001: 169–71; Tétreault 2000; Dazi-Héni 2002: 215–38). On the whole, however, political behavior in the Gulf statelets and Saudi Arabia is somewhat distinct from that in other oil-exporting states of the region. This distinctiveness is due not to regime type alone, as some would suggest (*inter alia* Herb 1999), but rather, I would argue, to the combination of relatively small population size, peculiar leadership structures (in the form of "family rule"), the virtual absence of indigenous nationalist movements, and the endogeneity of oil to – and the implication of the British in – state formation. See, as well, the provocative comment by Sluglett (2002: 150), "On voit bien que les systèmes politiques installés dans le Golfe n'ont rien à voir avec des lignées descendant des 'coutumes tribales traditionelles,' comme on l'affirme parfois, mais qu'ils sont une réinvention moderne issue de la reconnaissance par les Britanniques d'une famille particulière de 'souverains.'" ["We see that the political systems found in the Gulf do not have anything to do with dominant lineages issuing from traditional tribal roots with customary legitimacy, as is sometimes stated; rather, they are a modern reinvention stemming from the recognition by the British of the overriding leadership of one particular family." *Translation my own.*] In other words, the British conferred power on families of their choosing. For further elaboration, see below, chapter 7. On the significance of small size and the peculiarities of "family rule" see Salamé (1994: 84–111).

13   That is to say, where revenues from the sale of oil constitute at least one-half of total trade revenues.

14   The term "institutionalized state" should be understood in the Weberian sense: as distinct from a patrimonial state. An institutionalized state is one that is rule-governed and predictable, and in which office is both meritocratic and service-oriented. There is, as well, a clear delineation between the public and private spheres. In contrast, a patrimonial state is one in which nepotism and cronyism are avenues to power and promotion. There is little sense in which the powerful are rule-bound or accountable, and there is little, if any, distinction between the public and private spheres. Hence, corruption tends to be widespread and arbitrariness, common. Furthermore, sectarianism is prevalent: competing cleavage structures in society are manipulated and exploited by the state, largely for political purposes (Bellin 2005: 28–9).

constraint; the weakly institutionalized state becomes even more concerned with its political survival, and an environment of "catch as catch can" takes hold.

The second condition has to do with social cleavages at the inception of oil-based development. If, at that time, there are major societal groups which are weakly incorporated into the state – insofar as they are excluded by the regime from political and/or economic spoils – then political instability is more likely to ensue when there is an economic shock. This is because those groups which have suffered historically from marginalization are likely to be the hardest hit by an economic downturn. Disaffected, they may seize the opportunity presented by a weakened state and try to mobilize against it.

The third condition has to do with the way leaders respond to the challenges they face. If, in the face of an economic downturn, for example, the leadership fails to implement reforms and distribute resources in ways that appease social forces and incorporate those who have been marginalized, political instability will ensue. At issue is leadership choice at a "critical juncture:" a foundational moment in the political–economic development of the state, when choices of great consequence are presented to the leadership, and decisions have powerful effects on political institutions and outcomes (Collier and Collier 1991; Mahoney and Rueschemeyer 2003).[15] In contrast, those states that remain stable in the face of an economic downturn, or manage to re-equilibrate after a period of instability, do so largely because of astute leadership choices regarding the neutralization of domestic challengers.[16]

[15] The first two conditions, above, echo classic arguments about instability in resource-rich states with patrimonial systems. See, in this regard, van de Walle (1994: 129–57). As for the first condition, it brings to mind Ben Smith's (2007) central argument: that the timing of late development relative to access to oil wealth has an important bearing on the durability of regimes. When a regime's access precedes the initiation of late development, Smith insists, the regime is less likely to invest in strong institutions – preferring to distribute patronage. Thus, it has a lesser chance of survival than a regime which, without access, was forced, at the outset, to forge bargains and make concessions. My argument, as we will see below, is distinct from Smith's in that it zeroes in on agency, while still acknowledging the relevance of structure. It is not the timing of oil's insertion into the domestic political economy that matters most, in my view, but rather the capacity of leaders to make effective choices regarding the distribution of resources at moments of leadership challenge. In effect, my work gently confronts Smith's historical–structural argument by placing agency up front.

[16] Rodrik (1999a) argues that the variation in economic performance in the aftermath of an external shock derives from the ways in which societies react to the shock, and specifically to the social conflicts that emerge. On one level, the comparative dimension of my book can be read as an application of Rodrik's thesis to political outcomes.

I suggest that the variation in stability in Algeria and across regimes can best be explained by the decisions of leaders at critical junctures. To be sure, leadership decisions are shaped by a host of variables, not least among them the institutional underpinnings of the state. The latter provide part of the structure – those regularized patterns of behavior – within which leaders operate; and structures both constrain and enable the maneuverability of actors.

Structure and agency, or the challenge of leadership

In Alfred Stepan's study of the Goulart regime in Brazil (Stepan 1978a: 110–37), the author underscores the attributes of political leadership as an enabling factor for regime breakdown. He suggests that while macro-level variables, having to do with the social and/or economic context, may strain a political system, it is "the qualities and style of leadership" that bring those strains "to a crisis point" (120).[17] In his view, a leader incites breakdown when, in the face of important challenges, s/he fails to both build on whatever support s/he already has and prevent opposition to him/her from growing.

In my efforts to explain the enigmatic case of Algeria and respond to the general questions presented above about the variation in stability in oil-exporting states, I, too, emphasize the importance of leadership – that "relatively neglected variable" in comparative politics (Stepan 1978a: 111). Indeed, I insist upon the integrated roles of structure, context, and leadership choice in fashioning outcomes. No doubt, structures – composed as they are of cultures, social institutions, and resources – powerfully shape choice; they provide the framework within which actors make decisions, and the resources they may draw upon to achieve their objectives.[18] Leadership, therefore, is not only about acumen; it is, rather, "that constrained place where imagination, resources, and opportunity converge" (Samuels 2003: 6).

Leaders have at their disposal an array of resources with which to meet their goals. From the outset, they must have information: about the resources that are available to them, about the strength and character of the resource base of social forces, about preferences. Keen perception and acuity do play an important role in choice. For one, leaders must

---

[17] This point is made, as well, in Mahoney and Snyder (1999: 13), in their discussion of the "funnel strategy" for exploring the combination of structure and agency in the study of regime change.

[18] For illuminating discussions about the relationship between structure and agency see Sewell (1992); Hays (1994).

recognize how far they can go in distributing which resources and to whom, as well as anticipate the effects of their distributive activities. They must also be able to think creatively about how best to utilize the resources at hand. Furthermore, they must know how to push the limits of the possible or, as Richard Samuels (2003: 5–6) writes, "stretch the constraints" imposed by the structure that envelops them.[19]

Some degree of good fortune may play a role in the successful achievement of goals: the context may favor it, or there may be a sudden, fortuitous change in the domestic or international environment. But the importance of vision and of will, combined with the ability of individuals to exploit opportunities housed in constraints, does have considerable influence on the success of strategic choice, even though these variables may be difficult to operationalize.[20]

All political leaders invest resources in the creation, consolidation, and reform of institutions. They also distribute resources among their populations so as to effect status, authority, and wealth. In these and related ways, they engage in the critical tasks of state-building, while gaining support and securing compliance with their goals (Ilchman and Uphoff 1969: 86).

The notion that institutional endowments carry transformative powers for development has a long tradition, elaborated by Weber (1968 [1904–11]), Polanyi (1944), Gerschenkron (1962), Hirschman (1977), North (1981), and Ertman (1997), among others. The comparative institutional approach (Evans 1995) builds upon that tradition, identifying differences in the way states are organized and connecting those differences to variations in developmental outcomes.[21] In recent years, the approach has been applied, in part, to either single or paired oil-exporting states (Chaudhry 1997; Luong 2003; Vandewalle 1998).

---

[19] In his very influential *A Bias for Hope* (Yale University Press, 1971), Albert Hirschman introduced the notion of "possibilism:" the idea that opportunities for development and change can be found by creative actors even in conditions of scarcity.

[20] To wit, decisions can be considered "effective" only if they achieve their objectives, and the achievement of objectives can be determined only after the fact. Nonetheless, *post hoc* analysis can provide lessons for the future. For example, it can demonstrate what sorts of strategies worked, within what contexts, for leaders in their past efforts. This sort of exercise may be of value in that, rather than offer a recipe for success, it could provide leaders with the sense that they could, indeed, make a difference and offer insights into how they might do so. (I am grateful to Bill Liddle for helping me think through these ideas.)

[21] Thelen (1999: 390), for example, describes historical institutionalism as "a perspective that examines political and economic development in historical context and in terms of processes unfolding over time and in relation to each other, within a broader context in which developments in one realm impinge on and shape developments in others." For variants of comparative historical analysis, see Mahoney and Rueschemeyer (2003).

Some scholars suggest that dependence on subsoil assets, which provide quick profits and require primarily material resources rather than extensive human cooperation for their extraction, tends to discourage the development of good governance and consensual political processes that result from bargained outcomes between state elites and the mass of society (de Soysa 2002). Others find this claim problematic, since there are oil-exporting states, such as Norway and the United States, where "good governance" is not in doubt.[22] Furthermore, there are non-oil-exporting states that suffer from similar problems to oil exporters (Berman 1998; Clapham 1985; Englebert 2000). What appears non-trivial, however, is that because the presence of significant external revenues tends to discourage leaders from investing in the building of strong institutions and enhances the patrimonial inclinations of rule,[23] oil, implicitly and invariably, places a premium on good governance and appropriate leadership choices.

The argument and its underpinnings

In contrast to analyses of oil-exporting states that locate the explanation for political outcomes in structural variables – in the oil sector itself, for example – I suggest that to make sense of Algeria's trajectory (of "stability," instability, and re-stabilization), we need to explore the state-building experience. We must highlight not only the (historical) context, but also the choices made along the way regarding the development of institutions and the incorporation of competing cleavage structures into the domestic political economy. In essence, these choices have to do with the distribution of resources and their consequences (Boix 2003). Just as distributive concerns – regarding who has (how much of) what resources, for what purposes, and with what likely

---

[22] Note, however, that Norway and the United States are considerably different from most "oil states" in the developing world. For one, the discovery of North Sea oil occurred well after the inception and consolidation of Norwegian development, while the United States imports oil and enjoys a diversified economy. Second, both countries had competitive manufacturing sectors prior to the development of their mineral resources. Third, the United States has been able to isolate some of the worst effects of oil booms in three states of the union, without them having much impact elsewhere. Hence, the rest of the country has enjoyed the benefits of booms, while only the three producing states have suffered the costs. (I am grateful to Tom Naylor for bringing this last point to my attention.)

[23] This is the case because oil rents nurture a sense of overwhelming abundance and well-being. Moreover, in the "rentier" state, distribution, rather than administration and extraction, is the focus of government. For a provocative challenge to this idea, see Dunning (2008); Haber and Menaldo (2007).

effects – lie at the heart of the choice of political institutions, so the decisions of leaders regarding the distribution of resources in the aftermath of an economic shock play a major role in establishing outcomes: political stability or instability.

It is at the inception of oil-based development and with the availability of important rents that the leadership makes consequential decisions about the form and strength of political institutions. Whether and how to incorporate competing cleavage structures, for example, is a decision with far-reaching effects. For one, the marginalization of one or more key social groups and their exclusion from economic or political spoils provide fertile ground for dissent. When domestic dissent coheres with a favorable "opportunity structure," within the context of a weakly institutionalized state, key social groups may be mobilized relatively easily.

The resilience of leadership in the face of domestic challenges is critical for outcomes as well. Its capacity to respond effectively and in a timely fashion to popular unrest may not only mitigate dissent and impede mobilization, but also, in doing so, shore up regime legitimacy. Similarly with the capacity of leadership to respond to an (exogenous) economic shock and adjudicate distributional conflicts effectively by, for example, providing opportune political "rewards." Offering "rewards" – such things as recognition, participation, and the like – to gain support or acquiescence at difficult moments may dampen the frustration of popular expectations and protect against instability.

Both the inception of oil-based development and the occurrence of economic shocks are the critical junctures – foundational moments – in the trajectory of the oil-exporting state and for its political stability. At those junctures, the leadership makes momentous decisions about how to distribute resources. In this way, it (re-)defines the shape of political institutions and impacts outcomes.[24] It is up to leaders to manage foundational moments in a salutary fashion, to strengthen support for the regime and its policies, neutralize opposition, and promote stability. Given the structural and institutional challenges, leadership choice is, I argue, the most consequential variable in the elaboration of political outcomes.[25]

[24] In this book, I use the term "institutions" to refer, simply, to formal and informal socio-political arrangements. While the historical institutionalist tradition views institutions as the "enduring legacies of political struggles" (Thelen 1999: 388), others have noted that institutions can be created from above, virtually by fiat, via the decision of leaders (Hertog 2007: 548).

[25] Scholars have remarked that the relative success of Botswana in managing its diamond wealth and developing its economy has had much to do with having a capable and

To sum up, in formulating my explanation for Algeria's checkered experience with regime stability and, in comparative context, the variation in stability in oil-exporting countries in the aftermath of an economic shock, I build upon sectoral analysis – specifically, the rentier state/ resource curse literatures – and the comparative historical approach. I move beyond predominantly structural variants of the former by underscoring the importance of leadership choice in political outcomes. There may be a greater propensity for conflict in countries where the government has access to important financial resources from external sources, as quantitative studies of the "resource curse" suggest (Collier and Hoeffler 2001; de Soysa 2000; Greif *et al.* 2002; Ross 2004; Snyder 2006). Nonetheless, oil rents are not the proximate cause of instability, nor are patrimonial systems of rule.

Besides, for an economic shock to provoke domestic crisis, conditions must be in place internally. As Goodwin (2001: 25–6) indicates with regard to the emergence of revolutionary movements, the "political context" must favor it. Hence, the context – as it relates, in my cases, to institutions, historical legacies, social cleavages, actors and their policy decisions – must be elucidated. While oil rents impose structural challenges to political–economic development, it is the environment they come into and the ways they are exploited – in other words, the manner in which structure and agency combine – that matter when exploring outcomes.[26]

Toward comparative analysis

To reiterate, my principal goals in writing this book are the following: first, to explain the enigma of Algeria – why the domestic political

---

committed leadership, and participatory and regulatory tribal institutions, alongside a fairly homogenous society. See, for example, Acemoglu *et al.* (2003: 80–119); Clapham (2004: 89). For a different view, see Dunning (2005: 460), who suggests that where there are no "nonresource bases of economic power," challenges to the authority of those in power are few, weak, or nonexistent. In Botswana, the major nonresource economic base, cattle ranching, is controlled by the same ethnicity that controls the state and the diamond sector.

A counter example is that of the Ahijo government (1960–82) of Cameroon. The president froze the state's oil revenues and kept them outside the country. This appeared as a judicious leadership choice insofar as harmful Dutch Disease effects were attenuated (van de Walle 1994: 141). Unfortunately, President Ahijo's appropriation of these revenues in his own personal accounts meant that the domestic economy could not benefit from them at all. (I am grateful to Nicolas van de Walle for this clarification.)

[26] For rich discussions of combining structure and agency, see Dessler (1989); Mahoney and Snyder (1999).

economy unraveled so acutely, and how the regime eventually managed to regain its power and hegemony; second, to extend the argument about Algeria to explain why some oil-exporting states break down and undergo regime change, while others remain stable, and still others manage to restabilize after a period of acute instability; and third, to examine whether and how oil has mattered for political outcomes in Algeria, and for the variation in outcomes in oil-exporting states in the Muslim world more generally.

Given this set of goals, I am drawn naturally to the "rentier state" and "resource curse" literatures. Initially formulated to explain the economic development of oil-rich Iran (Mahdavy 1970), the rentier state framework has been elaborated and applied to other oil-rich countries of the Gulf region and North Africa (Beblawi 1987; Crystal 1990; Luciani 1987; Vandewalle 1988, 1998). The framework – Middle East Studies' contribution to comparative politics (Anderson 1987) – has also been applied to oil-rich countries outside the Middle East and North Africa (inter alia, Clark 1997; Englebert and Ron 2004; Karl 1997; McSherry 2006; Yates 1996).

Because of the initial regional focus to a framework that I build upon and seek to refine, I have chosen to study a sample of cases from different parts of the Middle East and North Africa, but also to stretch cautiously beyond, to Muslim countries outside the region. The purpose of this type of case selection is to both confront the regional focus and get beyond regional, ethnic, and historical specificities. Moreover, selecting a sample of countries in which Muslims constitute at least 90 percent of the population allows me to control for cultural variables somewhat, despite acknowledged differences in the practice of Islam across the cases.[27] Had I included a Latin American case – Venezuela or Mexico, for example – I would have had to address the possible impact on outcomes of Spanish–American culture.

---

[27] Surely Iran is distinct in that it is the only country in the sample where the vast majority of the population (90%) is of the Shi'a, and not the Sunni, tendency in Islam. In Indonesia, the Muslim faith of the population has been referred to as "syncretic:" a strong mystical/spiritual tradition, that borrows from Hinduism, Buddhism, and animism, is joined to the practice of Islam in the archipelago. (On Islam in Indonesia, see Geertz (1971); Hefner (2000).) In Saudi Arabia, Wahhabism – related to the Hanbali school of Islamic thought – is practiced; unlike the Maliki and Hanafi schools, found in Algeria and Iraq, respectively, it is deeply conservative and literalist.

I tend to agree with Nonneman (2001: 144) and others, that political culture plays some, albeit indeterminate, role in outcomes. Indeed, there is no such thing as "an overarching Arab–Islamic political culture." Besides, Islam is both a binding agent and a source of division (Murphy 2001: 24). Rather than insist on culture, it may be more appropriate to underscore that political behavior is shaped by context; and while culture is a part of the context, so are several other variables.

To be sure, Indonesia is an outlier of sorts in my sample. It is not a Middle East/North African state, nor does it have an Arab population.[28] Furthermore, by the early 1990s, Indonesia could no longer be considered an oil-exporting state since it had become a net importer of oil to meet domestic needs. Of the five countries, Indonesia had, as well, the most diversified economy and an important non-oil export sector. (It may well be that the country did not suffer from the 1986 oil shock as did the other cases precisely because its economy was not nearly as dependent on oil exports as were the others.) Furthermore, the economic shock Indonesia experienced toward the end of the 1990s was not induced by a sudden decline in the price of oil, as with the other cases in earlier periods; rather, it resulted from the region-wide Asian financial crisis that began in the summer of 1997 with the collapse of the Thai baht.[29] Despite these differences, comparing four countries that share numerous commonalities, and adding one semi-outlier, allows me to explore the variation in outcomes in otherwise "most similar" cases, and examine the relative significance for outcomes of oil dependence, oil-inspired shocks, and regional specificity.[30]

To summarize, four of the five cases are from the Middle East/North Africa region; all five are predominantly Muslim countries with authoritarian systems and patrimonial structures, and three of the five have predominantly Arab populations. All experienced powerful economic shocks in the form of the oil booms of 1973/4 and 1979/80, and one or more of the following: the decline in international demand for Middle Eastern oil in 1976/7, the severe oil price downturn and world recession of the mid-1980s, and the Asian financial crisis of the late 1990s (Table 1.2). Political unrest peaked in the wake of economic crisis. Furthermore, all have enjoyed considerable external support from Western governments and organizations: support that has been linked, in large measure, to resource endowments.

Nonetheless, Iran and Indonesia experienced regime breakdown and change (albeit in the wake of two vastly different shocks), Algeria

---

[28] Three of the five cases have predominantly Arab populations, while a fourth – Iran – has an Arab minority.

[29] On the Asian financial crisis see Pempel (1999); Radelet et al. (1998).

[30] Algeria and Iraq have been compared in terms of both their industrialization strategies and the populism of the FLN and the B'ath Party. See Addi (1990); Chaudhry (1999). Following the Islamic Revolution of 1979, Iran and Saudi Arabia were compared as well; there was much speculation about whether revolutionary fervor would take hold in another deeply religious society next door. See Munson (1988). For an instructive comparison of Indonesia and Iran in terms of regime durability, see Smith (2007).

Table 1.2 *Impact of economic downturns in Algeria and the comparators*

Country	% Change in GDP and in p.c. GNI, 1975–9, 1984–8, 1996–8												
	1975	1976	1977	1978	1979	1984	1985	1986	1987	1988	1996	1997	1998
Iran	5.4	16.9	-1.1	-11.0	-7.9								
		19.8	1.9	-7.7	-3.6								
Indonesia	6.1	5.9	8.6	9.2	7.1	7.2	3.5	6.0	5.3	6.4	7.6	4.1	-13.1
		9.7	11.1	14.0	14.0	9.8	4.5	6.0	6.4	8.3	8.2	5.1	-13.4
Algeria						5.6	3.7	0.4	0.7	-1.0			
						6.0	3.9	-0.5	-0.7	-0.2			
Iraq						11.8	3.9	-9.5	9.2	-0.6			
						...	0.0	-6.9	18.0	8.7			
Saudi Arabia						-3.1	-4.3	5.1	-4.0	8.2			
						-5.1	-6.8	1.7	-6.4	6.5			

Source: World Bank: World Development Indicators; Economist Intelligence Unit: Country Data; UN Statistics Division, select years

and Iraq underwent regime crisis and re-stabilization, while Saudi Arabia has enjoyed regime continuity without much upheaval. In explaining the variation in stability, I suggest that while there are differences among the cases in terms of both institutional foundations and the incorporation of competing cleavage structures, the most consequential difference concerns the ways in which leaders responded to domestic challenges and the strategies they adopted to shore up their incumbency and defuse opposition. As with Algeria, leadership decisions at critical junctures matter most for explaining outcomes.

Alternate explanations

Some may argue that other factors explain the variation in the stability of oil-exporting states. Among them: (1) the ratio of oil revenues to population size; (2) regime type; (3) the role of the international community; (4) the prevailing distribution of power between regime and opposition; (5) the degree of repression by the state. First, the higher the ratio of oil revenues to population size, the better equipped the state may be for managing crises of distribution. Hence, stability derives, in this view, from a powerful "cushion effect" in the form of sufficient funds with which to purchase consent and buy time. Second, the greater the degree of power sharing and internal dispute resolution in a regime, the greater the degree of regime stability. The idea here is the commonsensical one that regimes which promote consensual politics are more likely to endure than those which do not (Herb 1999). Third, the greater and more sustained the interest of the international community in a particular oil-exporting state, the more likely it is to intervene in ways that shore up the regime and avert civil unrest. A foreign power may choose to abandon a beleaguered regime in crisis, or it may decide, rather, to reinvigorate it through different means of support (Brownlee 2002b). Fourth, the stronger the regime – in terms of its capacity to achieve its goals – relative to forces of opposition, the greater the likelihood that it remains stable. Regimes that possess effective means for extending their domination and control are best equipped for neutralizing an opposition and promoting stability. Fifth, the more severe the constraints on popular collective action, the more stable the regime and the system remain. When government repression deters most forms of popular mobilization, the regime thereby preserves itself (Bellin 2004).[31]

---

[31] Michael Ross (2004) argues that repression helps maintain oil-rich regimes through crises; it serves to diminish the risk of regime failure.

I contend that the above five factors – and related hypotheses – may indeed shape the context, but they do not determine outcomes. They are secondary in their impact to leadership choice. I respond to each of these factors briefly below and return to them in greater detail in the final chapter.

First, the mere availability of funds matters less for outcomes than what regimes choose ultimately to do with them.[32] For example, although per capita GDP underwent a change of −10 percent in Saudi Arabia following the 1986 price shock, as compared with −2 percent in Algeria, the Saudi regime retained domestic peace, while the Algerian regime did not. The Saudi regime did so, in large measure, by drawing down government reserves and using those funds to keep social subsidies in place. In this way, it eased the burden on society.

Second, sharing power and resolving disputes internally would contribute to the stability of *any* regime – monarchical or not, dynastic or not. One need not be a dynastic monarchy to ensure regime stability, just as one need not be a sultanistic regime to provoke breakdown (Brownlee 2002a: 491).[33] Suharto of Indonesia, by no means a dynastic monarch, maintained stability for close to three decades despite a host of daunting challenges – not least among them that the population he ruled numbered roughly 200 million and was comprised of more than

---

[32] Consider that in 2006, the Algerian government had upwards of $70 billion in reserves for a population of 35 million. At that time, more than 40 percent of the population was living below the poverty line, according to the Algerian *Conseil National Economique et Social* (CNES). This proportion was greater than what it had been in the twenty preceding years, when per capita government revenues were significantly less.

[33] An anonymous reader's provocative suggestion begs a response. S/he has written that key to Saudi Arabia's stability may be the fact that it is a dynastic monarchy that was "consciously designed from the start as meshing with local political and social culture." Although I note (in chapter 7, below) that the Al Sa'ud regime has a degree of "historical depth," and this provides it with strong institutional foundations relative to Algeria and the other comparators, we need to be cautious about referring to the process of state-formation in Saudi Arabia as one of "meshing with local political and social culture." Indeed, the Al Sa'ud were one of several "households" which competed to rule the Arabian Peninsula. It was largely through conquest, followed, to be sure, by clever bargaining, that this particular household prevailed (Vassiliev 2000). While no doubt representing embittered minorities, the Shi'a, Hejazis, and those who worked in the oil fields would not likely describe their experience as evidence of "meshing" (Al-Rasheed 2002; Abir 1988; Vitalis 2007). As for the significance in the Saudi ethos of tribes and tribalism as a form of political organization, it may be especially important to the royal family. The insistence on a culture of tribalism has enabled a single household – the Al Sa'ud – to evolve into a "tribe" many thousands strong within a couple of generations. (I am grateful to Tim Mitchell for this important observation.) In addition, the focus on tribes and tribalism has allowed large numbers to feel they belong, and others to feel excluded. Tribes do function as a (potential) threat to the regime – hence, they have to be kept satisfied – but also a (potential) source of mobilization for the monarchy. However, tribes have not been at the core of Saudi state-building. See, in this regard, Al-Fahad (2004: 35–76).

200 ethnic groups, living in an archipelago of about 12,000 islands. Moreover, within the Al Sa'ud family, which touts the role of consensus in decision-making, there have been bitter struggles for power (Gresh 2002: 209). A result of these struggles has been that the "House of Fahd" has emerged victorious; it has done so through the effective use of a particular set of strategies.[34]

Third, the role of external actors has effects far too varied to make overarching claims. The intervention of foreign powers can shore up a regime in crisis, but it may just as well de-stabilize a regime. In Algeria and the four comparators, the presence of the international community has been noteworthy, but in no case, except for the United States' intervention in Iraq in 2003, has it been decisive for outcomes.

Fourth, the organizational strength and mobilizational capacity of an opposition is in part a function of (prior) leadership decisions regarding the distribution of resources and the shape of institutions. Indeed, opposition movements do not emerge in the absence of an enabling opportunity structure (Kurzman 2004). This being the case, relative power is also derivative of the intersection of choice and context.

Finally, repression can deter explicit opposition to the state, but it cannot preclude it altogether. Even the most repressive regimes have not been able to ward off political violence completely, as demonstrated by Saddam Hussein's Iraq. Moreover, the suggestion that the regime of the Shah of Iran succumbed to instability and breakdown because it was not repressive enough ignores, if nothing else, the twenty-year history of SAVAK brutality.[35]

---

[34] In his illuminating review article of authoritarian monarchies in the Middle East, Lucas (2004: 111) writes that "how a regime uses its resources is an important variable, as the spectacular failure of the Shah demonstrates." He goes on to say, "[H]ow resources are used, however, is also a factor of the type of regime." He then contrasts dynastic, "linchpin," and sultanistic monarchies. In response, I would submit that authoritarian regimes – whether monarchies or republics – with patrimonial features use resources in remarkably similar ways. This, I suggest, is certainly the case in the countries of the Middle East and North Africa. See, in this regard, fn.2 above, and Leveau and Hammoudi (2002). Moreover, with only one example of a sultanistic monarchy in the contemporary Middle East (Iran) – or, is it a monarchy that, toward the end of the Shah's reign, demonstrated sultanistic tendencies? (Katouzian 1998) – we are hard-pressed to evaluate Lucas' statement. On the deficiencies of the concept of sultanism, see Young (1999: 165–8).

[35] See, for example, Baraheni (1977). SAVAK (Sazman-e Amniyat Va Ettela'at-e Keshvar) – the Organization for Information and State Security – was created in 1957 with the help of the United States (CIA) and Israel as an agency for monitoring and repressing (potential) opponents of the regime; it was especially focussed on preventing the revival of the Tudeh and the National Front parties.

Methodology

I explore the questions posed above by first providing a detailed analysis of the state/nation-building experience of Algeria from the emergence of the Algerian nationalist movement in the 1920s through the civil war which began in 1992. The focus throughout is on three variables: (i) institutional development and its relationship to oil; (ii) the incorporation of competing cleavage structures in the domestic political economy; and (iii) the decisions of leaders (regarding the distribution of resources) at critical junctures.[36] Then, to enrich and extend the arguments advanced for Algeria, and to reinforce analytic points, I introduce comparative evidence from four other cases, focussing on the same set of variables.

Historical analysis of Algeria, followed by brief cross-case comparisons and within-case comparisons over time, are the principal methods employed (Mahoney and Rueschemeyer 2003). The historical narrative of Algeria is used to trace the interaction of agency and structure – to demonstrate, for example, how structural factors may strain the domestic political economy, but those strains are either mitigated or exacerbated by actors – while explanations for the genesis of particular structures rely on choice and contingency.[37]

Algeria's trajectory is described and analyzed in four chapters, through a combination of primary research and secondary literature. The causal variables are identified and, when appropriate, changes to them are traced. Because of the importance of path dependencies in my argumentation, process tracing is carried out through a historical narrative that is punctuated by a focus on "critical junctures:" foundational moments, or turning points, in the political–economic development of the state, when choices of great consequence regarding institutional arrangements are presented to the leadership.[38] The choices made set the country along a particular trajectory (Collier *et al.* 1991).

As noted above, the inception of oil-based development and the occurrence of (exogenous) economic shocks constitute the critical junctures in the trajectory of the oil-exporting state and for its political stability. In Algeria, oil-based development began in the mid- to late 1960s; it began in

---

[36] These variables relate to the conditions, noted above (pp. 10–11), that favor political instability.

[37] See Mahoney and Snyder (1999: 13–17) on combining structural and agential factors in the study of regime change: their "funnel strategy" proceeds from the macro-political level, eventually "funneling downward" to the micro-political. Akin to the methodology I employ, it demonstrates that the combination of structural, institutional, and agential factors provides the greatest explanatory power for political outcomes.

[38] See Bennett and Elman (2006: 250–67); Capoccia and Kelemen (2005); Goldstone (2003: 47–50); Pierson (2003: 195–7); Thelen (2003: 217–21).

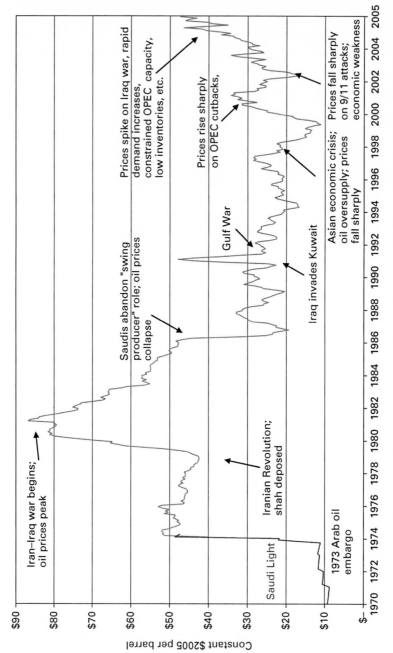

Figure 1.1 Major events and real world oil prices, 1970–2005 (prices adjusted by CPI for all urban consumers, 2005)
Source: EIA

the mid-1950s in Saudi Arabia, the late 1950s/early 1960s in Iran and Iraq, and the late 1960s in Indonesia. The shocks which these countries were exposed to include the oil price booms of 1973 and 1979/80, the downturn of 1976/7, and the bust of 1986. For Indonesia, the Asian financial crisis in the 1990s was another – and the most debilitating – economic shock[39] (figure 1.1).

Critical junctures are analyzed with three goals in mind: first, to understand what the stakes and circumstances were at that moment of leadership challenge; second, to learn how leaders responded; and third, to elucidate the longer-term impact on outcomes of the choices made. In this way, key features of institutional development are brought to the fore, as are the preferences of leaders and social forces.[40] To wit, the process tracing method helps me link constraints created during critical junctures to the resolution of later social conflicts, and to future outcomes.

Structure of the study

The book is organized thus: I begin, in chapter 2, by examining the theories that underpin this research agenda. First, I explore the literature on the impact of natural resource wealth on economic and political development. Second, I explore literature on regime breakdown and the onset of violence within states. I end this discussion by considering the linkages between natural resource abundance and political instability.

Next, I begin the study of Algeria. I explore its trajectory from the colonial period through the civil war in four chapters: chapter 3 addresses the period up to independence in 1962; chapter 4 discusses political–economic developments during the Ben Bella and Boumedienne regimes; chapter 5 focuses on the Benjedid era and the lead-up to civil war; chapter 6 explores the strategies employed by the regime in the 1990s in an effort to re-conquer power.

Following that, I move on to the comparators. I compare them to Algeria in chapter 7 in terms of the three variables that define this study: institutional development and its relationship to oil, the incorporation of competing cleavage structures, and the decisions of leaders at two critical junctures. I conclude in chapter 8 with a summary discussion of Algeria's trajectory. I reflect on what that country's experience teaches us about the stability of resource-rich patrimonial systems, the

---

[39] No doubt post-Gulf War sanctions represented an additional shock for Iraq.
[40] A variant of this research design was first enunciated in Lowi (2000); it appeared in published form in Lowi (2004).

contingency of oil, and the integrated roles of structures and actor choice in political outcomes. I then proceed to an exposition on the variation in outcomes in oil-exporting states, and the significance of the comparisons regarding the capacities of states to remain stable in the face of economic shocks. Finally, I address some of the alternate explanations for outcomes.

2   Natural resources and political instability

Natural resources and the political economy of development

With the division of the international economic order into exporters of manufactured goods and exporters of primary products, the former have been associated historically with relatively high growth and development, while the latter have been associated with relatively slow growth and skewed, if not under-development (Lewis 1977). If one considers natural resource availability alone, one finds that resource-deficient countries have fared far better than their resource-abundant counterparts in terms of income distribution and gross national product (GNP) growth. Between 1960 and 1990, for example, the per capita incomes of resource-deficient countries increased 2–3 times faster than those of resource-rich countries, and the gap in growth rates widened significantly from the 1970s (Auty and Mikesell 1998; Sachs and Warner 1995). Indeed, quantitative research has confirmed that there is a negative relationship between natural resources and economic growth. Of the resource-rich, the mineral-driven countries have been among the weakest performers. Furthermore, the resource-rich countries as a whole tend to be more prone to policy failures which, in turn, provoke growth collapses.

Given that capital scarcity – conventionally thought of as the source of economic backwardness – is not a significant factor in economies driven by high-value resources such as petroleum, how can we explain the relatively disappointing performance of this category of states? Development economists and political economists have offered a variety of explanations for this so-called "resource curse": the idea that natural resource wealth – especially hard-rock minerals and hydrocarbons (petroleum and natural gas) – functions as a constraint, rather than an asset, for development (Auty 1993; Ross 1999).

There are economic, political, and sociological explanations for the unsatisfactory performance of resource-rich countries. Explanations focus upon external or internal factors. External factors have to do with the impact on the domestic economy of international economic forces and a country's position in the international economy, while internal factors concern domestic structural and institutional features, and the impact of oil (rents) on them. Within the category that highlights external factors, there are two prominent explanations. First, Dutch Disease, which tends to afflict economies with booming resource sectors, weakens the competitiveness of non-booming tradable sectors.[1] Second, primary products are subject to greater price volatility in the international market than are manufactured goods. In the absence of export diversification, price volatility can provoke growth collapses (Auty 1998). As for the category of explanations that focuses on internal factors, the most prominent underscore the importance of either factor endowments or the relative mismanagement of rents in influencing performance outcomes.[2]

Alongside the research on economic performance has been a growing interest in political outcomes in resource-abundant states. Recent quantitative work on political violence, for example, has demonstrated a positive relationship between natural resource wealth, or the degree of dependence of government revenues on the export of a single resource, and domestic conflict (Collier and Hoeffler 2004; de Soysa 2000; Fearon and Laitin 2003; Greif et al. 2002; Ross 2006).[3] A related set of quantitative studies investigates the tendency of resource-abundant states to have authoritarian, or non-democratic governments (Wantchekon 2002; Ross 2001). In general, much of this literature suggests that political instability – in the form of civil unrest – is more prevalent in environments characterized by resource abundance, especially of the mineral variety, than those characterized by resource

---

[1] A booming economic sector is one that, in contrast to a lagging sector, experiences positive growth.

[2] For Adam Smith (1776), rent is unearned income or profits "reaped by those who did not sow." According to Amuzegar (1982: 817 fn. 3), economic rent is "a special, and fiscally speaking unearned, reward to the least-cost producers of a commodity in temporary short supply. Thus, due to the relatively low costs of extracting a barrel of crude in some oil-rich countries compared to the expenses of oil extraction elsewhere (or the costs of alternative sources of energy), the low-cost producers are able to anticipate and reap "windfall" profits from the sale of their oil." In the case of natural resources, therefore, economic rent is represented by the gap that exists between the value of the resource and the cost of extracting it. See, as well, Eifert et al. (2003).

[3] For variations on the type of resource and its connection to conflict see Le Billon (2001), Ross (2004, 2003), Snyder (2006a). For examination of the mechanisms that could link resources to conflict see Fearon (2005), Humphreys (2005).

scarcity.[4] Why this may be so remains to be explained. Given that most of the quantitative studies in this area are less concerned with explaining political outcomes and more concerned with elucidating the propensity for conflict in different kinds of political orders, what they offer in the way of explanation remains suggestive.[5]

For example, Greif *et al.* (2002) propose that "governments less constrained by financial imperatives feel less constrained as well in their treatment of citizen tax payers, and citizens, once free of their contract with their rulers, revert to predation and conflict." Auty (1997) suggests that since resource-rich countries have a greater tolerance for conflicts over rents than do resource-poor countries – insofar as "rents ... offer a natural magnet for political competition" (Auty and Gelb 2000: 7) – this fosters the emergence of factional states that promote sectional interests. Building upon that thesis, Auty and Gelb (2000) submit that resource abundance is more closely associated with predatory than with benevolent/developmental states, and the former are more closely associated with political instability than are the latter. Collier and Hoeffler (2001) suggest, rather, that it is the opportunities for natural resource predation that provoke conflict in resource-rich environments.[6]

In fact, efforts to explain political outcomes in resource-abundant countries are surprisingly few.[7] Until recently, those that existed tended to piggy-back onto explanations for economic outcomes: in short, unsatisfactory economic performance has negative political consequences.[8] Others, that relied upon sector-based analysis (Karl 1997; Shafer 1994) or the rentier state framework (Yates 1996) and ventured explicitly into explanations for political instability, ran into problems tracing causal relationships.[9]

In this chapter, I first outline the various economic and political explanations for outcomes in resource-abundant states. Second, I explore the literature on the causes of political instability and regime breakdown.

---

[4] This does not negate the finding of the project directed by Thomas Homer-Dixon (1991–3) that identifies resource scarcity (and the inequitable distribution of the scarce resource) as one of several factors in inter- and intra-state conflict.

[5] However, see Dunning (2005) for a game-theoretic analysis of leadership decisions to encourage economic diversification in resource-dependent countries and the relationship to political stability.

[6] For qualifications to that thesis see *inter alia* Snyder (2006a).

[7] However, see Dunning (2008), Englebert and Ron (2004), Lowi (2004), Okruhlik (1999), Smith (2007).

[8] To be sure, the notion that fiscal crisis, for example, encourages political instability and possibly regime change is standard in comparative politics. See *inter alia* O'Donnell (1973), Kurth (1979), Haggard and Kaufman (1995), Gasiorowski (1995).

[9] See below, pp. 36–7.

Finally, I offer my own thesis regarding the linkages between natural resource wealth and (in)stability, with, again, special reference to oil exporters. I reiterate the central argument of this study: that it is not oil wealth that determines political outcomes, but rather the combination of local factors and the decisions of leaders. The discussion in this chapter provides an important backdrop for the study of Algeria that follows.

Economic explanations for outcomes

Most of the studies by (neoclassical) economists defend the "resource curse" hypothesis by locating the explanation for the relatively poor performance of oil exporters in the peculiarities of booming sectors in general, and the Dutch Disease syndrome in particular. First used to describe the Netherlands' experience with large inflows of North Sea gas export revenues in the 1970s, Dutch Disease refers to two effects that tend to follow resource booms: the first is the appreciation of the real exchange rate, because of the sharp rise in exports; the second is the tendency of a booming resource sector to draw capital and labor away from manufacturing and agricultural sectors, thus squeezing production in those sectors by raising their production costs. Together, these effects provoke a decline in the export of agricultural and manufactured goods, and an increase in both imported items and the production (and cost) of non-tradables – such as physical infrastructure and social capital.

There has been considerable debate about the applicability of Dutch Disease to the experiences of oil-exporting countries. Some scholars maintain that its relevance is limited to full-employment economies, such as the Netherlands and Norway (Karshenas 1994; Amuzegar 1999: 191), while others claim that its most consistent finding is the decline of agriculture in a highly diverse set of oil-exporting LDCs (Chaudhry 1997: 186). Still others insist that the condition described by the term Dutch Disease is neither evidence of a "resource curse," nor particularly unhealthy: the shift in capital and labor toward booming sectors simply implies a change in a country's comparative advantage (Davis 1995). That being said, the Dutch Disease argument is instructive insofar as it elucidates the emergence in the economy of a structural bias against diversification. Nonetheless, the uniform outcomes it suggests contrast sharply with the considerable variation in strategies and in performance found in high-absorption oil-exporting LDCs.[10]

---

[10] See below, fn. 12.

Recent studies have shown that governments can offset the impact of Dutch Disease, if they so desire. They can save the temporary windfalls or invest them outside the country, as Kuwait, Norway, and Venezuela have done, and in so doing sterilize their short-term effects on the macro-economy (Gelb et al. 1988; Neary and van Wijnbergen 1986: 10–11).[11] They may, as well, offset the pressures against investment in the tradable sectors either by initiating industrialization programs, as did Algeria, Indonesia, Iraq, and pre-revolutionary Iran, or by targetting rural development, as did Indonesia and, initially, the Islamic Republic of Iran. For the low-absorption, low-population oil exporters such as Libya and the Gulf states, however, the application of the Dutch Disease hypothesis is even more tenuous, given that there exists no significant non-oil economy to develop.[12]

Indeed, Dutch Disease is not inevitable. As long as national governments implement policies to rein in private consumption and investment expenditures, and adopt productive investment programs in the non-oil tradable sectors, its effects can be minimized, if not averted (Gelb 1986: 57; Sachs 2007: 181–6). A country's economic performance in the aftermath of a resource boom/external price shock is influenced, to a significant degree, by the policies followed by its government (Neary and van Wijnbergen 1986: 10–11).

Consider the case of Indonesia, for example. In 1978 and then again in 1983, following boom periods, the government devalued the rupiah. The aim was precisely to prevent exchange rate appreciation that would discourage non-oil exports. To be sure, the devaluations boosted the non-oil tradable sector significantly: manufactured exports increased by 260 percent after the first large devaluation (Gelb et al. 1988: 221). Several Indonesia scholars insist, however, that the turn to prudent economic policies followed from the near financial hemorrhage and colossal embarrassment created by the Pertamina crisis of 1976 – in which the state oil company had accrued debts of more

---

[11] For further detail see Davis et al. 2001. For an insightful examination of how to enhance the overall effects of resource funds see Humphreys and Sandbu 2007.

[12] The low-absorption/low-population oil exporters are countries such as Kuwait, Libya, and Saudi Arabia, which have very large reserves of petroleum relative to population size. As a result of this favorable relationship, they tend to have balance of payments surpluses and very high per capita GNPs. In contrast, the high-absorption/high-population oil exporters are countries as diverse as Nigeria, Iran, Gabon, Algeria, Mexico, Venezuela, Ecuador, and Indonesia, where the relationship between population size and oil reserves is relatively unfavorable. Compared with the low-absorption states, they are capital deficient and have low per capita GNPs. Nonetheless, their opportunities for non-oil economic activity are far superior while, because of their relatively inferior reserves per capita, the need to diversify their economies away from oil is far more urgent.

than $10.5 billion that it could not pay back (Bresnan 1993: 164–8). Whatever the impetus for the policy of restraint, the Indonesian experience highlights the importance of local factors and the decisions of political leaders. Indeed, natural resource wealth does not, in and of itself, determine outcomes.

If there are mechanisms whereby resource-abundant states can mitigate the effects of Dutch Disease, what can they do to cushion their economies from the potentially catastrophic effects of price volatility and the general decline in the terms of trade for primary products, which, for mineral exports, are among the most volatile (Auty 1993; Gelb 1986: 55)?[13] Here, policy prescriptions stress the need for states to reduce their dependence on natural resource exports by diversifying their mono-economies, abolish protectionist policies,[14] and promote more open trade. In this way, they avoid the risk of growth collapse (Auty 1998: 11–12; Sachs and Warner 1995).[15]

In many oil-exporting states, foreign borrowing has often been the preferred remedy for the slackening of growth; it has also been encouraged by (foreign) banks, recognizing in high-valued natural resources "obvious collateral." Nonetheless, foreign borrowing has proven to be a temporary palliative: when easy access to credit combines with boom-driven and often inefficient government spending, excessive indebtedness results. As we will see most vividly in the case of Algeria, continued borrowing merely postpones the problem of adjustment and eventually intensifies the growth collapse (Auty 1998: 35).

Among the economic explanations for performance outcomes that focus on internal factors, the factor endowments argument is, perhaps, the most straightforward.[16] It suggests the following: the richer a

---

[13] Recent research sheds doubt on the (traditional) terms of trade argument as it relates to natural resources. See, for example, Cashin and McDermott (2002). I am grateful to Ellis Goldberg for bringing this to my attention.

[14] Recall the so-called "Prebisch hypothesis," associated with Raul Prebisch and Hans Singer in the 1940s and 1950s, and later championed by the United Nations Economic Commission in Latin America. It advocated state-led import-substitution industrialization to counter dependency on natural resource exports. The received wisdom is that this strategy foundered virtually everywhere it was attempted (Sachs and Warner, 1995: 4–5). For a compelling dissenter's view, see Rodrik (1999b: 68–77).

[15] However, Dunning (2005) makes the interesting observation that while diversification may be important for the economic health of resource-dependent countries, it can be politically destabilizing for those in power. He suggests that in some cases – such as Zaire under Mobutu – incumbents resist diversifying their economies, or they choose to de-diversify, precisely to protect their incumbency.

[16] For a thoughtful variant that stresses the importance of local endowments – for example, the size of the market, transportation costs, location relative to major markets, etc. – for development outcomes, see Goldberg et al. (2008). They point out that Saudi Arabia

country's "package" of factor endowments, the more "balanced" its growth and development are likely to be. It should be expected, therefore, that oil-exporting states such as Algeria and Venezuela – with relatively small populations (30–35 million), few natural resources, little arable land (roughly 3 percent), and proximity to world-class manufacturing regions with which they must compete – would have relatively poorly diversified economies. Indonesia, Nigeria, and to a somewhat lesser extent Mexico, with very large populations (close to, or greater than 100 million), rich soils (arable land constitutes 17 percent, 37 percent, and 13 percent of total land area respectively), and abundant natural resources, would have the most diversified economies. And countries like Iran, with moderate-size populations (70 million), some arable land (8 percent), lots of minerals, and some degree of isolation from other major manufacturers, would lie somewhere in the middle.

While economic performance in several of the oil-exporting states does meet the predictions of the factor endowments approach, the latter cannot account for outcomes in "deviant cases," such as Nigeria and post-revolutionary Iran. Until recently, Nigeria's political leadership has consistently failed to diversify the economy away from its overdependence on the capital-intensive oil sector, which provides 20 percent of GDP, 95 percent of foreign exchange earnings, and about 65 percent of budgetary revenues. Furthermore, the largely subsistence agricultural sector has failed to keep up with rapid population growth – Nigeria is Africa's most populous country – and the country, once a net exporter of food, has been importing food for several decades (Lewis 2007). As for the Islamic Republic of Iran, the mullahs in power paid relatively close attention to economic diversification in the initial years, at least insofar as the rural sector and agricultural development were concerned (Behdad 1996: 99–111).

Moreover, the factor endowments argument cannot clarify variations within each of the three categories of oil-exporting states. For one, direct government misallocations go a long way to explaining economic growth differences between countries with similar endowments, as do other contextual features. In sum, the factor endowments argument, as with Dutch Disease, fails to capture, or even consider, political and institutional processes that may shape behavior and outcomes. Indeed,

and Alaska have experienced high per capita incomes but low growth because they have a small domestic market and therefore few spillovers from oil wealth into other forms of economic activity. In contrast, Iran today and California in 1900–40 (the period of the gold and oil booms) have/had a large and growing internal market, such that Iran is suggesting that it may cease to export oil altogether within a generation, and California experienced increased industrialization and continued economic growth as a result of spillovers.

the limitations of economistic approaches underscore the importance of institutions and government policy – or leadership choice – in economic performance (Lowi 1997; Rodrik 2003).

Political explanations for outcomes

In contrast, political explanations for outcomes in resource-abundant states often engage a statist or institutionalist perspective. The most prominent are situated within the rentier state framework that was first employed to discuss the case of Iran under the Shah (Mahdavy 1970; Beblawi and Luciani 1987). The framework posits that when governments gain most of their revenues from external sources, such as resource rents or foreign assistance, they are freed from the need to levy taxes. As a result, states become less accountable to the societies they govern, and more autonomous in their decision-making and behavior. Moreover, awash with capital, their principal activity is distribution and not the promotion of productive activities, while the availability of rents diverts attention away from wealth-creating activities and into rent-seeking activities.[17] The state tends to become highly interventionist, while the political legitimacy of ruling elites rests upon the uninterrupted distribution of rents.

These characteristics have, according to the proponents of the framework, several effects on domestic economic and political life (Beblawi 1987; Boone 1990; Chaudhry 1994; Shambayati 1994; Yates 1996). First, because such states have a weakly developed extractive capacity, they lack the information they need to formulate sound development strategies. Second, being increasingly autonomous from society, they are ignorant of and insouciant to the preferences of their populations.[18] Third, since these are "allocation" and not "production" states, the state sector grows in size and importance – often becoming bureaucratically weak and highly inefficient. Neither human capital development nor entrepreneurship is encouraged, and "rent-seeking," often in alliance with the state, is key to social mobility. The availability of rents provides

---

[17] Rent reorients economic incentives toward competition for access to oil revenues and away from productive activities, especially in nontransparent environments characterized by uncertain property rights and weak rule of law. Private individuals, politicians, and corporations have strong incentives to exploit opportunities for capturing these rents – often by manipulating political mechanisms of various sorts.

[18] These seven effects reflect the conventional wisdom regarding the rentier state (Moore 2004: 306–8); they do not apply to all resource-rich states without variation. For example, several of the Gulf statelets, plus Saudi Arabia, have become increasingly attentive to social preferences (see above, chapter 1, fn. 12), while Indonesia during the 1970s boom years maintained an extractive capacity of note. See below, chapter 7.

an incentive for individuals and social groups to compete for proximity to state power, or to try to capture government policy to maximize their respective shares. Fourth, because resource-rich states use indirect redistribution to allocate rents, those rents become a key mechanism for promoting and consolidating state power, and purchasing loyalty. In this way, they tend to impede the formation of independent social groups that could make demands upon the state. Misallocations are, indeed, common. Fifth, unpredictable resource windfalls adversely impact macro-economic management because of relative price changes and fiscal distortions.[19] Sixth, windfalls – akin to manna from heaven – in the hands of heavily centralized governments function as a built-in impediment to reform, for they encourage the perception of overwhelming abundance and well-being. Seventh, both the centralization of government and the absence of effective regulatory structures nourish patrimonialism and corruption, which have a negative impact on the rule of law and the transparency of rent distribution.

Surely, several of the characteristics and effects noted above and attributed to "rentier states" are common to many post-colonial regimes. For one, low regulatory penetration and bloated bureaucracies are features of various developing country administrations. Moreover, the fragmentation of civil society is commonplace in African countries, but can be found, as well, in Latin America, the Middle East, and Asia (*inter alia* Rotberg 2004; Widner 1994; Zartman 1995).

Beyond its general observations about states that are heavily dependent upon external rents and despite efforts to trace causal relationships, the rentier state framework has been stretched to explicate contradictory trajectories and outcomes. Oil rents have been pointed to as the cause of political quiescence (Crystal 1990), but also the rise of opposition (Okruhlik 1999); political instability (Karl 1997), but also stability (Hertog 2006); the turn to democratization (Levine 1978), but also the persistence of authoritarianism (Crystal 1990; Vandewalle 1998).[20] Indeed, one of the few phenomena for which oil rents are, unequivocally, the proximate cause is the enhancement of state autonomy during

---

[19] For a lucid discussion of the sources of and problems with the volatility of income see Humphreys, Sachs, and Stiglitz (2007: 6–8).

[20] With regard to the contradictory linkages between oil and democratization on the one hand, and oil and authoritarianism on the other, note that of all oil-exporting LDCs between 1945 and 1975, only Venezuela became more democratic; the others either became less democratic, or did not change much at all. Indeed, several Latin Americanists have argued that Venezuela's democratic experiment derives from its oil revenues, which financed the organization of middle- and working-class groups (Philip 1994: 147; Auty and Gelb 2000: 1).

pre-boom and boom years. This has been demonstrated in empirical studies of an array of oil-exporting LDCs.[21] While Auty and Gelb (2000) are indeed correct in saying that given the marked differences in contexts, the fact that resource endowments have contradictory effects is not in the least bit surprising, this does beg the question of the utility of unidimensional forays into causality.

Jill Crystal, in her work on Kuwait and Qatar (1990) – two low-absorption, low-population oil-exporting states – shows how oil rents were instrumental in weakening the links between state and society, increasing the power of the state, and de-politicizing society. Employing a classic rentier state framework for what are "pure distributive states," Crystal demonstrates quite convincingly that the distribution of oil rents in these desert statelets purchased quiescence, and promoted clientelism and the persistence of authoritarianism.

Terry Karl (1997) seeks to explain why the oil booms of 1973–4 and 1978–9 led to economic stagnation and political turmoil in many oil-exporting states. Following on the heels of Michael Shafer (1994), she suggests that the characteristics of a country's leading export sector influence the state's capacity to promote economic development, and that resource abundance tends to weaken state institutions. She claims that oil booms are destabilizing, and argues that the greater the increase in government spending immediately after the rise in prices, the greater the degree of instability. While her claims with regard to the effects of oil windfalls on state behavior and state capacity are well illustrated by her account of Venezuelan oil politics and echo insights of the rentier state framework, her claim that oil booms *per se* produce instability does not stand up. Not only does she fail to explain the causal relationship between the increase in government spending in the aftermath of a price shock and political instability, but Karl provides no compelling evidence that the instability experienced in Algeria, Iran, Nigeria, and Venezuela between 1974 and 1992 derived from the boom, rather than from some other phenomenon or set of phenomena.[22]

---

[21] See, for example, Crystal (1990), Chaudhry (1997), Karl (1997), Katouzian (1981), Robison (1986), Watts (1987).

[22] Besides, as Ross (1999: 318) rightly points out, it is not terribly surprising that, given what we know about historical experience and political development, these four states would undergo some degree of instability during any eighteen-year period in the latter half of the twentieth century. Algeria had only recently emerged from eight years of war for its independence, following 130 years of colonial rule; Iran had undergone an acute leadership crisis in the 1950s and persistent, yet strongly opposed, foreign intervention during much of the century, prior to the 1979 revolution; Nigeria had been wracked by ethnicized politics, plus a secessionist war, since its independence in 1960; and Venezuela was trying

Sectoral arguments of the sort presented by the rentier state and resource curse literatures do contribute to our understanding of economic performance and political outcomes, and provide an important backdrop for the study of development in oil exporters. However, several of the earlier contributions to the literature fell short in explaining outcomes insofar as they implicitly assigned far too much weight to oil rents, and insufficient weight to such things as historical legacies, institutional foundations, the choices of leaders, or even cultural peculiarities. The implied suggestion was that oil-exporting states evolve as they do because of oil, and not because of "predatory" governance, brittle institutions, inappropriate policies, or something altogether unrelated to oil.

Still other contributions from the "first wave" of research on the rentier state maintained that oil revenues spawned a set of effects, but as with Karl's (1997) work, failed to prove that those effects issued from oil, and neither preceded it nor issued from something else.[23] Indeed, the words of caution from Juan Linz (2000: 154) regarding resource-rich "sultanistic" states ring true: "it would be a mistake to consider such regimes as the inevitable result of the economic structure, ignoring many other factors contributing to their emergence and stability."

In effect, without factoring agency, cultural peculiarities, and historical legacies more systematically into their analyses, earlier studies of the resource curse could not account for some of the very interesting variations among oil exporters in terms of both strategies and performance, nor could they provide compelling explanations for political outcomes. As Kiren Chaudhry rightly points out: "oil exporters vary not only in their levels of dependence on oil revenues, but also in the mix of endowments and historical legacies that condition policy and political outcomes" (1997: 188).

More recently, the acknowledged variation in outcomes in natural resource exporters along a range of dimensions has spawned

---

desperately to maintain a highly controlled and very fragile democratic arrangement while legacies of authoritarian rule, administrative inefficiency, and foreign company involvement remained prominent.

[23] Herb (2005) introduces an important corrective: "Rentier states tend to be located in regions ... where states, rentier or not, typically suffer from generally unsatisfactory political outcomes." He argues that region has a stronger negative effect on democracy than does the degree of "rentierism" – the proportion of rent-derived income in government finances, combined with the tendency for distribution to take precedence over production as the principal task of the state. As he points out, the squandering or misallocation of oil wealth in many rentier states is not necessarily due to the fact that the wealth is from oil. Had the wealth come from another source, it may well have been squandered or misallocated as well, and political development may not have been impressive either.

"conditional theories" of the resource curse. Contributions from the "second wave" have been attentive to the impact of pre-existing institutions on outcomes (Chaudhry 1997; Jones Luong and Weinthal 2001; Smith 2007), for example, and other contextual features (Dunning 2008; Englebert *et al.* 2004; Le Billon 2005), suggesting that institutional quality mediates the relationship between mineral wealth and outcomes. Nonetheless, apart from a few rare examples (see Vandewalle 1998; Dunning 2005), the quality of governance and the nature of leadership choice have remained relatively understudied.[24]

There has been, of late, a flurry of research on the resource curse, focussing on such topics as the relationship between natural resource wealth and civil war (Collier and Hoeffler 2001; Humphreys 2005; Ross 2006), resource wealth and democracy, resource wealth and regime durability. Quantitative studies of political development, linking authoritarian tendencies or the failure to democratize to oil, indicate statistically robust relationships (Ross 2001; Wantchekon 2002; Herb 2005).[25] Causal mechanisms to explicate the relationships have been suggested, but the more detailed empirical analysis remains to be done.

Other quantitative studies demonstrate that oil-exporting states are not particularly prone to instability and failure (Boix 2003), despite suggestions from the "first wave" of rentier state literature and more recent scholarship on civil war (Fearon and Laitin 2003).[26] Smith (2004) highlights a trend of regime durability, despite the volatility of the revenue base, and suggests that statecraft in the form of strong institutions is key. His statecraft hypothesis echoes the findings in Lowi (2000, 2004), who, via a qualitative study of a single case, places the explanation for outcomes within the framework of the creation of the modern nation-state and the institutional foundations that inhere.

Smith (2007) builds upon this framework and argues that the persistence or breakdown of regimes depends on the timing of access to oil rents relative to "late development." Documenting the experiences of Iran and Indonesia through the end of the 1970s, he suggests that the availability of (oil) rents and the existence of an organized opposition at the inception of

---

[24] This is the case not only in studies of oil-exporting states, but also within the discipline of political science more generally and comparative political economy in particular. For the importance of leadership as a variable in explaining outcomes within states, see Stepan (1978: 110–37) and Samuels (2003), and between states, see Byman and Pollack (2001: 107–46).

[25] For a dissenting view, from quantitative analysis, see Haber and Menaldo (2007).

[26] In my study of Algeria (Lowi 2005), I find only an indirect link between oil wealth and civil war.

late development impact institutional arrangements, hence political outcomes. Similarly, Karl (2007: 273) indicates that the relative success of Norway with the resource curse demonstrates that "the problem of managing oil wealth is essentially a problem of historical sequence: good institutions must be in place prior to the exploitation of oil."

While I, too, am sensitive to the exigencies of time – hence my focus on decisions at critical junctures – I note that neither statecraft nor "good institutions" are accidents of history. Rather, they are functions of the careful marrying of the skill of human agents – Machiavelli's *virtu* – with the structure, context, or circumstance – *fortuna* – that agents find themselves in. To be sure, the very creation of an institution, with its own set of opportunities and constraints, is itself an act of agency (Hargrove 2004: 582). Of course structures and institutions matter in explaining political outcomes, but they, and the context of which they are a part, do change, and they must be considered alongside and in conjunction with agency.[27] This is the case because agents, leaders, human individuals, as opposed to unmediated social forces, are the actual movers of history.

Having said that, we need to encourage this new crop of qualitative studies that combines structural and institutional variables, and refine them with the explicit addition of agential variables. In this way, we may gain a keener appreciation of the interesting variations among oil exporters in terms of strategies, performance, and outcomes: variations that derive largely from the peculiarities of time, context, and leadership choice.

Finally, structural-Marxists argue that it is the structure of international capital markets and the integration of the oil-exporting state in those markets that determine political outcomes. In this view, politics follows markets. In his analysis of the crisis in Indonesia in 1998–9, Richard Robison (1999) argues that the groundwork for regime breakdown and change lay in the mid-1980s, when there was a major shift in global capital markets in response to global recession.[28] International liquidity dried up and capital-importing countries were dealt a hard blow. With the fall in the international price of oil and the drying up of

---

[27] With respect to the centrality of context in the explanation for outcomes, the cautionary note in Engelbert and Ron (2004) is instructive: "No matter how tempting natural resources might be and how they may exacerbate ongoing instability and armed conflict, they are unlikely to stimulate civil war on their own unless the political context is already unstable." Under certain conditions, oil provides incentives for civil war, while under different conditions, but in the same country, it supports the consolidation of state power.

[28] "Why Indonesia is Unraveling in the Wake of the Asian Crisis," Comparative Politics Seminar, Department of Politics/Woodrow Wilson School, Princeton University, February 25, 1999.

concessional loans, the Indonesian state was forced, for the first time, to borrow private capital with short time horizons. When loan payments became due in the 1990s – coinciding with the downward spiraling of the rupiah – the domestic economy unraveled. With economic collapse came political instability.

A similar argument can be made for Algeria, with one caveat: that its interaction with international capital markets had, since independence, consisted primarily of short- to medium-term loans from international banks (Corm 1993: 23). Problems emerged in Algeria in the early 1980s when the price of oil began to fall and debt repayments fell due. They intensified with the more dramatic price downturn in 1986 and the absence of new sources of borrowing. Thus, it was a fiscal crisis, prompted by international structural change, that, in the cases of Indonesia and Algeria, provoked instability.

This is a compelling argument insofar as it highlights the deeply vulnerable condition of (single-)export economies and the profound impact of international structural change on domestic policy, institutions, and outcomes.[29] However, as with dependency theory, to which it is related, the argument plays down the significance of domestic-structural and agential factors in shaping outcomes. For an exogenous shock to provoke a domestic crisis, conditions must be in place internally. Hence, internal conditions, including the choices of key actors, need to be elucidated.[30]

To be sure, actors choose from among alternative possible responses to the set of conditions they face: conditions that, themselves, provide a structure and impose constraints. In responding as they do, actors contribute to fashioning the outcome that eventually results. Choosing a different response to the same set of conditions could provoke an altogether different outcome.

Furthermore, by disregarding domestic-structural, institutional, and agential factors in the explanation for outcomes, the possibility that states could implement policies of adjustment in the face of adversity is implicitly denied. There is, indeed, no room for choice in this framework. Thus, an international-structuralist analysis offers no more than a partial explanation for political instability in oil exporters.

---

[29] Recall that crude oil prices increased more than fifteen times between 1973 and 1980, and fell by close to 80 percent between 1981 and 1986. Prices increased more than 400 percent between 1987 and 1990, and fell around 50 percent between 1991 and 1994 (Amuzegar 1999).

[30] Fn. 27 above. For example, in the mid to late 1980s, the Algerian state refused, because of national pride, to reschedule its foreign debt. It preferred to cut down on food imports, creating shortages of various essential items.

Sources of instability and regime breakdown

In the 1950s and 1960s, the experiences of an array of new states plainly revealed that the tasks of state- and nation-building on the heels of, at times, protracted and brutal anti-colonial struggle posed enormous challenges. In a classic article, Clifford Geertz described the nature of the challenges thus: now organized into states, nationalist movements had to "define and stabilize their relationships both to other states and to the irregular societies out of which they arose" (1973: 238). Indeed, the post-independence trajectories of new states have depended, in large measure, on the internal relationships among state authorities, national elites, and popular groups.

During the heady initial years of independence and state-building, widespread violence often accompanied the rapid changes that these societies were undergoing. Revolutions, coups, riots, and civil wars erupted across the developing world. Trying to explain the instability and violence became something of a cottage industry in academia. Initially, scholars rested their analyses upon broad single factors. They focussed primarily on the opposition to the state – its motivations and behavior – and downplayed the role of state institutions (*inter alia* Gurr 1970; Galtung 1964; Huntington 1968; Tilly 1978).

To "bring the state back in" to analyses of the conditions that provoke instability, violence, and regime breakdown, Theda Skocpol (1979) explored structural relationships. In developing her theory of revolution, she insisted that particular structural features of states, in conjunction with international pressures, precipitated regime breakdown. However, she, and her cohorts (Paige 1975; Eisenstadt 1978; Trimberger 1978), ignored agency-related variables in their analyses. They considered such things as leadership, ideology, and culture[31] as either inconsequential or driven by – indeed derivative of – prevailing structural conditions (Goldstone 2001: 42; Mahoney and Snyder 1999: 6).

For Goldstone (1991), three conjunctural conditions lead to instability and ultimately, regime breakdown. First, the state loses its legitimacy vis-à-vis society; it has failed, for a variety of reasons, to accomplish the major tasks it has set for itself and promised to society.[32]

---

[31] Although related to agency, culture – as a system of knowledge, values, and practices – is grounded in structure. Indeed, it should be thought of as a type of (social) structure insofar as it tends to remain stable over time and imposes constraints. However, culture, like structure, also allows for change: it can be adapted and transformed (Hays 1994: 57, 72).

[32] The legitimacy of the state may also be undermined by defeat in war or particularly repressive rule, but also by its "squandering or neglect of cultural resources"

More often than not, a fiscal crisis lies at the core of this condition and is the very first step in the collapse of the state.[33] Second, because elites and popular groups deny the legitimacy of the state, they withdraw their support. Third, elites have the resources to mobilize support for change among disaffected popular groups which are, themselves, prepared to take action. In conjunction, these factors challenge the regime. Whether or not they provoke breakdown, however, hinges squarely upon resilience: how the leadership responds to the challenges it faces.

Those states that are prone to political crisis in the form of popular mobilization in opposition to the regime are typically "closed or exclusionary, organizationally weak (or suddenly weakened), and repressive authoritarian regimes" (Goodwin and Skocpol 1989: 495–8). Within the category of authoritarian regimes, those that have patrimonial structures are often singled out for their vulnerability to instability and breakdown (Weber 1968: 231–2; Eisenstadt 1978; Bratton and van de Walle 1997: 61–96). And as the literature on democratic transitions has demonstrated (Geddes 1999; Haggard and Kaufman 1995), authoritarian regimes are more prone to breakdown during economic crises.[34] This is, not surprisingly, because the social effects of economic crisis erode the regime's legitimacy, and domestic dissent in response to economic crisis could, under certain circumstances, be mobilized to bring down the regime. No doubt, growth collapses are invariably periods of high risk for domestic political stability (Hegre 2003). Indeed, the popular explosion in Algeria in 1988 and the Iraqi invasion of Kuwait in 1991 were both preceded by growth collapses, while regime breakdown in Iran in 1979 and in Indonesia in 1998 coincided with or followed on the heels of a growth collapse as well.[35]

A closer look at the unfolding of domestic political crises elucidates that not only structural factors – and certainly not regime characteristics alone – but also a variety of conditions related to institutional and

(Goldstone 2001: 12–14). Alternatively, the success or failure of a state relative to performance can be measured by its success or failure at supplying public goods: such things as security, freedom (to participate or be recognized), but also education, jobs, etc.

[33] In his study of revolutionary crises, Goldstone (1991) suggests that the roots and timing of "distributive shocks" have to do with institutional resilience, or its absence, in the face of the convergence of high population growth, state fiscal crisis, food shortages, and increasing prices. For the conditions under which rapid population growth is problematic see Goldstone (1999).

[34] Geddes (1999: 7) specifies her conclusion thus: "Single-party regimes ... tend to be brought down by exogenous events rather than internal splits....Personalist regimes are also relatively immune to internal splits, except when calamitous economic conditions disrupt the material underpinnings of regime loyalty."

[35] See below, chapter 5, pp. 112–15 and chapter 7. Another very colorful example of this phenomenon, from a resource-rich state that is not a major oil exporter, is that of Zaire. See Ndikumana and Emizet (2005: 63–87).

agential variables are linked, and in a variety of ways, to political instability, regime breakdown and change. As Goldstone (2001: 43) notes, the outcomes of regime crisis and civil unrest are profoundly affected by, if not partially dependent upon, decisions of "leaders, foreign powers, and popular forces, and of interactions among them."

Natural resource wealth and regime breakdown

Because of the singular importance of oil revenues in total government revenues, all oil-exporting states – no matter the regime type – are shaken when there are drastic and irremediable changes to revenue flows.[36] With the focus of government activities on distribution, unanticipated resource contraction can be thought of as a "distributive shock." Where distribution has been instrumental in camouflaging social cleavages and the inequalities that inhere, material changes brought on by "distributive shocks" bring latent social conflicts to the fore.[37] Without the resources to paper over inequities and deep divisions, there no longer exists an effective brake on civil unrest. The contraction of distribution frustrates expectations, exacerbates grievances and social conflicts, and increases the mobilization capacity of society against the state. It is in this sense that oil, although by no means the agent of political instability, may appear to be the instrument that, with its depletion and in the absence of judicious leadership decisions, unleashes instability.

However, neither economic crisis nor societal dissent in the face of economic crisis pre-determines outcomes. And despite the findings of the transitions literature and studies of patrimonial systems, oil-exporting states are not especially prone to regime breakdown during economic crises (Smith 2006). What impacts outcomes is precisely how leaders – and especially those leaders of weakened states – respond to economic challenges (van de Walle 2001).

The nature and degree of leadership resilience is key. Some authoritarian regimes manage economic crises in ways that mitigate dissent and stave off political unrest. Others fuel unrest by scorning social preferences, and eventually succumb to political upheaval. Still others respond initially in ways that exacerbate hardship, tease tensions, and fuel mobilization against the state. They may thereby lose their grip on power, only to reassert their hegemony after a period of

---

[36] On Norway see, for example, Listhaug (2005).

[37] I borrow the term "latent social conflict" from Rodrik (1999: 386). According to him, it indicates "the depth of preexisting social cleavages in a society, along the lines of wealth, ethnic identity, geographical region" but also class, language, or other divisions.

re-equilibration – during which they find ways to both extend political resources and remain in power – following the threat of regime break-down. Outcomes turn on leaders' decisions relative to the particular context – the "structured" environment composed of resources, institutions, social systems, and social forces – they find themselves in.[38]

As a rule of thumb and as we will see in the pages that follow, it is in the interest of political leaders to extend "political resources" in the face of economic crisis and the absence of material resources. By distributing scarce "public goods" – such things as (political) participation, (ethnic, cultural, ideological) recognition – and thus investing in institutions, leaders may promote stability.

Moving beyond the transitions literature, the recent failed state literature offers useful conceptual tools for understanding the variation in (in)stability in oil-exporting states in the wake of an economic shock (Esty *et al.* 1998; Rotberg 2003, 2004).[39] It privileges agential variables in its analysis, since state failure is about not responding to popular discontent or accommodating political challenges effectively. As noted in Rotberg (2003: 10): "(F)ailure is preventable, particularly since human agency rather than structural flaws or institutional insufficiencies are almost invariably at the root of slides from weakness (or strength) toward failure and collapse." Fateful decisions at critical junctures can either force states over the edge, or restore them to a level of equilibrium.

The failed state literature drives a wedge into analyses in which natural resource abundance determines outcomes. It, in conjunction with some of the more recent theorizing about regime breakdown, reinforces the significance of both context and leadership choice in explaining the variation in stability in the aftermath of an economic shock. And it is both context and leadership choice that inform the analytic framework of this study.

---

[38] See Mahoney and Snyder (1999) for an outline of three different types of integrative research strategies, synthesizing agency and structure, in empirical work on regime change. For an effort to combine agency and structure in the comparative study of revolutions in Iran, Nicaragua, and the Philippines, see Parsa (2000). He explores structures, but also collective actions by (and the interests and ideologies of) major actors.

[39] Rotberg (2003: 21–2) identifies three signals of impending breakdown: 1) rapid decline in income and living standards; 2) the regime withdraws and withholds political goods – freedoms, participation, recognition – while hoarding privileges for itself and those closest to it; 3) the level of violence increases.

Part II

Algeria and its discontents

3   From conquest to independence

The weakening of the state and the onset of civil violence in post-colonial settings must be understood within the framework of the creation of the modern state. The establishment of institutions that impose rules, resolve internal conflicts, distribute rights and resources, integrate disparate communities, and enunciate a policy direction and a shared sense of purpose remains the principal and most consequential challenge for the modern state. Where imperial domination prevailed, legacies remained that would color the state- and nation-building experience in diverse ways. The more intense the foreign occupation and control, the more destructured the domestic society and its mechanisms of social regulation. This has made the unification of territory, the choice of institutions, and the centralization of power and authority that much more complicated.

Algeria had been a settler colony.[1] As of 1848, the French government transported thousands of European nationals across the Mediterranean to settle in the new colony and establish themselves there indefinitely as *bona fide* residents. In 1962, just before independence, the settler community constituted 10 percent of the population; there were European families in Algeria which had lived there for more than 100 years. Moreover, while there was, in colonial Algeria, a European sphere and an indigenous sphere, the Europeans dominated politics and the economy absolutely.

In 1962, 90 percent of the European community left Algeria *en masse* over a period of six months. It left behind an impoverished institutional environment. On the one hand, French settler colonialism had had a profound impact in the social, economic, and political realms; not only had it practiced economic subjugation and cultural domination, but it had also encouraged regionalism and ethnic favoritism. On the other hand, Algerian nationalism, which featured, in the first decades of the twentieth century, a fairly diverse political community in terms of ideology

---

[1] On the particularities of settler colonies, see Elkins and Perdersen (2005).

and interests, came to be hijacked over time by the crudest, most militarized, and least "democratic" elements of the indigenous population.

As Crawford Young (1988) so eloquently explained in discussing the
African colonial state, the dominant nationalist elites reflected their
former occupiers in important ways: with their narrow social base and
dubious legitimacy, they constricted the arena of political debate
and relied on coercion for maintaining order. They denied political –
and cultural – pluralism, ignored justice and merit as criteria in the
distribution of resources, and purposefully excluded important social
groups from political and economic spoils. Given the leadership structure
and the weak political culture it revealed, those in power failed to create
institutions to resolve internal conflicts effectively.

In this chapter, I begin the analysis of the state- and nation-building
experience of Algeria. I follow the country's historical trajectory during
the colonial period, from the arrival of the French imperial power in 1830
until its departure in 1962. The focus throughout is on institutions and
their development, competing cleavage structures and their incorporation, and the choices of leaders at critical junctures. First, I consider the
French conquest and the initial Algerian response. I discuss the impact of
colonialism in the social, economic, political, and cultural spheres. Next, I
outline the emergence and development of the Algerian nationalist movement from the first decades of the twentieth century through the end of
World War II. I continue the discussion of Algerian nationalism, focussing on the critical period from 1945 to 1954, when the movement was
marred by intense internal struggles. Following that, I describe the seizure
of power, after the Soummam Congress of 1956, by the most "militarized"
of the nationalists, and their systematic elimination of contesting nationalist voices. I explore the consolidation of power by the militarized core
and its hijacking of the Algerian revolution from 1958 until independence
in 1962. I conclude with an analysis of the period in terms of institutional
foundations, the "idea of the nation," competing cleavage structures, and
their implications for the future of the independent state.

1830–71: the conquest

On the eve of the French occupation, Algeria had been governed since the
sixteenth century from a distance by the Ottoman empire, represented
on the ground by the Ottoman *dey*. It was, however, the weakening of
Ottoman-controlled Algeria and especially the latter's financial problems – a crisis of payments in its international transactions – that was the
avowed justification for the French conquest of 1830 (Ageron 1979;
Lacoste *et al.* 1960: 234–46).

While a financial dispute between the French crown and the Ottoman *dey* lay at the heart of the conquest, foreign interventions in Ottoman Algeria had continued since 1815 in an effort to hamstring the country economically and militarily, and thereby further weaken Ottoman control (Lacoste *et al.* 1960: 188–96).[2] Nonetheless, the *prise d'Alger* was also facilitated by the fact that well before 1830, Ottoman authority over roughly two-thirds of the country had evaporated progressively in the face of the significant power and influence of a variety of *sufi* brotherhoods and *marabouts* (Vatin 1974: 104).[3]

When France under Charles X invaded Algeria in 1830 and forced out the Ottoman *dey*, it found a country of roughly 3 million inhabitants including Arabs, Berbers, Jews, Turks, Black Africans, and *khouroughli* (Turko–Arab stock), living in both urban agglomerations (5–7 percent of the population) and rural environments (93–95 percent), and engaging in a variety of economic activities. Among these groups, with their varied backgrounds and sometimes conflicting interests, the principal bond was Islam; albeit of different forms, Islam was the religion of 99 percent of the population (Lacoste *et al.* 1960: 217–28).

To its initial consternation, the French invading power faced stiff, armed resistance from both Arab and Berber populations. Indeed, the era of conquest would continue for more than forty years. For much of this period, the strongest and best organized resistance came from *sufi* brotherhoods and tribal confederations, from rural but mostly mountainous zones. Most notorious among the resistance movements was that led by the *emir* 'Abd el-Qader, a towering figure of the traditional elite and *Qadiriyya* brotherhood. 'Abd el-Qader fashioned his struggle as a *jihad*, to prevent the believers from suffering the domination of Christian infidels.

For seven years, from 1832–9, 'Abd el-Qader worked to extend his authority throughout land not controlled by the French. Within that "realm," he sought to create a form of centralized state power that included an army to fight the French, as well as a centralized financial organization and system of taxation. Having gained sovereignty throughout much of the west and center of Algeria – recognized by France through the 1837 Treaty

---

[2] For example, the French blockade of Algeria's maritime links to Constantinople had several important effects. First, it meant that the Ottoman government in Algiers could no longer acquire military reinforcements. Second, it re-oriented Algerian commerce to land routes (i.e., from Constantine to Tunisia, from Tlemcen to Morocco). This attenuated internal conflicts and accentuated the administrative decentralization of the country (Lacoste *et al.* 1960: 196).

[3] Linked to Sufism, a *marabout* is a "holy man" – one who is infused with *baraka*, or divine grace, is recognized as just and spiritual, and tends to have an extensive following, which includes disciples.

of Tafna – 'Abd el-Qader was effective not only in bringing together heterogeneous populations for the purpose of resisting the French conquest, but also in putting into place structures that could unify these diverse groups (Lacoste *et al.* 1960: 272–91).

As of 1839, the French under Marshal Bugeaud reneged on the treaty they had signed two years before and launched an all-out war against 'Abd el-Qader. Over a period of eight years, France transferred a third of its entire army onto Algerian soil to put a once-and-for-all stop to 'Abd el-Qader and the political and economic order he had constructed. Through a combination of horrendous "scorch and burn" tactics and brutal repression, French forces finally destroyed the infrastructure and economic potential of the *emir*'s proto-state, terrorized the populations into submission, and forced 'Abd el-Qader's flight and eventual exile in 1847 (Lacoste *et al.* 1960: 298–309).

The conquest of Algeria was not complete: several other millenarian movements followed, leading the struggle in the name of Islam.[4] It would take another fifteen years, from 1850 until 1865, to crush resistance movements that had emerged among the Berber populations of the mountainous Grand and Eastern Kabylias (Lacoste *et al.* 1960: 310–15). Then in 1871, in response to both the extension of colonization with its profound social consequences and the passing of two highly divisive pieces of legislation, yet another insurrection was upon the French forces.[5] Beginning in the region of Constantine and quickly spreading to Kabylia and other parts of the country, this armed uprising (sometimes referred to as the Moqrani or Rahmaniya insurrection) was the last to take place before 1954. It demonstrated the extent of both the Algerians' refusal of foreign domination and the French determination to hold onto Algeria for their own purposes, by whatever means. After ten months of fighting, the defeated Algerians suffered severe punitive measures, in addition to profound social dislocation and absolute economic dependency (Lacoste *et al.* 1960: 331–43).[6]

Colonialism and its impact

It was only after the military campaigns of 1871 and roughly forty years of fighting and devastation that colonization triumphed. The Algerian

---

[4] In so doing, these movements of resistance confirm the historical usage of Islam as a political resource.

[5] On the *Senatus Consulte* and the *Crémieux decrees* see below, p. 52.

[6] There were deep divisions in France over the "Algeria question." For many years, the French government was undecided as to how far to go. Its indecision was often interpreted by the military as license to proceed as it saw fit. As for the settler population, it was determined to hold onto the colony (Vatin 1974: 112–31).

people and their traditional leaders had been defeated and humiliated. The indigenous population was pushed off the best lands, which were placed under European control for European profit. European settlement continued unabated, as did European domination over political, economic, and even religious life. Algerian culture and society were radically disrupted, and traditional ways of life disintegrated.

If we consider land tenure, which was the basis of social organization and economic activity in what was then a predominantly rural society, the changes wrought by the French occupation were enormous. In the northern portions of the country parallel to the Mediterranean coastline, where European emigrants were settled en masse, the very best lands were expropriated from the indigenous populations. This practice had begun in the 1840s with the *cantonnement* policy of the French government; it amounted to squeezing tribes into a small portion of their traditional land and seizing the best part of it for settler-agriculturalists.[7] At the end of the century, tribes were left with only 10 percent of their communal lands (Lacoste *et al.* 1960: 363–4; Ruedy 1992: 83). By 1919, close to 1 million hectares had been granted to individual settlers, while another 6 million were transferred to the public – that is, French government – domain (Ruedy 1992: 94–5).[8]

In addition to being located on the most fertile land, European farms tended to be considerably larger in size and equipped with more modern technology – hence producing far larger yields – than those remaining in Algerian hands. More often than not, those Algerians who had lost their land were forced to work as wage laborers on European farms. The proletarianization and pauperization of the rapidly growing Algerian peasantry, and the resultant destruction of traditional social units, intensified as European settlement expanded and settlers' demands for arable land increased. Families, no matter their size, were expected to make do on smaller and smaller plots (Ageron 1979: 216–20; Bourdieu 1961: 120–1).[9] Their impoverishment became even more pronounced when European agriculture in Algeria shifted in the 1880s to viticulture. Then, as of the turn of the century, and in response to the growing constraints on the

---

[7] For the European emigrant, settlement and land acquisition in Algeria were guaranteed sources of social mobility. Settlers who had been small peasants or laborers in Europe could become land owners in Algeria and employers of wage laborers (Ageron 1979: 94–9).

[8] For a detailed picture of rural colonization including the different types of land acquisition and development strategies, portraits of settler-agriculturalists, and the perks of the enterprise, see Ageron (1979: 72–99).

[9] Quoting from various politicians of the time, Ageron (1979) and Bourdieu (1961) provide evidence that some of the colonial laws pertaining to land were conceived purposefully to destroy the fundamental structures of the economy and the traditional society.

quality of rural life for indigenous populations, migration to Algerian cities and European capitals began in earnest.

Wine production and export, 90 percent of which remained in European hands, quickly became the most lucrative of agricultural activities, and the profits it promised invigorated and intensified colonisation (Ageron 1979: 106–17). Note that viticulture was geared exclusively to the external arena; its internal market was restricted to the European population of roughly 600,000 at the turn of the century (as compared with about 4 million Arabs and Berbers). Not only was this economic activity alien to the indigenous population, but its importance in terms of production and revenue magnified the distorted nature of the Algerian economy as an agricultural commodity-extracting hinterland for the European metropole (Lacoste *et al.* 1960: 384–92). Nonetheless, the industry developed into the largest employer of manual labor; it became a principal source of sustenance for Algerian families.

In the spheres of political life and civil liberties, the regime meted out to the indigenous population was equally severe, although it was selective, depending on one's particular affiliation: Jews were considered the best of the lot, while Berbers were superior to Arabs. In essence, the French colonizers elaborated an institutionalized system of legal discrimination in the civil, fiscal, juridical, and political domains. The obvious purpose of many of the policies and pieces of legislation was not only to maintain the indigenous population in a position of perpetual inferiority vis-à-vis the settlers, but also to create divisions and distinctions within the indigenous population itself, so as to both inflame social conflicts and rule more effectively through the classic *divide ut imperes*.

Among the most insidious rulings were the *Senatus-Consulte* (1865),[10] the *Crémieux Decree* (1870), and the *code de l'indigénat* (1870s). The *Senatus-Consulte* stipulated that the Algerians were French subjects, not citizens. To enjoy rights of citizenship, they were required to renounce their Muslim civil status and agree to live under French, rather than Islamic, law. As this, to a Muslim, was equivalent to apostasy, few Algerians requested naturalization, preferring the status of civil and political inferiority relegated to non-citizens (Ruedy 1992: 75–6; Vatin 1974: 118). In contrast, Jews were treated as *bona fide* Frenchmen. Via the *Crémieux Decree*, this tiny minority was granted naturalization upon request. While for years, many Jews had resisted the French colonial effort alongside Muslims, most of them readily accepted French citizenship

---

[10] On the first *Senatus-Consulte* (1863), which affected tribal landholding and destroyed the traditional social structure, especially the position of tribal leaders, see Lacoste *et al.* (1960: 370).

(Lacoste 1960: 336). To add insult to injury, Muslims were subjected to the humiliating regime of exception known as the *code de l'indigénat*; it would survive in different forms until World War II. A list was composed of infractions that were not illegal in France but were both illegal and punishable in Algeria when committed by Muslims. It included such offenses as refusing to answer questions posed by an official, traveling without a permit, forgetting to declare a family birth or death, refusing to fight forest fires, or speaking disrespectfully about the French government (Ageron 1979: 24–5).

While both Arabs and Berbers were subjected to the regime of exception, the dominant French view was that Berbers were superior to, and could be more easily assimilated than, Arabs. Smacking of racialist prejudice, positive traits of pride, courage, curiosity, industriousness, and austerity were attributed to Berbers, in what came to be a "Kabyle myth," while Arabs were characterized as the very opposite.[11] The aim of the dichotomization of Algerian society was to marginalize the Arabs, win over the Berbers, and proceed with the Frenchification of Algeria and its deeper integration into metropolitan France (Ageron 1979: 138–44).[12] To the misfortune of the French, however, their efforts would backfire: the Kabyle Berbers were the first to engage in anti-colonialist agitation. They figured among the most prominent of Algeria's nationalist leaders.

Finally, the geography of French colonization itself was to have an enormous impact on Algerian culture, and on the formation of anti-colonial national consciousness (El-Kenz 1997: 323–47). Algeria was implicitly divided into three distinct zones. The northern portion of the country, a strip about 100 kilometers wide along the Mediterranean coast, comprised the better part of the colonial economy and society, and was controlled by the settlers. Here were the largest cities, rich coastal plains, most of the economic infrastructure, as well as the farms that were engaged in modern export agriculture. Here lived the vast majority of the European settlers, surrounded by more than half of the indigenous population. It was here that colonial policy was the most aggressive. The local elite was educated in French and gradually assimilated

---

[11] Note that the name "Kabyle" derives from the Arabic word *qba'il*, or tribes. When the French arrived in Algeria in the 1830s, the Arabic term was used by urban populations to refer to hillsmen and mountain dwellers. While the French tended to use "Kabyle" to refer to Berber populations wherever they were found, it eventually came to signify the Berbers of the Djurjura, Biban, and Guergour mountains, just east of Algiers, as distinct from the Chaouia Berbers of the Aurès mountains in the southeast, the Mozabites of the Mzab in the northern desert region, and the Tuareg of the central desert zone.

[12] For a fascinating study of ethnic stereotyping in colonial Algeria and the "Kabyle myth," see Lorcin (1999).

European – or rather, French – culture; French became the idiom for all who could read or write. Nevertheless, the vast majority of the indigenous population, who were turned into wage laborers, remained illiterate, and more so in Arabic than in French.

The second zone – the central portion of the country – extended from the High Plateaux to the steppe and was administered by France. Colonization was organized around sheep-raising and extensive cereal-growing domains. As there were far fewer settlers in this zone, the impact on the colonized population was significantly less. The third zone included the vast desert region to the south – an area populated primarily by nomadic tribes. In this region, governed by soldiers living in garrison towns, the colonial presence was minimal. Because French culture was far less in evidence, the Arabic and Berber languages and traditional culture were able to persist. In sum, the territorial effect of colonization created geo-cultural distinctions within indigenous society which would fuel antagonisms within Algerian nationalism and the independent state.

The nationalist (re-)awakening

As of the first decades of the twentieth century, muffled criticism of various aspects of French colonial policy could be heard from both the *évolués* and the *vieux turbans* of urban Algerian society. Representing two nascent, yet already distinct, trends in Algerian nationalism, the *vieux turbans* was a small group of traditional, largely religious leaders from within the urban bourgeoisie who defended the institutions of Islam and opposed innovation, while the *évolués* constituted a narrow elite of relatively privileged Algerians, educated in French schools and in "French ways," who worked within the "French sphere" in Algeria. The "Young Algerians," as the *évolués* called their movement with its foundation in 1912 – reminiscent of the "Young Turks" – were openly assimilationist. Of secular and liberal inspiration, and somewhat removed from the Algerian masses, they advocated the emancipation of the Algerian people, but within the French nation and as equals of the French.[13] Among their demands were equitable taxation and political representation, and the extension of education. The conservative *vieux turbans* denounced these modernists as young, gallicized non-believers and renegades (Ageron 1979: 227–44).

---

[13] Indeed, the most influential political figures within the movement, Omar Bouderba and Dr Benthami, were both French citizens (Ageron 1979: 239).

With the passing of the highly controversial *Jonnart Laws* of 1919,[14] the "Young Algerians" split into two: (i) a more radical wing led by Emir Khaled, the grandson of Emir 'Abd el-Qader, that favored naturalization with the retention of Muslim personal status, and fought for full Muslim representation in the French parliament (Ageron 1979: 285–8); (ii) a conservative and increasingly assimilationist wing, led by Dr. Benthami, which advanced limited demands of the Algerian population within the colonial framework. Each of these wings would lay the groundwork for more prominent nationalist tendencies that would emerge in the inter-war period and dominate the political landscape in the decades leading up to independence.

The enormous discrepancy between the Algerians' duties to the French colonial power and their rights, especially in the wake of their involvement in the war effort alongside the French, prompted a new *prise de conscience*. The mid-1920s witnessed the emergence of distinct nationalist movements with considerable followings. The movements came to represent four currents within Algerian nationalism. First, the francophone and francophile *Fédération des Elus Indigènes*, that developed out of a reconstituted "Young Algerians," represented the modernized, Frenchified elite. Under the leadership of Dr. Bendjelloul and then Ferhat Abbas, this movement of secular, bourgeois liberal reformists favored assimilation with equal rights for Algerians and indigenous representation in the French Parliament. It advocated, as well, the idea of an Algerian nation federated with France (Ageron 1964: 320–2). In 1944, Ferhat Abbas split from Dr. Bendjelloul and the more conservative *élus*. He organized a new political movement – the *Amis du Manifeste et de la Liberté* (AML) – to support the 1943 *Manifesto of the Algerian People*,[15] propagate the idea of an Algerian nation federated with France, and create a broadly based, conservative national movement, proning non-violent resistance to oppression (McDougall 2006: 74–8; Ruedy 1992: 144–8).

---

[14] The *Jonnart Laws* were promulgated in the aftermath of World War I in an effort to reward Algerians for their participation in that war within the French ranks. They were a set of reforms that, among other things, provided electoral rights to some 43 percent of the adult male Algerian population. In this way, they instituted a separate college of non-French voters, composed of a select group from the indigenous society.

[15] The *Manifesto of the Algerian People* was a document drafted by Ferhat Abbas in 1942 and presented to the French authorities as the political program of the *élus*. It was the first enunciation of their adoption of the idea of political independence for Algeria (Ageron 1979: 559–63). In his memoirs, Hocine Ait Ahmed (1983: 25), in reflecting on the significance of the *Manifesto*, writes that it was a direct response to the Allied war effort: the Algerian people would support the Allies on the condition that, in exchange, the right of the Algerians to express themselves freely and democratically regarding their future would be respected.

Second, the Islamic Reform Movement, led by Abd al-Hamid Ben Badis (and his successor after 1940, Muhamad al-Bashir al-Ibrahimi), advocated the return to and purification of Islam in order to strengthen the religious and cultural foundations of the Muslim nation. In this way, it was believed, the community could defend itself against French policies of assimilation.[16] Deeply influenced by the teachings of the *Nahda*, or Islamic renaissance thinkers – Mohamad Abduh, Rashid Rida, and Jamal al-Din al-Afghani (Merad 1967: 31–7, 214–26, 372–3) – the Reformers conceived the movement as a party of the Islamic reformation and Arab culture. It was a religious, but also a national, party, and touted the slogan, "l'Algérie est notre patrie, l'Islam est notre religion et la langue arabe est notre langue." With the creation in 1931 of the *Association des 'Ulama Musulmans Algériens* (AUMA), the methodical implantation of the movement throughout Algeria began in earnest. As it functioned in Arabic, it was much more closely linked to the indigenous masses than was the *Fédération des élus* (Merad 1967: 118–44). However, while its primary concern was the protection of the Arab–Islamic personality of Algeria, it came to favor, as did the Fédération, autonomy for Algeria within a union with France. As such, there was an important element of solidarity between the two movements (Ageron 1970: 333; Merad 1967: 188–91).

Third, the *Etoile Nord-Africaine* (ENA) reflected a secularist tendency within Algerian nationalism, that espoused a kind of working-class populism combined with vaguely Islamic overtones. The movement was founded in Paris in 1926 by Algerian migrant laborers with a Kabyle majority.[17] It was influenced, in its early years, by the French communist party and trade union movement (Ageron 1979: 349–50). The ENA quickly came to be identified with Messali Hadj, a Tlemçani of humble (*Khouroughli*) origins, who, before embarking on a life of militancy, had been intrigued by Emir Khaled's analysis of the Algerian condition, but was disillusioned by his political prudence (Stora 1982: 40–1). Messali demanded, for the very first time, the independence of Algeria. His political program included the departure of the army of occupation and the constitution of a national government with Arabic as the official language. In the economic and cultural spheres, he stressed egalitarian themes such as the nationalization of banks, mines, the railroads, and

---

[16] The Reformers were fundamentally opposed to *maraboutism* – loosely defined as sainthood, or the "cult" of holy men, often associated with Sufism – and its prominence in Algerian religious life (Merad 1967: 58–76, 229–34). For a rich discussion of the place of the Muslim reformers, followers of Abd al-Hamid Ben Badis, in Algerian nationalism, see McDougall (2006).

[17] On Algerian labor migration to Europe, see Ageron (1979: 526–32).

public services, the extension of social insurance to all Algerians, programs to benefit the peasantry and return land to them, and free and
compulsory education in the Arabic language (Stora 1982: 69–71). In
1937, the French government dissolved the ENA. In reaction, Messali
created the *Parti du peuple algérien* (PPA) and transferred its headquarters
from France to Algeria. The PPA remained the most active and most
visible of Algerian nationalist movements until it was banned in 1939
(Stora 1982: 146–87). Messali Hadj would become the most prominent
activist of the period prior to the inception of the War of Independence,
with by far the largest following.[18]

Finally, there was a very small and relatively insignificant Communist
Party in Algeria. It was closely tied to the French Communist Party and
was internationalist in its outlook. Its position regarding Algeria, and
colonies in general, reflected its geopolitical concerns: most notably,
fascism in the 1930s, US imperialism in the 1940s. Throughout this
period, it remained quite isolated in Algerian society. Moreover, its relations with the other nationalist movements were consistently hostile
until the late 1940s, when it abandoned its commitment to an Algeria
within a French union, and rallied behind the nationalist demand for
total independence (Ageron 1979: 379–86, 596–601).

As the political spectrum outlined above indicates, there had been
considerable ideological diversity within Algerian nationalism. In fact,
because of the marked differences among the movements – in terms of
class base, interests, programs, and tactics – it would be more correct to
talk of "nationalisms." For the most part, relations among the four
currents were adversarial, characterized by competition to enlarge political constituencies. Nonetheless, there had been some dialogue, especially
in the earlier period, that is, before 1945.[19] Messali and Abbas, for
example, maintained a regular correspondence between 1933 and 1936;
Messali adhered to a revised *Manifesto* in 1944, and the PPA remained
linked to the bourgeois reformists for a short time thereafter (Harbi 1980:
27–9; Stora 1982: 105, 188–91). Moreover, Messali adhered to the
arabo–islamism of the 'Ulemas.[20] The followers of Abbas and Ben
Badis, bourgeois modernists and bourgeois traditionalists respectively,
advocated similar political arrangements, and conferred over tactics and

---

[18] For an incisive discussion of Messali Hadj and "messalism," see Harbi (1980: 14–30).
[19] The years from the emergence of clearly defined nationalist movements in the 1920s to
the triumph of Algerian nationalism in 1962 can be divided into two more-or-less distinct
phases, with the second phase beginning in the mid-1940s when the population was more
radicalized and the arena of political debate became increasingly constricted.
[20] On Messali's links to and use of Islam, see Stora (1982: 108–18).

agendas.[21] Messali and the communists had been associated before parting ways, once and for all, over the Blum-Violette Bill of 1936.[22] None of the movements, however, had what we might call a *projet de société* – a coherent vision of the political future of the country, a program for the construction of the state and nation.

The radical turn

By 1945, Algerian nationalism had moved into a far more confrontational phase. The combination of the defeat of Vichy France, the dire economic conditions in Algeria, and the continued incarceration of Messali Hadj forced the change. Until then a more or less urban-based phenomenon, the struggle now included the peasantry, and the movement took on a popular, populist, and increasingly revolutionary form. In May 1945, mass demonstrations in Guelma and Sétif, calling for the independence of Algeria and the liberation of Messali, turned into open insurrection and a bloodbath when colonial forces fired on the crowds. Reverberations throughout the country led to widespread uprising and more severe repression. Over a two-week period, as many as 40,000 Algerians died (Ageron 1979: 572–5; Ruedy 1992: 149–50).[23]

Hocine Ait Ahmed, then a PPA militant and later one of the *chefs historiques* of the Algerian revolution, describes a movement in crisis in the aftermath of the May catastrophe (1983: 72–8, 82–7). The leadership was deeply divided, increasingly remote and authoritarian, and tended to improvise on strategy. On the one hand, the leadership made all decisions, with neither consultation nor clarification. On the other hand, it was divided between those, led by Dr. Lamine Debaghine, who favored armed struggle and the immediate creation of a military wing, and those, led by Messali Hadj, who wanted to win over the people first and have the PPA participate in parliamentary elections (Harbi 1980: 35–6).

Not only was Messali skeptical that the time was right for armed struggle, but he felt strongly that there had to be civilian control over the military wing. Although Messali did create the *Mouvement pour le*

---

[21] On the differences between the two, see Yefsah (1990, 27–8).

[22] The Communist Party had joined Leon Blum's Popular Front in France in 1936. The Blum-Violette Bill was a proposal to grant citizenship to about 25,000 Algerian évolués. Of the four movements, only the "messalists" rejected it (Ageron 1979: 449–66).

[23] Harbi (1980: 29–30) suggests that the degeneration of the demonstrations of 8 May was in part the responsibility of the PPA leadership; it had provided no precise direction to the demonstrators. Furthermore, a schism had emerged within the leadership: some called for armed struggle, while others hesitated. In his memoirs, Ait Ahmed (1983: 33–45) makes clear that during this period, the leadership's contact with the "street" and with PPA militants was often absent, delayed, or ambiguous.

triomphe des libertés démocratiques (MTLD) in 1946 as a front organization for the then-outlawed PPA, and Debaghine got his way with the
formation of a secret paramilitary structure – the *Organisation spéciale*
(OS)[24] – the two factions became increasingly polarized and hostile. At
the end of 1949, in fact, Messali had Debaghine, who had been secretary-
general of the PPA since 1940, excluded from the party for allegedly
sowing dissent (Harbi 1980: 67).[25] It had become impossible to question
authority or discuss tactics.

The first critical juncture in the development of the Algerian nation
turned precisely on the question of identity: how should the nation be
conceived and who were its constituents? In the late 1940s, a group of
PPA activists raised the issue of the Berber dimension of Algeria and of the
nationalist movement. It called for an open forum within the PPA to
discuss matters related to ideological and political perspectives, including
the recognition and integration of *berberité* ("berberness") into the idea of
the Algerian nation. This group demanded, as well, that the role of Islam
in politics and in the movement be addressed in a public debate. It
objected to what it perceived as increasingly religious overtones in the
party rhetoric. Was Algeria an Arabo–Muslim country? Should it be
defined by the Arabic language and the Muslim religion? For the purpose
of such discussions, the group requested a party congress.

The leadership, however, showed no willingness to address these
issues. It considered them both divisive and reflective of the interests of
the colonial power (Ait Ahmed 1983: 76–85; Harbi 1980: 59). As a
pretext for suffocating debate, the leadership insinuated that the latter
risked dividing the movement and thus could play into the hands of the
colonizers. Presenting a façade of unity was thought to be far more
important than addressing differences (Hadjeres 1998). The leadership's
response to the internal cleavages exposed a determination to hold onto
power even through demagoguery, and eliminate what were perceived as
competing power centers.

Recall that the precursor of the PPA, the ENA, had been founded in
France by migrant workers, a majority of whom were Kabyles. This early
experience with activism, and implantation in a foreign country where
there was exposure to multiple political currents, nurtured somewhat

---

[24] The initial mandate of the OS was to explore the possibilities for armed struggle. Its early
leaders included Hocine Ait Ahmed and Ahmed Ben Bella. Note that around the same
time (spring 1946), Ferhat Abbas created a new party, the *Union démocratique du manifeste
algérien* (UDMA).
[25] From 1937 to 1946, Messali Hadj had been either in exile or in prison. During his
absence, Dr. Debaghine led the PPA. With the liberation of Messali and the creation of
the MTLD in 1946, Messali re-imposed himself as leader (Stora 1982: 201–5).

greater political sophistication among the nationalists from Kabylia than among those from other regions. Furthermore, Berber particularism in Algeria, be it of the Kabyle, Chaouia, Mzab, or Touareg communities, has been more or less pronounced. In the case of the Kabyles, it has been especially so in the political sphere.[26]

As noted above, Berber particularism was exploited by the colonial power in an effort to distance the Berbers from the Arabs. In contrast, the most militant Algerian nationalists used particularisms not to distance themselves, but rather to demand a more inclusive nationalism and conception of national identity.[27] For them, defining the Algerian nation by the Arabic language and the Islamic religion defied the complexity of the sociological landscape. Instead, they defended the notion of an Algerian Algeria (*l'Algérie algérienne*). Moreover, they contested the authoritarian tendencies of the PPA leadership and the exaltation of Messali Hadj (Harbi 1980: 62). Thus, they insisted not only that Algeria was an Arabo–Berber country and that the Berber language, Tamazight, had its rightful place alongside Arabic, but also that internal party politics had to be democratized in order for the party to retain its legitimacy and lead the people to independence. The foundations and objectives of Algerian nationalism had to be redefined democratically.[28]

The PPA–MTLD leadership reacted promptly to what it referred to as a "Berberist plot" (Ait Ahmed 1983: 178–92; Harbi 1980: 60–7). It initiated a witch-hunt, and excluded from the movement the main spokespeople for the "Berberist" position, whom it accused of regionalism,[29]

---

[26] It may be that Kabyle particularism derives, in part, from the harsh physical environment – a rugged mountainous zone of high altitudes – that demanded a strong constitution and defensive attitude. This has fostered a strong sense of identity, pride, communal solidarity, and attachment to place.

[27] There was, however, a minority faction within the "Berber nationalists" which did advocate a form of Berber separatism (Harbi 1980: 65).

[28] Around this time, three university students, members of the PPA–MTLD – Mabrouk Belhoucine, Sadeq Hadjres, and Yahia Henine – wrote and published a document entitled *L'Algérie Libre Vivra*, under the collective pseudonym Idir El-Wattani. The document dealt precisely with the national question – including the impact of colonialism on the Algerian identity. In addition, it elaborated principles of the anti-colonial struggle which the authors identify as nationalism, revolution, and democracy. Because of the fratricidal climate of the time, the document circulated only clandestinely and briefly. As political debate was not tolerated, the document disappeared as soon as the "berberist" tendency lost out, without having been discussed. Excluded from the PPA, the three authors joined the Communist Party and, later, the FLN. (I am grateful to Mohamad Harbi for drawing my attention to this important text and providing me with a copy of it, and to Sadeq Hadjres for sharing his personal recollections of this period.)

[29] Harbi (1980: 60) points out that regionalism had always been an important component of Algerian nationalist movements. Reflective of the strength of tribal social structure that

cultural sectarianism, and divisiveness. It called them "plotters" and "agents of colonialism" (Belhocine 1987: 131).

By resolving the crisis – that derived from the refusal of the leadership to discuss fundamental issues related to the Algerian identity – through coercion and the settling of accounts, the more conservative wing of the PPA–MTLD leadership inaugurated what would become a tradition – of silence, conspiracy, and arbitrary exclusions.[30] Quoting Ait Ahmed, the head of the OS, who himself would be pushed aside: "Désormais, les mythes idéologiques, l'embrigadement des masses et le terrorisme politique tendront à constituer les trois mamelles du populisme algeriens" (1983: 188) [From then on, ideological myths, indoctrination of the masses, and political terrorism would constitute the three prongs of Algerian populism (translation my own)].

As identity-related issues were closely linked to political matters having to do with leadership and direction, the crisis that came to a head in 1949, and its resolution, bore heavy consequences for the future of Algerian nationalism. First, it destroyed the hopes of allowing a radical nationalism to develop independently of religious faith. Second, it brought the struggle to democratize the nationalist leadership to an impasse. Third, by excluding so-called "berberists," it not only weakened the radical wing of the PPA–MTLD, but also eliminated from the movement some of its most thoughtful and politically astute militants; instead, it promoted those who kow-towed to the leadership. The unfortunate results of favoring deference to authority – that sometimes went hand in hand with mediocrity – would be felt during the course of the war of liberation (Harbi 1980: 66–7).

The *crise berberiste* was perhaps the most critical juncture in the development of Algerian nationalism. More so than any other episode, it set the stage for what would follow. On the one hand, it brought to the fore issues that had not been treated before and would remain unresolved: Who are we and what do we want to achieve together? What kind of nationalism for the liberation of Algeria? And where do we look – toward the West (Europe) or toward the East (the Islamic world)? On the other hand, from then on, the denial of debate, the commitment to the most conformist position, and the resolution of crises through naked force were the distinguishing features of political life, reflecting, in fact, the poverty of politics. Increasingly, the heterogeneity of the Algerian cultural and political landscape was denied and forced underground.

---

preceded colonization, regionalism and other "symbols" of weak national integration were exacerbated by a variety of colonial efforts: among them, the division of the country into different zones of occupation, noted above (pp. 53–4).

[30] In analytical terms, this was, as noted by an anonymous reader, "path dependence down a slippery slope."

The *crise berberiste* was intimately linked to another crisis within the nationalist movement. Cloaked as a dispute over tactics, it was in essence a struggle for leadership. Recall that as of the late 1940s, the PPA–MTLD was torn by dissension over whether to fight for independence from France through revolutionary means, advocated by the OS and the followers of Debaghine, or through legalistic strategies, advocated by Messali Hadj and the Central Committee. Then, with the weakening of the party after the crisis of 1949, the expulsion of Debaghine and others, and the dissolution of the OS, a conflict escalated between Messali and the Central Committee. The latter accused him of authoritarianism and of trying to impose a personality cult (Harbi 1980: 97–9; Ruedy 1992: 154). By the early 1950s and in an effort to hold on to power, Messali had come around to the position that the only solution to the Algerian predicament was armed struggle (Harbi 1980: 87). The "centralists," however, remained committed to a reformist strategy.

By the spring of 1954, Messali Hadj was no longer recognized as the undisputed leader of the PPA–MTLD. In fact, the Central Committee had him and his followers expelled from the political bureau. In light of this split, a third force, the *Comité révolutionnaire d'unité et d'action* (CRUA), composed of young nationalists who had been deeply affected by the massacres of May 1945, emerged from within the PPA–MTLD, ostensibly to bridge the gap between the two antagonistic factions (Harbi 1980: 90–107). Initially, the CRUA represented an alliance between "centralists" and "activists." Within no time, the "activists," partisans of immediate armed insurrection, regrouped and joined forces with the external delegation of the MTLD, some of whom were former OS militants (Stora 1992: 134–6; 1982: 220–2).[31]

The CRUA seized control of the nationalist movement, marginalized much of the former political elite, created the *Front de libération nationale* (FLN), disbanded itself, and launched the Algerian Revolution.[32] With the creation of the FLN on November 1, 1954, armed struggle was imposed as the only means to bring down the French colonial enterprise. Ferhat Abbas, the 'Ulemas, the Communist Party, and even the "centralists" were condemned for both their insistence that independence could be achieved through successive stages and their attention to "social" issues. Indeed, the FLN's program was to take up arms and act first, and address all other matters later. Whoever refused to adhere to its

---

[31] Mohamed Boudiaf was one of the original CRUA activists, while Hocine Ait Ahmed, Ahmed Ben Bella, and Mohamed Khider joined from Cairo (Harbi 1980: 115).

[32] For a fascinating portrait of the founding members of the FLN, see Harbi (1980: 115–18).

program was considered "the enemy": "If you're not with us, you're against us."

Acceptance of political pluralism, recognition of culture and competence, and the creation of institutions to resolve internal conflicts – all of which had been part of the platform of the "centralists" – were categorically denied (Harbi 1980: 114). Instead, a political culture of *beni oui-ouisme*[33] – the silencing of debate, the insistence upon conformity and acquiescence, and kow-towing to the leadership – the institutionalization of the FLN (Horne 1977). While the leadership has always presented November 1, 1954 as the major turning point in Algeria's political development, it was, in fact, a manifestation and consolidation of the politics that had been put into place in 1949.

The monopolization of power and myth-making

At the urging of Abbane Ramdane, most political tendencies dismantled their own movements and rallied behind the FLN soon after its creation (Harbi 1980: 132–42).[34] Messali Hadj, however, would not. By the end of the decade, his movement – renamed the *Mouvement national algérien* (MNA) – was completely overwhelmed by the FLN. Messali himself was treated as a traitor and his followers were systematically eliminated (Stora 1982: 239–81).

The FLN was, as its name suggests, a "front" organization: as it was meant to include all nationalist tendencies, it reflected, in principle, a plurality. In practice, the plurality was concealed. This was despite the fact that Abbane Ramdane had insisted that there should be dialogue among all political forces within the FLN, without according autonomy to any of them (Harbi 1980: 142). The "front" closed within itself all potential intra-elite conflicts in an effort to remain the sole interlocutor of France, impose armed struggle, and maintain an external façade of unity. Politics was quickly replaced by the myth of a "popular will," of which the FLN was the exclusive representative and protector.

[33] On the origin of the term, see Ruedy (1992: 88).
[34] McDougall (2006: 140–3) suggests that the Reformist 'Ulama did not dissolve the AUMA, but instead, "… included themselves alongside, or rather 'at the head of' the Front …" until the Association was finally decapitated by the FLN during the spring and summer of 1957.

Harbi (1980: 128–9) notes that while Ben Bella and Boudiaf wanted to make of the FLN the organization of the former members of the OS, Abbane, a nationalist of Kabyle origin, was committed to transforming it into a large movement representing *all* nationalist tendencies.

Nonetheless, the victory of the "activists" ushered in a period of struggle among the founders of the FLN themselves. In theory, power was shared among five *wilaya* leaders – Mustafa Ben Boulaid (I), Mourad Didouche (II), Belkacem Krim (III), Rabah Bitat (IV), Larbi Ben M'hidi (V) – plus Mohamed Boudiaf, all of whom remained in Algeria (and referred to as "internals"), and the three former OS members – Ahmed Ben Bella, Hocine Ait Ahmed, Mohamed Khider – who were in exile ("externals").[35] In practice, however, this was not the case. First, there was very poor and irregular communication and coordination among them, because of both geographic distance and the increasing autonomy of the five *wilaya*s.[36] Second, there was constant bickering among them about the relative power of the "internals" versus the "externals." Finally, the rapid emergence and prominence of Abbane within the "internal" leadership laid bare the vacuity of the supposedly collegial nature of rule.

At the behest of Abbane and Krim, the Soummam Congress was held in the summer of 1956 (Harbi 1980: 173–84; Stora 1992: 146–8; Yefsah 1990: 45–50). It was convened in order to resolve some of the problems that had surfaced related to the conduct of the revolution: first, the leadership struggle between the "internals" and "externals," and between Abbane–Krim and Ben Bella–Boudiaf; second, the need for a defined political program and the creation of structures; and third, the poor material conditions of the ALN (*Armée de libération nationale*) forces.

The Soummam Congress was a critical juncture in the institutionalization of the revolution: a historic moment when the direction of the movement and its leadership could have been transformed, but the opportunity was lost with the elimination of Abbane Ramdane. Instead, the Congress ushered in an era of more vigorous internal struggles. As for a political program, the commitment to national liberation through armed struggle was reiterated at the Congress and, with Abbane at the helm, so was the primacy of the "internals" over the "externals" and the political over the military. However, in terms of these latter two points, the Congress would eventually prove to have been a dismal failure. In a formal sense, the political arm of the nationalist movement assumed control of the insurrection; in practice, the FLN had no existence independent of the ALN. Moreover, the Soummam platform remained silent about a nation-building program: How should the devastated Algerian society be revitalized? How – that is, according to what doctrines and norms – should

---

[35] Together, these nine figures are referred to as the *chefs historiques*.

[36] *Wilayism* refers to the tendency of the politico-military commands of the five *wilaya*, or zones (into which Algeria had been divided for the sake of conducting the revolution), to behave as autonomous units, obeying no designated central authority.

modernization proceed? And while the platform did embrace the inclusion within the Algerian nation of non-Arab communities – Berbers, Jews, Europeans – that, too, quickly proved to be empty rhetoric.[37]

Regarding new structures for the conduct of war, the Congress created the *Conseil national de la révolution algérienne* (CNRA) and the five-member *Comité de coordination et d'exécution* (CCE), roughly equivalent to legislative and executive powers respectively. One year later (July 1957), and despite the vehement opposition of Abbane Ramdane who himself was a member of the CCE, the CNRA enlarged the latter to include five colonels – Abdelhafid Boussouf, Lakhdar Bentobbal, Mahmoud Cherif, Belkacem Krim, and Omar Ouamrane – and only four "politicals" (Yefsah 1990: 53).[38] A tiny "hard core," mobilized by facile populism and militarism, had hijacked Algerian nationalism. Its hegemony was guaranteed by its symbiotic relationship with the military wing – the ALN. Indeed, from virtually its inception, the FLN was no more than a front for the ALN; ultimate power resided in the ALN.[39]

The primacy of the military over the political and the predilection for masking or physically liquidating alternate voices or potential power centers remained emblematic of political life and the pursuit of national liberation. Consider, for example, the fate of Abbane Ramdane. He was a true nationalist: not only had he orchestrated the alliance among the different movements soon after the FLN was created, but also, at the Soummam Congress in 1956, he re-traced the boundaries of the districts and regions of Algeria so as to eliminate linguistically homogenous zones (confidential interview: July 5, 2000). He insisted on creating a movement characterized by pluralism, in which people of merit and skill, such as Ferhat Abbas of the AML and Tawfiq al-Madani of the Reformist 'Ulemas, had their place (confidential interview: March 8, 2001). He was outspoken in his rejection of the increasing militarism of the FLN leadership and of the continued practice of exterminating opponents.[40] He felt strongly that the populist insurrection promoted by the

---

[37] Note that the first president of independent Algeria, and each one thereafter, has proclaimed the Arabo–Islamism of the state. As for the incorporation of the European population, OAS (*Organisation de l'Armée Secrète*) operations on the eve of independence put an end to the likelihood that large numbers of Europeans would remain in Algeria, or be encouraged to do so. For details, see Ruedy (1992: 184–6).

[38] The four "politicals" were: Ferhat Abbas, Lamine Debaghine, Abdelhamid Mehri, and Abbane Ramdane.

[39] As we have seen above, many of the founders of the FLN were themselves politico-military leaders of the different *wilayas*, or zones, and enjoyed the title of "colonel."

[40] For him, the military was no more than a tool for struggle. In fact, Abbane is said to have announced that there should be no military rank above colonel and that at independence a classic army would be created (interview: Hocine Zahouane, March 23, 2001).

leadership was detached from the national movement, while the latter itself was in a state of crisis. The solution, he felt, was to politicize what was essentially a military apparatus and forge a close alliance with civilian forces.

Abbane Ramdane was executed in 1957 by his co-revolutionaries. While Abdelhafid Boussouf was, according to most sources, the henchman, all five colonels of the second CCE – including Mahmoud Cherif, Belkacem Krim, Lakhdar Bentobbal, and Omar Ouamran – eventually assumed responsibility for his death.[41] Hi assassination was a severe blow to Algerian nationalism.

In the aftermath, real power devolved for some time upon Krim, Bentobbal, and Boussouf. Whatever remained of the relative power of a political apparatus – supposedly, the FLN – faded completely: the colonels were in command and would remain so. An alliance with civilian forces was subordinated, once and for all, to the preponderance of the military (Harbi 1980: 195–205; Horne 1977: 223–30). From then on, the principles of collegiality, transparency, and accountability – that had been accepted implicitly or explicitly at the Soummam Congress – fell by the wayside (confidential interview: March 8, 2001).

The heterogeneity of the political elite and the continuous internal power struggles belied the creation of a tightly knit organization. After six years of war, the FLN had failed at building meaningful political institutions and developing successful ways to handle intra-elite conflict. It remained, as William Quandt suggests, "a segmented structure consisting of numerous competing and often hostile subgroups" (1969: 126). With no clear political platform and no agreement regarding the general orientation of the revolution or strategies for dealing with problems related to the conduct of war, conflicts remained highly personalized (Harbi 1980: 171). As the war progressed, the political elite became increasingly fragmented and fratricidal.

The revolution betrayed

In September 1958, the FLN announced the creation of a provisional government – the *Gouvernement provisoire de la République algérienne*

---

[41] According to Horne (1977: 228–9), the five colonels had decided to rid themselves of Abbane so that they could assume control of the movement uncontested. See, as well, Harbi (2001: 242–3). Others have suggested that Abbane's high-handedness and moralism, but also his detachment from the realities of the Algerian countryside, were responsible for his downfall. See, *inter alia*, Roberts (2003d: 47–52). Whatever their motivations, Abbane was lured to Morocco, where Boussouf was stationed, in the company of Krim and Cherif, and it was there that he was killed. For an in-depth study, see Mameri (1988).

(GPRA) – with its headquarters in Tunis. In terms of composition, the GPRA represented a broadly based executive: Ferhat Abbas, founder of the AML, was president, Ben Bella, a former leader of the OS and prominent "external," was vice president,[42] Dr. Debaghine, the former MTLD centralist, was Foreign Minister, and Tawfiq al-Madani, of the Reformist 'Ulama, was Minister of Culture and Religious Affairs. Nonetheless, the militarist "triumvirate" that had dominated the second CCE – Krim, Bentobbal, and Boussouf – held the main positions of power.[43] No sooner was it formed than new axes of conflict emerged. Most important among them was that between the GPRA and the military: a power struggle that would escalate over time, becoming a veritable crisis of leadership within the FLN in the spring of 1962, reaching a climax by late summer (Harbi 1980: 321–76; Haroun 2000).

At the heart of the conflict was, as before, the relationship between the political and the military. In fact, the General Staff, created by the "triumvirate" and with Colonel Houari Boumedienne – Boussouf's close collaborator from *wilaya V* – in command, rejected the authority of the GPRA over the ALN, even though the "triumvirate" was a part of the GPRA. It would not even recognize the legitimacy of the GPRA and the CNRA, the only two existing political institutions. In contrast, the GPRA's "official" position was that the political monopoly of the FLN had to be preserved and that the binational *Executif provisoire*, created in April 1962 to oversee the transition to independence, was the only institution with the authority to discuss the future of the country.[44] Nonetheless, by supporting the General Staff, the "triumvirate," which constituted the *Commandement interministeriel de guerre* within the GPRA, had implicitly conceded to it military authority and, ultimately, political power.

So severe was the rift that Ahmed Ben Bella and the General Staff insisted on the creation of a Political Bureau to replace the GPRA. In response, the GPRA tried to assert its authority by firing Boumedienne

---

[42] He had been in French detention from October 1956 to March 1962.

[43] They held the Ministry of the Armed Forces, the Interior, and Communications/ Intelligence (Horne 1977: 316). A second GPRA, that excluded Abbas and others, was formed in 1960 and enjoyed greatly diminished authority. Within one year, its membership was altered again (Ruedy 1992: 174, 182, 184–6).

[44] Negotiations between the French government and the GPRA began at Evian in May 1961 and reconvened in February 1962. A final agreement was signed on March 18, formally recognizing the independence of Algeria and ushering in a ceasefire. The agreement led to the creation of a twelve-member Provisional Executive, composed of representatives of the FLN, European settlers, and pro-French Algerians (Ruedy 1992: 184–6). Another crucial issue addressed in the Evian accords was the French acceptance to give up its claims to the oil-rich zones in the south of the country.

and two other top officers of the General Staff, but the officers denied its authority to do so. This led to open polarization and, especially following the proclamation of Algeria's independence on July 3, 1962, a frenetic struggle for power. The General Staff and Ben Bella who, at the time, were on the Moroccan and Tunisian borders, entered the country and established themselves at Tlemcen in the west, forming what came to be called the "Tlemcen group." At the same time, most members of the GPRA retreated to Tizi Ouzou, in the heartland of Kabylia in the east, and formed the "Tizi Ouzou group" (Haroun 2000: 124–64). To wit, not only power and personality, but also ethnic and regional affiliations proved to be factors in this split.

Then, in the absence of effective political institutions to govern an independent state or mechanisms for creating such institutions, the small and narrow group of "externals" – the five-man, self-appointed Political Bureau, with Ben Bella at the helm – opposed the provisional government (GPRA) outright. After a few days of full-scale war, it seized power with the support of the external ALN and its General Staff. Although it was based on the borders and cut off from the *maquisards* (guerilla fighters) inside, the external ALN was nonetheless the most cohesive institution within the nationalist movement.

The GPRA crumbled and Ahmed Ben Bella, who had been either in prison or outside the country since 1950, asserted his leadership through the force of arms, excluding from power those who had led the struggle in his absence. The revolution was betrayed (Harbi 2001: 356–68). On September 25, 1962, the GPRA and the Provisional Executive remitted their powers to the National Constituent Assembly that had been drawn from a list of candidates chosen by Ben Bella, Khider, and the Political Bureau. Three days later, Ben Bella became Algeria's first president, and Houari Boumedienne, the prominent ALN colonel, his Minister of Defense.

Conclusions

If we consider some of the major turning points in the development of Algerian nationalism – the *crise berberiste*, the CRUA seizure of the movement in 1954, the distancing of Messali Hadj, the elimination of Abbane Ramdane, and the confiscation of power by the *Armée de la frontière* in 1962 – a pattern becomes evident. Pluralism is denied, the educated are mistrusted and marginalized, and conflicts are personalized, motivated by a lust for power and resolved through brute force. No doubt, the weak political culture that is the crux of this pattern had its roots, in part, in the destructuring and fragmentation of Algerian society by the colonial power.

The French, through their social and economic policies, had blocked the emergence of "modern" Algerian elites. The few who did exist had been co-opted into the European sphere, rather than be allowed to function as "modern" elites within the indigenous sphere. Produced primarily by the French army and administration, those elites were essentially praetorians:[45] they were motivated largely by the goal to "conquer the state apparatus" (confidential interview: January 7, 1999). As for the even smaller and more sophisticated elite, who manifested social democratic tendencies and was represented by Ferhat Abbas, its members were de-legitimized by their francophilia and their "liberalism."

As there were virtually no solid, indigenous structures in colonial Algeria – apart from the family, tribe, mosque, and *zawiya* – there was virtually no center around which a national movement could constitute itself. Without either a bourgeoisie or a self-conscious working class, and with a peasantry that was completely overwhelmed by its social and economic dislocation, the national movement tended to crystallize around poles – such as the Kabylie or the migrant community in France – and around individuals; in this way, it reflected the fragmentation and atomization of Algerian society (confidential interview: August 3, 2001). This tendency was exacerbated by the very nature of the Algerian revolution: a protracted, highly decentralized war – patterned on the *wilaya* system – both inside and outside the country, and enjoying mass mobilization. With numerous "commanders" on the ground, each responsible for his particular fiefdom and empowered by his relative status and following, the context was not conducive to identifying a single "national" leader and extending support to him. Rather, the potential for multiple, highly competitive, and mutually antagonistic power centers was great.

This combination of factors fostered a heightened sense of cultural, regional, and individual distinctiveness – not simply vis-à-vis the French, but also vis-à-vis each other. As a result, factionalism was promoted, while the development of a truly national identity and a commitment to the democratic regulation of politics were discouraged. In the absence of regulatory mechanisms, dissent was simply eliminated and opponents were purged.

---

[45] Praetorianism refers roughly to the seeking of personal advantage through violence. Often applied to the caudillo regimes in Latin America, a praetorian state is one in which the military tends to intervene in government and may, in fact, dominate political structures and institutions. See Perlmutter (1969).

Apart from a dedication to greater rights and representation for the Algerian people, principles, class interests, and social projects played little, if any, role in the elaboration of Algerian nationalism. Almost invariably, the burning issues had nothing to do with ideological questions or principled positions, but rather with the leadership of the movement: who would be in control? There was virtually no talk about the Algerian "nation" – its nature and constituents – and at least until the mid-1940s, there was little attention to ethnicity, as the Kabyle nationalists shared the same religion as their Arab compatriots.

It was only for a brief moment in 1949 that crucial questions related to the construction of the Algerian nation were raised: Who are we, and what do we want to achieve together? What kind of nationalism for the liberation of Algeria? And where do we look – toward the West (Europe) or toward the East (the Islamic world)? As Algerian nationalists could not agree, the issues raised by these questions were terrifying: they were perceived as potential sources of division and disintegration, but also the loss of the monopoly of power by the leadership. Hence, they would remain suppressed and unanswered. Nonetheless, these questions would re-emerge, in increasingly violent forms, time and again, before culminating in civil war (1992–2002). In the poignant words of one historian of Algeria, "once 'the nation' was freed, its meaning would remain to be fought over" (McDougall 2006: 143).

The weakness of a truly national Algerian identity was glaring. For one, regionalism remained a powerful force, often loaded with value-based assumptions or prejudices. The Kabyles, for example, were true nationalists vis-à-vis the French colonial power; however, they were considered regionalists – and ethnocentrists – vis-à-vis arabophone Algerians. In 1949, Arabs accused prominent Berbers, such as Hocine Ait Ahmed, of being "berbero-materialists" or of supporting fellow Berbers out of ethnocentrism alone, while Berbers accused Arabs of mistrusting them because of their ethnicity. As for Ferhat Abbas and his followers, they had the misfortune of being bourgeois liberal urbanites, a highly discredited combination in the nationalist movement as it evolved and came to be dominated by rural, lesser educated, confrontational "clans."[46] To wit, the clannishness and nepotism of Algerian nationalism, derivative of a leveled, deculturated, but also historically tribal society, figured

---

[46] See Hugh Roberts' (2007: 21 fn.4) note regarding the misuse of the word "clan" in Algerian politics. While clan denotes "extended family," there is not necessarily any kinship affiliation within Algerian factions, as tribes had long been destroyed. Hence "faction" is the more appropriate term in the Algerian context.

prominently, contributing to the poverty of politics and the weakness of "national" identity.

Recall that from the late-1920s through 1954, Algerian nationalism took various forms and was, at the outset, a largely urban phenomenon. To some degree, the movement(s) reflected the diversity of Algerian society, composed of traditionalists and "modernists," migrant workers and bourgeois professionals, Arabs and Berbers, cultural nationalists ("indigenists") and francophiles, liberals and communists. However, given that the vast majority of the Algerian population was rural, the orientation of the countryside was crucial for the evolution of the movement. With the destruction of the traditional rural economy, rural society was uprooted. While many of the traditional ways of life were thrown into disarray by the social and economic dislocations, uprooting tended to intensify the conservative, narrow, and "clan"-based relationships of the rural populations with the rest of the country and to political mobilization. At the same time, it radicalized ambitions.

Furthermore, the massive internal migration from the countryside to the cities in search of sources of livelihood had a threefold impact. First, the cities became very important centers of activity for the Algerian population. Second, the cities were overwhelmed by a demographic explosion. Third, the insertion of rural society into domestic politics was highly destabilizing, for the former arrived with its clientelistic, nepotistic, and "clan"-based views. Indeed, it was in part because of the ruralization of the cities that Algerian nationalism could be so easily hijacked. To paraphrase Mohamad Harbi: in 1954, the shepherds came down from the mountains ... and they brought with them their guns (interview: January 7, 1999). A minority tendency within the movement took control; it did so through the force of arms.

The reliance on force, the denial of diversity, and the silencing of debate, that were emblematic of political life as of 1949, nurtured the militarism of the Algerian political leadership – or rather, the continued domination of Algerian nationalism by highly authoritarian, militaristic elements that would eschew the demands of nation-building. The implantation and reinforcement of militarism are evident if we consider only three features of the period of the war of liberation.

First, the regional structure of the FLN/ALN, composed of *wilayas*, itself had a military character, with the leader of the *wilaya* assuming the title of colonel, even though he enjoyed political responsibilities as well. Second, the more "political" and better educated of the nationalist leaders were systematically pushed aside, either by the French or by their fellow Algerians. Hocine Ait Ahmed and Mohamad Boudiaf, whose plane was hijacked by the French in 1956, spent several of the remaining war years in prison; Larbi Ben M'hidi was captured and killed by the French,[47] and Abbane Ramdane was executed by his co-revolutionaries. With these figures removed from the scene, it became increasingly difficult to confront the militarized core. Finally, the army, established on the borders of Algeria and benefitting from the enlistment of Algerian deserters from the French army – many of whom had been trained in Indochina – would, through force and superior military competence, seize power in 1962. The (external) ALN would triumph over the interior of the country and over the *wilaya* guerilla fighters who, despite having no formal training, were closely connected to and supported by the people, and suffered the greatest losses.

It is not surprising, therefore, that at the heart of the militarism that would come to monopolize Algerian political life, there was, despite the rhetoric, a visceral distrust and suspicion of the people. The latter was borne out, at least in part, by the leadership's alienation from the Algerian population. The failure, or refusal, to tackle fundamental and profoundly complex issues related to the construction of the nation followed suit. Indeed, the poverty of politics was reflective of the weakness of "legitimate" power and its replacement with force and by force.

The myths of unity, of the absence of social differentiation and ideological, regional, and linguistic particularisms, were to persist in the FLN "party-nation" – in its rhetoric and programs. The people were sacralized and idealized, the state was deified, and Islam and Arabism were integral to the official conception of the nation.[48] Through its obsession with popular unity and some notion of a popular will, the leadership masked the real complexity and diversity of the deeply divided Algerian society. Thus, the challenges presented by the rich dichotomies within Algerian society – urban–rural, Arab–Berber, francophone–arabophone–berberophone, "Europeanized"–"traditional" – and the equally rich nuances between and within them, were categorically denied and ignored. Moreover, the mode of struggle for liberation both derived from and contributed further to a political culture that promoted confrontation (and violence), rather than negotiation (and regulation), in order to resolve problems.

No doubt because of the way in which the FLN had come to dominate political life, Algerian regimes have viewed diversity and difference as profound threats – potential agents of disintegration of their exclusive

---

[47] See the description by Ben M'hidi's "confessed" hangman, General Paul Aussaresses, in the latter's memoirs of the Battle of Algiers (2001).

[48] See the text of the Tripoli program, adopted by the CNRA at its congress in Libya (May 27–June 7, 1962), in *Annuaire de l'Afrique du Nord*, vol. 1, 1962, pp. 683–704.

monopoly of power. Moreover, because of the obsessive and instrumental insistence on "the people," successive governments have been under pressure to provide "rapid but also egalitarian access to … material benefits" (Roberts 1984: 7). Indeed, the official discourse had created the illusion, and the expectation, that all would benefit from the revolution, without distinction.

4   The elaboration of a system

Introduction

On the eve of independence, Algerian society displayed severe dislocations. There were close to 3 million people in *centres de regroupement*
("regroupment" or internment centers), over 300,000 refugees outside the country, and about 400,000 in prisons. Of a population of
10 million, 70 percent were rural and 30 percent urban. During the
war years, more than 3 million, of a total of 8.5 million rural Algerians,
had been displaced. Between 1954 and 1960, roughly three-quarters of
a million people fled to the urban areas; the urban population increased
by 67 percent. It would increase again when the French gave up the
internment centers, since about half of those in the camps would go to
the cities and establish themselves, most often in *bidonvilles* (shanty
towns). Indeed, at independence, 55–65 percent of the urban population were migrants from the countryside who, in the cities, represented
the bulk of the unemployed and underemployed (Ruedy 1992: 214;
Bennoune 1988: 89–93). As John Ruedy (1992: 190) has indicated,
"[I]t was with millions of impoverished, uprooted, culturally deprived,
and bewildered ex-peasants that independent Algeria would begin
the difficult task of restructuring itself."

Over a four-month period, just preceding and immediately following independence, 90 percent of the European population – roughly
1 million people – abandoned their homes and workplaces and fled
Algeria. They represented most of the private capital, as well as the
professional, technical, and managerial expertise in the country.
Algeria sorely lacked highly skilled labor, an entrepreneurial class, and
technological know-how (Vandewalle 1988: 27–8). Within one year,
industrial output plummeted, investment in the country fell by more
than 200 percent, GNP contracted by 35 percent, and about 70 percent
of the active male labor force was unemployed or underemployed
(Bennoune 1988). The economy was in dire straits.

At independence, there was a weak and tiny Algerian private
sector, composed of an old bourgeoisie that had been involved in the

tea, coffee, and sugar trades during the colonial period, and had links to the international market (interview with an Algerian economic historian: June 27, 2000). Shortly after independence, this bourgeoisie was joined by some *anciens combatants* who had been given money by the state so that they could get started in business and stay out of politics.[1]

The private sector was quickly undermined by the Ben Bella regime. With no social roots, the regime feared the emergence of independent social forces. As for the *anciens combatants* turned businessmen, they did not epitomize a capitalist class with entrepreneurial skills. Rather, they remained rich through commissions from and close financial ties to the state: ties that were cemented through marriage. Indeed, by the mid- to late 1960s, the private sector was essentially a part of the state, even though there was scant acknowledgement of its existence (Dillman 2000; confidential interview: July 1, 1999).

Human capital at this time was feeble as well. Although the population, of roughly 10 million in 1962, with a growth rate of 3.4 percent per annum, provided an important labor force, illiteracy hovered around 90 percent. Roughly 1,000 people (or .01 percent of the population) had a university education; there were 400 Algerian students at university in Algeria, and only 4 Algerian engineers who had been formed by the French system (interviews, with former ministers/ technocrats: June 26, 2000; June 29, 2000). Nonetheless, in the late 1950s and early 1960s, several hundred Algerians had been sent abroad by the FLN or the GPRA to study engineering and economics. They would return to Algeria soon after independence to assume important positions in the administrations (confidential interview: July 1, 1999). They would form the technocratic corps, charged with building the "new Algeria."

---

[1] The most notorious of these "new capitalists" were Abdelhafid Boussouf and Messaoud Zeggar. During the war of liberation, Colonel Boussouf, commander of *wilaya* V (Oranie), became the head of intelligence services, known as the MALG (*Ministère de l'Armement et des Liaisons Générales*) in the GPRA. The MALG was the predecessor of what, after independence, has been called the *Sécurité Militaire* (SM). Recall that Boussouf was one of three individuals directly responsible for the assassination of Abbane Ramdane in Morocco in 1957 (see chapter 3, p. 66). As for Zeggar, he was Boumedienne's "shadow" advisor and representative, accomplishing many of his wishes behind the scenes, both inside and outside the country. He, too, had been affiliated with the MALG during the war years; his chief responsibility had been procuring arms, munitions, and explosives, and getting them to the ALN. See Taguemout (1994).

The challenges faced by the first government of independent Algeria were enormous. As the country had just emerged from 130 years of foreign domination and 8 years of brutal war that had ravaged all aspects of life and culminated in a fratricidal struggle for power, the leadership's principal tasks were threefold: first, to pacify the countryside; second, to win over the population and consolidate its own power; and third, to jump-start the devastated economy.

In this chapter, I follow Algeria's historical trajectory from independence in 1962 until the death of President Houari Boumedienne in 1978. In addressing the economic, political, and social challenges that leaders faced, the focus is on the character of the institutions that were created, as well as the decisions of leaders. While there were important differences between Presidents Ben Bella and Boumedienne, the choices they made regarding the shape of institutions, the distribution of resources, and the integration of competing social cleavages nurtured a fractured national identity and a divisive social and political landscape. In significant ways, politics and nationality in the first decades of the independent state reflected that which had been put into place in the post-1949 era – the "revolutionary decade."

First, I consider the consolidation of power and the creation of political institutions in the independent state. I note the emergence of both intra-elite and broader social conflict, and explore the methods of conflict resolution and arbitration adopted by the leadership. Second, I examine the redistributive policies of the Ben Bella and Boumedienne regimes. Massive redistribution cemented regime legitimacy and buttressed an ideology that glorified the people and the system. Additionally, it reinforced tendencies that had figured prominently in the 1950s: clientelism, regionalism, and nepotism. Third, I discuss economic development policy during the Boumedienne era. I focus on conflict within the policy community and Boumedienne's response to it. Fourth, I explore institutional developments and leadership choices during the boom period following the oil price shock of 1973 – a critical juncture for all oil-exporting states – and note the important socio-economic constraints they gave rise to. Finally, I return to the divisive issues of identity and nationality, and to the competing cleavage structures that were energized by institutional design. I note that in the face of growing social discontent in the late 1970s, the regime responded in a manner that would ensure its stability. Relying on distributive mechanisms, it was able to appease the population for some time at least. I conclude the chapter with an overview of the period in terms of leadership choice and the shape of institutions.

The consolidation of power, elaboration of institutions, and emergence of social conflict

In the immediate aftermath of the seizure of power in September 1962, Algeria found itself at a crossroads. In the absence of political consensus, the wartime FLN, propelled by personal ambitions, quickly disintegrated into factions. The struggle for power continued.

There was, at this time, a relatively small group of liberals, composed of the old bourgeoisie and a tiny group of *nouveaux riches*, and represented by Ferhat Abbas, who favored the creation of a multi-party system and a market economy. The vast majority of the political elite, however, were socialists of various tendencies. Some, like Sadek Hadjeres, shared sympathies with the former PPA or the Communist Party; others, like Boualem Bourouiba, were linked to the UGTA (*Union Générale de Travailleurs Algériens*); still others, among them, Mohamad Harbi, were "independent" Marxist intellectuals. The remaining *chefs historiques*, especially Hocine Ait Ahmed, Mohamed Boudiaf, and Mohamed Khider, advocated socialist goals, each with his own particular *cachet*. However great or small the differences among them, all members of the political elite reiterated the populist refrain that had surfaced in 1954 and would function as a persistent drone into the 1980s: "the people" – their needs and interests were invoked to justify every plan, policy, program, and piece of legislation (Ruedy 1992: 196–7).

As leader of the newly independent state, Ben Bella felt threatened not only by those whom he had alienated in his seizure of power, but also by those who had helped him take power (Yefsah 1990: 112). Initially, he sought to appease them by offering key positions in government: Ferhat Abbas was named President of the National Assembly, Mohamed Khider became Secretary-General of the Political Bureau of the FLN, and Houari Boumedienne was given the Ministry of Defense, while a member of his "Oujda clan," Ahmed Medeghri, became Minister of the Interior (Yefsah 1990: 99–100). Ben Bella made sure, as well, to have the different factions within the FLN – including the former UDMA (*Union Démocratique du Manifeste Algérien*) and the AUMA (*Association des 'Ulama Musulmans Algériens*) – represented in government.[2] Within no time, though, the heterogeneity of his government became a tremendous source of

---

[2] For example, Tawfiq al-Madani, of the former AUMA, was named Minister of Culture and Religious Affairs. However, no representatives of the former CNRA – such as Ben Khedda, Boussouf, and Bentobbal – were included in the first government (Harbi 1980: 375).

concern for him. He began maneuvering among the various factions, playing off one against the other in an effort to prevent the emergence of any independent power base. In effect, the institutional framework was one of personalist rule with military backing and a neutralized civil society.

The absence of consensus and the machinations of the leadership meant that the National Assembly could neither pass, nor even formulate, legislation. It was completely hamstrung, while the five-man Political Bureau remained the strongest institution of the country, alongside the ANP (*Armée Nationale Populaire*).[3] As for the FLN, and despite the ongoing proclamations glorifying the single-party state, it continued to have no existence as a political party independent of the wartime military and bureaucratic apparatus. It was replaced by, and became an instrument of, the increasingly powerful Political Bureau (Yefsah 1990: 79–100).

With no agreement among the major figures within the political elite as to the elaboration of patterns of authority and institutions of governance, Ben Bella began to concentrate power in his hands and take "direct control of virtually every autonomous political group within Algeria" (Quandt 1969: 206). In the winter of 1963, he brought the UGTA firmly under the control of the Political Bureau – much as he had done with the FLN – allowing it no independent voice and transforming it into his personal tool (interview with former UGTA leader: March 14, 2001). Around the same time, he contested the authority of the National Assembly to pass legislation or draft a constitution. Instead, he decided that the Political Bureau would draft the country's constitution.

In effect, Ben Bella quashed what little remained of tolerance for opposition, forced the disintegration of both the National Assembly and the Political Bureau, two institutions which he himself had created, and instigated the widespread alienation of elite members. Opposition to his increasingly despotic rule continued to grow (Yefsah 1990: 112–25). As early as the fall of 1962, Mohamed Boudiaf resigned from both the Political Bureau and the National Assembly. He created the *Parti de la Révolution Socialiste* (PRS) to oppose what he perceived as preliminary steps toward the establishment of a dictatorship.[4] In the spring

---

[3] The Political Bureau was composed of Ahmed Ben Bella, Mohamed Khider, Rabah Bitat, Colonel Hadj Ben Alla, and Said Mohamedi.

[4] See the foundational tract of the PRS, written by Boudiaf and published in *Le Monde*, September 23–4, 1962 and reprinted in *Annuaire de l'Afrique du Nord* (1962: 713) under the heading, *Tract du Comité Provisoire de Coordination du Parti de la Révolution.*

of 1963, Mohamed Khider, who had been Secretary-General of the Political Bureau, resigned and went into exile, taking with him the FLN treasury. That summer, Hocine Ait Ahmed resigned from the National Assembly and organized a Kabyle-dominated party, the *Front des Forces Socialistes* (FFS), to oppose what he termed a "fascist dictatorship." He later called for armed struggle against the Ben Bella regime and led an ill-fated insurrection (Ait Ahmed 1964: 165–9, 180–204).[5] Also in the summer of 1963, Ferhat Abbas resigned as President of the National Assembly over the unconstitutionality of the hijacked Constitution.[6] He was immediately excluded from the FLN. By the fall of 1964, Boudiaf, Ait Ahmed, and Abbas were either in prison or under arrest.

There remained only two effective political forces in Algeria: Ben Bella himself, who was the head of state, head of government, and, as of Khider's resignation, Secretary-General of the FLN, plus the army with Colonel Boumedienne and his "Oujda clan" at the helm. All other (semblances of) political forces were mere phantom institutions. Ben Bella had not only prevented the development of institutional capacity, but he even impeded the institutions he had created from functioning as they were meant to (Quandt 1969: 204–11).[7] Given this constellation of forces, Ben Bella's days were numbered once he threatened to undermine the military's influence in politics (Yefsah 1990: 138).[8] On June 19, 1965, less than three years after taking power, Ben Bella was ousted in a bloodless coup led by Boumedienne, his closest ally and Minister of Defense, who accused him of arbitrary, personalistic rule.

---

[5] Note that the first to oppose Ben Bella were the three – Ait Ahmed, Boudiaf, and Khider – who had been with him since 1956, first on the hijacked airplane and then in prison. Moreover, Khider and Abbas had been with Ben Bella and Boumedienne in the "Tlemcen group" that, in 1962, had successfully contested the authority of the GPRA. See above, chapter 3.

[6] Abbas' letter of resignation was published in *Le Peuple,* August 8, 1963, p.1; extracts of the letter are reprinted in *Annuaire de l'Afrique du Nord* (1963: 843–4) under the heading "Extraits de la lettre de demission de F. Abbas."

[7] Several former members of Ben Bella's government spoke to this author about the president's ineffectiveness as leader and policy-maker: "He made lots of speeches, but he had no ideas." "Whatever ideas he expressed, he changed constantly" (interviews: July 5, 2000; March 8, 2001). "He could not accept criticism, interpreting it always as personal, rather than principled" (interview: March 15, 2001).

[8] When Ben Bella intimated that he was going to remove Abdelaziz Bouteflika – Boumedienne's close comrade within the "clan" (and the current President of Algeria (1999–) – from his post as Minister of Foreign Affairs, the final decision was taken to overthrow him (Mortimer 2006: 160). Hugh Roberts (2007: 8–9) writes that it was Ben Bella's appointment of Colonel Tahar Zbiri as Minister of Defense "behind Boumedienne's back" that catalyzed his ouster.

In power, Houari Boumedienne dismantled whatever political institutions and organizations had been established under his predecessor – a pattern that would be followed in varying degrees by every Algerian leader. The National Assembly, the Political Bureau, and the Central Committee of the FLN were immediately dissolved, the constitution was suspended, and presidential elections were abolished (Ruedy 1992: 207–8).[9] Nonetheless, Boumedienne upheld the stipulations of the 1963 Constitution that Algeria was a socialist state, Arabic the official language, Islam the official religion, and the FLN the sole legal party.

In the absence of a parliament, the most powerful political institution of the time was Boumedienne's own creation: the Council of the Revolution was dominated by the Oujda clan, his military entourage from the war years, and represented its interests. Of the twenty-six members at its inception, twenty-four had been military figures during the war. In effect, the army became the hegemonic national group: its involvement in politics was institutionalized and eventually, with the *Charte Nationale* and the new constitution of 1976, its role was backed by legislation. As for the Council of Ministers, the second political institution created by Boumedienne, one-third of the members had military backgrounds. To be sure, the key ministries, such as Foreign Affairs and the Interior, were held by military men (Quandt 1969: 251). Moreover, elites from the east of the country, and from the provinces of Batna, Tebessa, and Souk-Ahras especially, monopolized key positions in the army and in the civil administration, strengthening the clientelist, regionalist, and nepotistic tendencies of rule.[10] By 1975, however, and because of intra-elite cleavages, the Council's size dwindled to only nine members: independent voices had been weeded out (Vandewalle 1988: 92).

As for the FLN – supposedly the most powerful institution in independent Algeria – it was stripped of any real authority, despite much talk of the "party-state" and "party-nation." Instead of developing into a movement to mobilize mass support, it remained a symbol of the myth of national unity. Similarly with the labor union (UGTA) and the students' union (UNEA – *Union Nationale des Etudiants Algériens*): both were placed under the control of the ineffectual FLN

---

[9] The three organs would reappear, along with a new constitution, in 1976.
[10] The dominance of "easterners" would persist until the tenure of Bouteflika in 1998. Of the seven presidents Algeria has had since independence, only Ben Bella and Bouteflika came from the western part of the country. "Easterners" have been more prominent as prime ministers and heads of the FLN, as well (Werenfels 2007: 35, 146).

and expected to function as transmission belts for the "party line" (Bennoune 1988: 138).[11] With the armed forces constituting the backbone of the regime, the development of political institutions was woefully undermined.

Boumedienne worked toward consolidating control and constructing a highly centralized, bureaucratized authoritarian state, composed of the Oujda clan and a small but growing technocratic corps which had emerged as a secondary elite in the later years of the war of independence (Quandt 1969: 246–51). While the military exercised a monopoly over both political and coercive power, those with technical expertise were given important positions in the state apparatus, as part of the regime's ambitious development program. The technocrats, however, most of whom had been trained in the French system, had neither autonomy nor political power; they were held on a tight leash and were, in effect, little more than *"serviteurs mercenaires du pouvoir politique"*. Their status and maneuverability were absolutely dependent upon the inclinations of Boumedienne. Furthermore, by virtue of their status – however impermanent – and credentials, they were, for the most part, alienated from the Algerian population (interviews with former technocrats from the Boumedienne era: November 10, 2000; March 11, 2001).[12]

Developing the economy, building up infrastructure, and educating the population, at the same time as consolidating power and authority, became the major preoccupations of the leadership. By the end of 1967, after the attempted coup d'état led by Tahar Zbiri, Boumedienne was firmly in control of the state apparatus. Moreover, all mechanisms that could function as conduits for popular pressure

[11] The former communist party, renamed the *Parti de l'avant garde socialiste* (PAGS), acted as a substitute for the FLN, recruiting the youth into a parallel circuit. It was very active throughout the 1970s in the universities. Although nominally illegal, it was tolerated – if not co-opted – by the regime; in this way, it facilitated the regime's "policing" of student politics (Henni nd: 26). In their defense, (former) members of the PAGS claimed that rather than having been co-opted, they had rallied to the regime in 1971 ostensibly because of the latter's anti-imperialist and anti-American stance (Roberts 1988, reprinted 2003a: 13).

[12] Being predominantly francophone, many of the technocrats were uncomfortable speaking Arabic and some could not even read Classical Arabic. One of my interviewees – a well-known scholar – pointed out that in his forties, he spent six months in Cairo to study Arabic. The phenomenon of a removed or alienated elite is not unfamiliar today: several high-ranking ministers in the most recent governments (2000–8) – among them, President Bouteflika, Ministers Abdelhamid Temmar, Chakib Khalil, former Minister Bashir Boumaaza – spent many years outside the country, living in Europe, the United States, or the Gulf; is this a return to *l'extérieure qui domine l'intérieure*?

had been neutralized: "the strict control of popular behavior remained the rule" (Harbi 1984: 380).

The practice of silencing alternative voices – inaugurated by Ben Bella and reinforced by Boumedienne – became an integral part of the system. Recall that within less than one year after Ben Bella's seizure of power, five of the six remaining *chefs historiques* of the Algerian Revolution were either in exile or under house arrest. In exile, Ait Ahmed and Boudiaf would continue their opposition through their political parties. In their view, the military–authoritarian regime of Boumedienne did not offer a favorable alternative to Ben Bella's personalistic rule. Khider and Krim would be assassinated in Europe, under mysterious circumstances that have never been clarified. Mohamad Harbi and Hocine Zahouane, part of the intelligentsia of the wartime FLN who later assumed important positions in the Ben Bella government, were imprisoned for denouncing the coup of 1965. They, too, would eventually go into exile for the remainder of the Boumedienne period, at least.

Ferhat Abbas remained in Algeria after his release from prison, but was unceremoniously excluded from political life.[13] As his was the only credible alternative to the FLN, and no doubt because of his bourgeois background as well, he could not be integrated into the system that was put into place at independence. In fact, he was completely marginalized. Ferhat Abbas did not count in independent Algeria. Furthermore, none of his collaborators – members of the UDMA and former *Centralistes* – were given important jobs either (interviews with a *chef historique*: March 8, 2001; with a high-ranking technocrat of the Boumedienne years: March 11, 2001).[14] A politics of exclusion had become an essential feature of the system.

With the neutralization of the Party, the harnessing of nascent civil society organizations, and the muzzling of independent actors, Algerian society appeared to become increasingly depoliticized. External rents played an instrumental role in this process, egging on the already considerable patrimonial tendencies that characterized *le système* ("the system"), and the apparent complacency of society.

---

[13] No doubt his biggest mistake was to rally behind Ben Bella at Tlemcen and against the GPRA in 1962. By doing so, he compromised his beliefs and demonstrated that he, too, wanted to be on the winning side.

[14] Apparently, Boumedienne was particularly harsh with Abbas, as well as with Ben Khedda – both of whom were pharmacists and part of the bourgeois intelligentsia. That *paysan mesquin*, in the words of one interviewee, took away their pharmacies and denied them their means of livelihood (interview with a former technocrat of the Boumedienne period: November 10, 2000).

The politics of distribution

Until the mid-1970s, massive redistribution, made possible through the availability of oil revenues and abandoned colonial property, went a long way to purchasing social peace. Oil had been discovered in Algeria in 1957, and by the end of the 1960s it became the principal source of export income for the government.[15] Between 1966 and 1971, the oil sector and all other foreign concerns were completely nationalized. Oil rents, transiting through state-owned enterprises (SOEs) that controlled close to 80 percent of all economic activity, were invested in rapid growth via far-reaching development projects. They were earmarked, as well, for the provision of extensive social insurance: free, universal education and health care, as well as subsidized foodstuffs and public transportation. Many Algerians also came to enjoy virtually free housing.

As they fled Algeria during the spring and summer of 1962, Europeans tried to sell off their properties at whatever price they could fetch.[16] Algerians who had lived on the peripheries of cities during the colonial period simply entered the "European quarters" at independence and occupied the homes and shops of former settlers. These *biens vacants* – abandoned (colonial) property – as they were known, would quickly fall under the management of a special government office, the *Bureau national des biens vacants*. They were, for all intents and purposes, a form of rent that Algerians enjoyed and came to expect.[17] Until the early 1970s, much attention was paid to distributing and re-assigning the *biens vacants*.

Redistribution was carried out in a hierarchical fashion, with the regime granting privileged access to "old guard" militants, their allies, and those closest to the regime. Some of the most interesting *colon* real estate ended up in the hands of members of the Algerian

---

[15] The first major discovery of oil in Algeria was made in 1948 in the Sidi Aissa region in the pre-Saharan southeast. By 1958, the country's main oil field at Hassi Messaoud in the east central region was coming onstream. Gas production began in 1961 at Hassi R'mel, just 500 kilometres south of Algiers. While the country has the eleventh largest oil reserves in the world, it is particularly rich in condensates and natural gas; indeed, it possesses the world's fifth largest proven natural gas reserves. By the late 1990s, natural gas constituted 70 percent of Algeria's recoverable hydrocarbon reserves, and crude oil 30 percent (Entelis 1999: 13–15).

[16] According to the Evian Accords of March 18, 1962, detailing the terms of Franco–Algerian cooperation following independence, the French were not allowed to sell the land.

[17] Occupation and "ownership" were legalized only later, after a census was carried out and minimal, largely symbolic fees were paid to the state (interview with an Algerian sociologist: May 15, 2000).

military and bureaucratic elite, and especially the former *Armée de la frontière* (Lowi 2005). Eventually, what those in power did not keep for themselves or distribute to their cronies was simply occupied by individuals.

The regime's monopoly over distribution enhanced personal ties between the leadership and particular individuals. With this model to draw upon, Algerians were motivated to adopt social strategies that would bring them close to the regime, rather than form interest groups with like-minded cohorts. Proximity to leadership became the principal avenue to social promotion and access to resources; it was, in and of itself, a highly valued good (Roberts 1984: 28). Thus, the system of redistribution reinforced clientelism, which in turn bolstered the already strong collegial networks and regional ties that had carried over from the colonial period (Henni nd.: 40–50).[18]

The peasantry, constituting 70 percent of the population, never really benefited from the redistribution of colonial land. This was despite the profusion of socialist rhetoric, and the hyperbole about 1954–62 having been a "peasant revolution." The marginalization of the peasantry would have far-reaching consequences: it encouraged the rural exodus which persisted throughout the 1960s and 1970s.

Migration to urban areas was prompted by two factors: first, the failure of the regime to divide the most fertile abandoned agricultural land among the landless peasants and small peasants who had been expropriated during the colonial period, and second, the availability in urban areas of *biens vacants* – virtually cost-free housing – in addition to social services and employment. Migration from the countryside nourished urban demographic growth, which itself gave rise to an acute housing shortage, the extension of the *bidonvilles*, rising unemployment, and social discontent. By the mid-1970s, the politics of distribution would expose the contradiction between the discourse and reality of equality and inclusion. It would aggravate social conflicts which, by the end of the decade, would become intolerable and dangerous, eventually exploding ten years down the road.[19]

---

[18] As for its economic impact, the practice of distributing colonial property quickly froze the real estate market. In fact, the combination of rural exodus, the availability of subsidized food and housing in the cities, and the practice of squatting put a brake on all building activity, with profound effects on the dynamism and productivity of society (Henni nd.: 120).

[19] As we will see below (chapter 6), migrants from the countryside would constitute the majority of the rank-and-file of the Islamist insurgency in the 1990s. See, as well, Lowi (2005).

Not dissimilar from the experience with the *biens vacants*, Algerian workers spontaneously and collectively occupied and began to manage farms and factories that had been abandoned by their European owners and managers. No sooner had the *autogestion* (workers' self-management) movement gained momentum than Ben Bella quickly recognized it and adopted it as his own. For him, backing *autogestion* was meant to serve political ends: to both co-opt the relatively powerful labor movement, and gain workers' support at a time (1963) when the political landscape was turbulent and divisive (Lawless 1984: 159; Tlemcani 1989: 116–17). During the Boumedienne era, however, the self-managed sector would fall into oblivion: it comprised no more than one-eighth of the rural population and was relegated to the "authority" of the by then subdued UGTA, itself an appendage of the powerless FLN. By 1970, *autogestion* was completely overshadowed by the *étatist* development strategy.[20]

Massive redistribution nourished the state's egalitarian discourse and its legitimacy. Nonetheless, there was a general feeling at the time that Boumedienne was engaged in building the "new Algeria:" schools, hospitals, factories, highways, dams, pipelines, and the like mushroomed across the country. Hundreds of Algerian students were sent abroad every year to study, while thousands were trained in national institutions. In the international arena, Algeria was prominent in the non-aligned movement. The combination of redistribution and the perception that Boumedienne had a social project made the absence of political participation, as well as the plethora of austerity measures that accompanied the development strategy, tolerable for some time.

Developing the economy

At the end of the 1960s, Boumedienne turned his attention to developing the economy. By that time, he had secured his power base beyond the confines of the army and had few remaining uncertainties about the orientation of the regime. The already very strong and centralizing state quickly became a formidable power in the economic domain as well, in part through its appropriation of the vast hydrocarbon rents (Table 4.1).

---

[20] On *autogestion*, see Clegg (1972). Bennoune (1988: 123) points out that while in 1969, 12.8 percent of all industrial workers were employed by the self-managed sector, that figure declined to 4.7 percent by 1973.

Table 4.1 *Algeria: net hydrocarbon rent per capita ($)*

	Nominal	Real (base = 1999)
1965	10	75
1970	25	125
1975	190	725
1980	525	1075

Source: compiled from Aissaoui (2001: 30)

Boumedienne expressed a commitment to rapid growth through heavy industrialization, the gradual reduction of dependence on the oil sector, and the provision of social services with some attention to equity. In tandem with Belaid Abdesselam, his audacious Minister of Industry and Energy (1965–77) and former director of SONATRACH (1963–5), the SOE for the hydrocarbons sector,[21] he enunciated a three-pronged state capitalist strategy. It consisted of central economic planning, the nationalization of foreign capital, and the rapid development of the state sector.

As was common in post-colonial LDCs in the early years of independence, state capitalism was adopted because an indigenous bourgeoisie with capital to invest and entrepreneurial skill was lacking. The state was left to take the lead in economic activities. The strategy served regimes well insofar as it allowed the state to dominate the political arena so completely, while it enjoyed a monopoly over rents and their distribution. In the case of Algeria, state capitalism would be decisive for the country's economic and political development. Supported first by the successive waves of nationalization of foreign concerns between 1966 and 1971, and then by the creation of SOEs that controlled close to 80 percent of all economic activity, the image of a modernizing, developmentalist, and omnipotent state was consistently being revitalized and reinvigorated (Bennoune 1985; Jacquemot and Raffinot 1977).[22]

---

[21] On the birth of SONATRACH – the *Société nationale de transport et de commercialisation des hydrocarbures* – in 1963, see Aissaoui (2001: 63–71, 202–4) and Entelis (1999).

[22] The direction of the first state-owned enterprises was given either to military men or to former ministers or functionaries of the GPRA: the SNS (*Société Nationale de Sidérurgie*: National Steel Company) went to Ben Tobbal, SONACOME (*Société Nationale de Constructions Mécaniques*: Mechanical Engineering Company) to Mahmoud Cherif, and SONATRACH to Belaid Abdesselam (Yefsah 1990: 197 fn. 64).

State capitalism was combined with the industrial strategy that had first been enunciated in de Gaulle's 1958 *Plan de Constantine* for the economic development of Algeria.[23] The strategy was one of sectorally unbalanced growth with emphasis on industry over agriculture and investment over consumption. At the core of the strategy was the concept of *industries industrialisantes* – that is, the promotion of big, capital-intensive industries, such as those in the hydrocarbon, mineral, chemical, and heavy machinery sectors, which would spur economic growth through backward and forward linkages.[24] Financed through hydrocarbon reserves plus considerable borrowing from foreign sources, the strategy was to diversify the economy and make it self-sufficient (Entelis 1986: 113–14).

According to Ali El-Kenz, the fixation with this all-out development strategy – in which the Algerian population was deeply engaged through the severe austerity measures they were subjected to – was akin to "the continuation of the war of liberation," albeit on an economic plane. The economy became a way of circumventing politics, or better, a "way of engaging in politics by other means" (1997: 332). The rhetoric was one of total engagement, of both the state and society, in building the "new Algeria": an Algeria that would extricate itself, once and for all, from backwardness and dependence, and assume its proper place in the industrialized world.

The direction of economic development policy was conducted by Boumedienne himself. Until the eve of the first oil price shock, he worked with his Oujda clan and engaged, in a consultative role, key technocrats–ministers: Belaid Abdesselam (Industry and Energy) and Kemal Abdallah-Khodja (the Plan). Until roughly 1971/2 and the nationalization of the hydrocarbons sector, there was general agreement over orientation and strategy. After that time, however, the policy community began to unravel. The initial fissures were the result of a

---

[23] The *Plan de Constantine* contained de Gaulle's social and economic proposals to appease the Algerian nationalists. It included a fairly coherent economic plan – a five-year development program – for agricultural, infrastructural, and industrial development. Industrialization was to center around a few large-scale heavy industrial projects – most notably, a steel complex at Bône (Annaba) and oil refineries. Although the GPRA had rejected the Plan, the two major heavy-industry projects became centers of Algerian industrialization post-independence (interview with a former technocrat in the Boumedienne government: November 10, 2000).

[24] *Industries industrialisantes* was the brainchild of the French economist Gérard Déstanne de Bernis, who served as a consultant to the Algerian government and had trained several Algerian technocrats. He himself had been influenced by the thinking of two other economists: François Perroux (1955) and Albert Hirschman (1958). Linkages and growth poles, which figured prominently in the latter's thinking about development, were integral to Algeria's strategy (Vandewalle 1988: 109–11).

growing conflict between Abdesselam and Abdallah-Khodja over the method of development. Abdesselam, like Indonesia's B.J. Habibie, favored very big, expensive projects with visibility and much prestige. In contrast, Abdallah-Khodja, not unlike Indonesia's Nitisastro, found such projects extravagant, wasteful, and unsuited to the needs and capacities of an LDC like Algeria, with limited human capital resources.[25] He was convinced that Abdesselam wanted to do far too much, far too quickly (interviews with former technocrats in the Boumedienne government: July 7, 2000, November 10, 2000, December 13, 2000). By 1974, the differences between the two turned on not only development strategy and initiatives, but also the "functions and prerogatives" of their respective offices (Bennoune 1985: 200). Boumedienne's "project" was coming apart.

The oil price shock of 1973

In 1973, OPEC members used their leverage over the world price-setting mechanism for oil to quadruple world oil prices. The effect on the revenues of oil-exporting states was stunning: within the space of a few short months, oil-exporting LDCs saw their revenues triple or even quadruple (Table 4.2). The "oil shock" was a critical juncture for oil-exporting states: burgeoning revenues presented a new set of opportunities for late development in terms of policy direction, the shape of institutions, and the distribution of resources.

In Algeria on the eve of the oil shock, tensions surfaced within the political alliance at the core of the regime. Some sources maintain that the Oujda clan had become increasingly polarized between those who supported the *étatisme* of the regime and those who favored some degree of liberalization (Yefsah 1990: 255–8). It appears that personal jealousies and a power struggle were at the source of the intra-elite conflict. For one, the growing influence of Belaid Abdesselam – as exemplified by his relatively free hand in the heavy industry and hydro-carbons sectors, and the great esteem that Boumedienne seemed to have for him – rankled those who, over time, saw their own influence eclipse (interview with a high-ranking technocrat in the Boumedienne government: July 7, 2000). Ahmed Medeghri, for example, who had

---

[25] For example, Belaid Abdesselam promoted a project to create an Algerian automobile industry. This would be a boost to national pride, a symbol of sovereignty, and evidence of development. Abdallah-Khodja thought that this was unnecessary, beyond the country's resource capacity, and a waste of public funds. Belaid got his way and a car-building factory was established at al-Harrash. However, the factory ended up building wheelbarrows and cement mixers (confidential interview: March 11, 2001).

Table 4.2 *Oil revenues of select OPEC countries (US$ billions)*

	1972	1973	1975
Venezuela	1.9	2.8	7.5
Nigeria	1.2	2.0	6.6
Indonesia	0.4		3.9
Algeria	0.7		3.4
Libya	1.6	2.3	5.1
Iran	2.4	4.1	18.5
Iraq	0.6	1.5	7.5
Kuwait	1.7	1.9	7.5
Saudi Arabia	3.1	5.1	25.7

Source: compiled from Philip (1994: 153, 173)

been very close to Boumedienne and, as Minister of the Interior, quite powerful and respected, had deep concerns about aspects of the development strategy, as had (his co-clansman) Kaid Ahmed. Moreover, Medeghri was in conflict with Abdesselam and despaired that he no longer had Boumedienne's ear (Quandt 1969: 262; interview with former member of the Oujda clan: March 25, 2001).[26]

To be sure, Boumedienne's personal power and autonomy in relation to the rest of his government had grown considerably from 1971. Not unlike his predecessor, his rule became increasingly autocratic and personalistic. As he began taking initiatives and forging contacts outside the country without consulting his entourage, it became clear that he no longer had much use for the once all-powerful "old boys' network," composed of his closest collaborators (interview with a political sociologist: March 15, 2001).[27] By 1974, the Oujda clan had disappeared and Boumedienne embarked on a new trajectory (Yefsah 1990: 254–64).

[26] Medeghri was found dead in 1974. The cause of death, either suicide or assassination, has never been confirmed.

[27] Members of the Oujda clan were riled that Boumedienne was assuming the leadership style of his predecessor – a style which, in their view, had warranted a *coup d'état*. Besides, Boumedienne's independent decision-making in the foreign policy arena elevated his international stature significantly, while leaving his closest collaborators in the shadows (interview with former member of Oujda clan, March 25, 2001). Recall that Boumedienne hosted the first OPEC summit meeting in 1975, and presented, along with others, the platform for a New International Economic Order (NIEO) at the Sixth Special Session of the United Nations General Assembly in April–May 1974. Because of his central role in the call for a NIEO, he was elected president of the UN General Assembly for 1974–5 (Mortimer 1977).

With the spectacular growth in rents that accompanied the oil shock, Boumedienne, like several other leaders of oil-exporting states at this time, became euphoric about the possibilities presented by the new-found revenues. He now had the means to realize lofty ambitions for the country. He found in Belaid Abdesselam a kindred spirit; he too could not accept that there were limits to what was possible. The "Rasputin" of economic development, Abdesselam had impressive qualities: he was hard working, determined, and quite austere (interviews with former technocrats in Boumedienne government: November 10, 2000; March 10, 2001). Very quickly, he became a force to be reckoned with.

Like the Shah of Iran vis-à-vis his planners and Suharto of Indonesia vis-à-vis his technocrats,[28] Boumedienne no longer heeded the words of caution from his most adept economic advisors and especially, Kemal Abdallah-Khodja, Secretary of State for the Plan. Abdallah-Khodja's investment targets and projections concerning the economy's "carrying capacity" were considered far too prudent, while his suggestions that consumption demand had to be met and that some private investment should be tolerated ran contrary to the "new thinking" (Hassan 1996: 84, 100–1; interview with an economist who had been with the Plan: June 30, 1999). In this new environment of plenty, planners were dispensable.

Boumedienne relied increasingly upon Belaid Abdesselam, who advocated freeing up or borrowing whatever resources were required to realize the very costly industrial projects he himself proposed. Whenever there was a disagreement between the Ministry and the Plan, Boumedienne invariably arbitrated in favor of the former. It became increasingly difficult for the Planners to dialogue with Boumedienne (interview with high-ranking technocrat in Boumedienne government: March 11, 2001). Furthermore, Belaid was able to ignore rules and procedures stipulated by the Plan. For example, he had access to investment funds without having to go through the Ministry of Finance. And, through his intervention, SONATRACH, then directed by his protégé, Sid Ahmed Ghozali, was never audited (confidential interviews: June 30, 2000; March 10, 2001; March 25, 2001). There were, indeed, no limits to what was possible.[29]

---

[28] See below, chapter 7.

[29] For an illuminating discussion, from Belaid Abdesselam himself, about the struggles within the high bureaucracy over policy directions, see Bennoune and El-Kenz (1990: 421–2). For a scathing critique of Belaid, from someone who knew him well, see Hassan (1996: 58–60, 98–103).

Over time, the Algerian SOEs became increasingly powerful. They had immense projects and important monopolies; they enjoyed huge subsidies from the state, and their directors, who were appointed by presidential decree, had considerable autonomy in their own spheres of economic activity (Yefsah 1990: 197–8). Embedded in patron–client networks of the public administration, they became increasingly involved in the exchange of favors and other forms of social accommodation (Liabès 1989: 219). Among them, SONATRACH was in an especially privileged position because of the importance of hydrocarbons in state revenues.[30]

As with all the public enterprises, SONATRACH fell under the authority of the Ministry of Industry and Energy. However, because the Ministry was run by Belaid Abdesselam, and because he had been the first director of SONATRACH and had been instrumental in placing Sid Ahmed Ghozali as his successor, a symbiotic relationship developed between Belaid and SONATRACH, with both doing much as they pleased. For example, SONATRACH managed to avert a regulation that required SOEs to request funds from the Plan for spending outside the country. Instead, SONATRACH arranged with the Ministry – that is, with Belaid Abdesselam – to simply leave funds outside the country for use there (interview with a former high-ranking technocrat in SONATRACH: June 26, 2000). SONATRACH, in turn, served as a virtual bank for Belaid: whenever he needed funds that were denied him by the Ministry of Finance – which would happen regularly, as there were constant battles between the two – he would dip into SONATRACH's purse (confidential interview: July 7, 2000).

Thus, from the early 1970s, SONATRACH was something of a sacred cow in the Algerian political economy, and those who managed it were allowed to become (or at least to behave) virtually untouchable. It was from this time that the military-backed regime relied increasingly for its incumbency upon rents generated from oil and gas production, overseen by SONATRACH.

Although the Algerian economy grew tremendously after the first oil shock, major problems with pronounced distributional effects emerged in the mid- to late 1970s. Algeria was not alone in this regard: many oil-exporting LDCs that embarked upon heavy industrialization strategies during this period faced similar problems (Philip 1994:

---

[30] In terms not only of influence but also of size, SONATRACH was the most important of the SOEs. By 1980, it had 100,000 employees, while the SNS – itself quite large and influential – had just under 40,000 (Abdoun 1990: 24).

174–91).[31] First, huge sums had been invested in heavy industry without building the necessary infrastructure. Faulty planning resulted in the proliferation of plants that were either not used to capacity, or else produced more than the market could absorb (Entelis and Naylor 1992: 15). Second, the commercial monopolies linked to the SOEs created inefficiencies and shortages that encouraged corruption and contraband activities (interview with a technocrat in the Boumedienne government: March 11, 2001). Third, the agrarian reform program, despite the populist discourse, was a dismal failure; rather than break up large landholdings and redistribute plots in an egalitarian manner among the peasantry, the latter were forced into cooperatives. In the absence of incentives to produce and with living standards depressed, massive migration to the cities continued unabated, swelling the ranks of the urban poor. Moreover, since agricultural production failed to keep pace with population growth, the need for food imports intensified (Swearingen 1992: 127). Self-sufficient at independence, Algeria would import more than 60 percent of its food by the end of the 1970s; that figure would increase to 75 percent by 1990 (Swearingen 1992).

Fourth, with the tremendous growth in the size and number of cities, a natural population increase of 3.2 percent, and the drying up of the *biens vacants*, an acute housing shortage would galvanize social conflicts in an incontrovertible manner (interview with technocrat in Boumedienne government: March 18, 2001). Despite the counsel of technocrats, Boumedienne would not accept that investing in housing was imperative; industrialization had to have the state's undivided attention (interviews with high-ranking technocrats in Boumedienne government: June 26, 2000; July 7, 2000). Indeed, structural variables that the leadership chose to ignore, combined with the distributional effects of leadership choices, would contribute to the deepening, and the politicization, of social cleavages.

Identity and nationality

As leaders of the independent state, both Ben Bella and Boumedienne encouraged the Arabo–Islamism advocated initially by the Messalists and the 'Ulemas, propelled as they were by the "monolithic unanimism" of Ben Badis' slogan: "Algeria is my country, Arabic my language, Islam my religion." The assertion that Arabic was the official language and Islam the official religion was written into the constitution of

---

[31] See, *inter alia*, the case of Venezuela (Karl 1997: 101–37) and of Iran (Katouzian 1981). For "report cards" of OPEC members, see Amuzegar (1999).

1963. Boumedienne endorsed it upon his seizure of power in 1965, and had it included in all official documents, alongside the stipulations that Algeria was a socialist state and the FLN the sole legal party.

Whether this was a rhetorical device employed by secular regimes to distance themselves from the former colonial power, a cynical means to win favor among more traditional forces, or tangible recognition of the contribution that reformist Islam had made to the nationalist struggle was beside the point. Certainly, unanimism advanced the interests of those in power. As James McDougall (2006: 234) has written, quoting, in turn, Omar Carlier (1998: 134): "In the political culture of the new state ... the reformists' religious *tawhid* ('unicity') served as the model for a political community in which 'diversity of status and opinion is denounced as deviance ... Community is placed under the sign of unicity while society itself unceasingly produces diversity.'"

With the stroke of a pen, the Berbers, as well as the *"pieds noirs"* (who chose to remain), were formally excluded from the Algerian "nation," while religious traditionalists and reformists were, in the early years at least, co-opted by the state.[32] Before long, however, a "contesting Islam" gestated outside of the official Islam and among those (religious) forces who felt marginalized by the system, just as they had in the final years of the revolution (Willis 1996a: 38–49).

The affirmation of ethno–national purity reinforced the continued domination of the militarized core that had hijacked power in the most brazen fashion. It provided the regime with a sense of legitimacy, insofar as it allied itself explicitly to the majority and to those who had gained control of the nationalist movement during that critical period between 1949 and 1954. By appropriating Islam and asserting its own religious affiliation, the regime attached itself – at least in form – to the peasantry, the traditional backbone of Algerian society, and to its dominant world view.

Arabo–Islamism was essentially a continuation of the divisive policies pursued by the colonial power, albeit in reversed form; this time, the Arabs were favored over the Berbers.[33] In addition, the commitment to Arabo–Islamism whitewashed the nationalist slate of the enormous

---

[32] Algerian Jews had effectively excluded themselves when a majority of them accepted the divisive *Crémieux Decree* of 1870. For an analysis of their attachment to the "nation" see Stora (2006).

[33] "Arabo–Islamism" refers to: the preference for Arabs over non-Arabs (Berbers) and for Arabic over Tamazight and French in/by the Algerian state; the persistent efforts to arabise the educational system and other key spheres, and the concomitant denial of the Berber dimension of Algerian culture and society; and the insistence on a religious (Islamic) dimension to governance and social relations.

contribution of the Kabyle Berbers, both as initiators of Algerian nationalism in Europe in the 1920s and as prominent revolutionaries during the war of independence. And it failed to acknowledge – indeed, it snubbed – the important role played by a considerable number of French nationals in actively promoting the Algerian revolution, often at great personal risk.[34]

Hocine Ait Ahmed, who, as we recall, had been a key player in the *crise berberiste* of 1949,[35] did resurrect the notion of an inclusivist Algeria. In his role as member of the first National Assembly, he insisted that the Berber identity be integrated into the constitution of 1963, and that all political forces be welcomed into the government so as to build a truly democratic Algeria (Ait Ahmed 1964: 143–64). At the same time, he objected to the incorporation of Islam into the constitution, as the latter was a *political* document representing the *national* community.

It would not be until twenty-five years later, after the bloody riots of October 1988, that the Berber dimension of Algeria was finally incorporated into the constitution, even though Tamazight would not be recognized as an "official" language – but rather, a "national" language – and formal instruction of Tamazight would still not be tolerated.[36] Besides, recognition on paper could not conceal genuine marginalization, as the revolts in Kabylia in the spring and summer of 2001 so poignantly demonstrated.[37]

Adopted, no doubt in part, to mask social cleavages which the leadership perceived as divisive and threatening, the Arabo–Islamism of Algerian regimes would have important social consequences in years to come. On the one hand, it would encourage the emergence, in the early 1980s, of a vibrant Berber culturalist movement. On the other hand, it would empower Islamophiles, who had been maneuvering in the shadows during the Boumedienne era, and contribute to the emergence of a politicized Islam. In the ensuing years, both Berber culturalists and Islamists would rally increasing numbers of adherents among the excluded and disillusioned.

---

[34] Among them, no doubt, was Frantz Fanon, whose work as a medical doctor and political analyst brought the Algerian Revolution and the struggle of the FLN into European drawing rooms. See his *The Wretched of the Earth* (1963) and *A Dying Colonialism* (1965). See, as well, the work of the "*réseau Jeanson*," described in Hamon and Rotman (1979).

[35] Above, chapter 3, pp. 59–61.

[36] It is interesting to note that Kabyle Berbers have insisted that Tamazight be taught throughout the country as an integral part of Algerian culture (interview with Algerian sociologist: May 15, 2000).

[37] See International Crisis Group (2003b).

Ben Bella and Boumedienne encouraged the Islamic dimension of Algeria in part, as was suggested above, to "keep the peasantry in place"; if the leadership affirmed its ties to traditions, then the traditionalist popular classes would rally to its support (confidential interview: July 3, 2000). In general, however, both leaders developed a relationship to religious traditionalists that included a combination of concessions and restraints. Ben Bella, for example, flirted with both secular modernists, represented by Mohamad Bedjaoui, then Secretary-General of the government, and religious traditionalists, represented by Malek Bennabi, the editor of al-Qiyaam, the newspaper of *al-Qiyaam al-islamiyya* – the movement created by Sheikh Bashir Ibrahimi (formerly of the AUMA) and Abassi Madani in 1964[38]– even though the two were hostile to each other.

Boumedienne dissolved the *al-Qiyaam* movement in 1967 and made it illegal (interview with a representative of an Islamist organization: July 4, 2000). Nonetheless, in an effort to appear to Algerian society as the "true Muslim," Boumedienne built mosques and numerous institutes of Islamic studies, and provided them with ongoing financial support. In this way, he promoted the religious and social activities that went on there. By the end of the 1970s, the mosque had become a *ressource contestataire* – a resource for the expression of opposition to the state, in addition to being a site for the expression of religious faith (Moussaoui 2006). In this highly authoritarian environment, the mosque was, after all, the only forum where people could gather, exchange views, and debate. Furthermore, by appointing Ahmed Taleb-Ibrahimi, the son of Sheikh Bashir Ibrahimi – former president of the pre-Independence Association of 'Ulema – Minister of Education, Boumedienne handed over educational reform and arabization to the religious traditionalists; he did so in an effort to appease them.

Primary education had been arabised completely by the early 1970s, while a two-tier system was adopted in secondary and post-secondary schools (Balta and Rulleau 1981). Because of the massive illiteracy – over 90 percent in 1962 – and the fact that those who were educated tended to be more fluent in French than in Classical Arabic, the regime was forced to recruit arabophone teachers from abroad. Algerian schools became the dumping ground for the least qualified and most

---

[38] Campaigning on behalf of Islamic values and demanding official support for Islamic rituals and duties, *al-Qiyaam al-islamiyya* was evidence of the beginnings of a relatively clandestine "Islamism." Note that Abassi Madani would co-found the *Front Islamique du Salut* (FIS) in the 1980s, and Ahmed Taleb Ibrahimi, son of Sheikh Bashir, would support the FIS in various ways, and later create his own "Islamo–nationalist" party, *Al-Wafa* (Roberts 1988, reprinted 2003a: 9–11).

undesirable of the foreign unemployed. Egypt's President Abd al-Nasr, for example, routinely sent members of the opposition Muslim Brotherhood to teach in Algeria (confidential interview: July 3, 2000; interview with a representative of an Islamist organization: July 4, 2000). There they would not only teach Arabic, the language of the Qur'an, but also inculcate their interpretation of Islamic doctrine and practice (Roberts 1988 in 2003a: 11–12). Moreover, the only Algerians who, at independence, were literate in Arabic – and hence could be hired to teach in the Arabic track – were those who had studied in the *medersa*, or Qur'anic schools.

As for the French track, it was by far the more rigorous, and it attracted the best students from relatively comfortable backgrounds (interviews with two Algerian scholars: March 4, 2001). Given that the system created by Boumedienne – a modernizing, urban-biased social-ism with a technocratic bent – was one in which, increasingly, profes-sional training and formal education, preferably in French, became the prerequisite for advancement, those educated in the French track stood far better chances of acquiring gainful employment than their arabophone compatriots (interviews with technocrats in Boumedienne government: June 26, 2000; July 7, 2000).[39] Indeed, by 1977, there were demonstrations in the universities, staged by arabophone students who could not find jobs (interview with Algerian scholar: June 26, 2000).

Educational reform reflected not only the contradictions that lay at the heart of Algeria's political development, but also the question about identity that had arisen in the 1940s and remained unanswered: Where do we look – toward the West (Europe) or toward the East (the Middle East and the Islamic world)? Since the question was con-sistently avoided, or treated in a paradoxical manner, educational reform exacerbated social cleavages and nurtured "political Islam." Schools became the breeding ground for "Islamism," at the same time as they sought to provide Algerians with the tools for building a modern nation.

To be sure, schools were a microcosm of what was occurring at the national level: all ministries having to do with language, religion, and values – in other words, Education, Information, Culture, and Justice – were dominated by religious traditionalists, while those related to the economy and development remained the responsibility of secular modernist technocrats. Identity and development would be advanced by two different, and often hostile, groups. Rather than integrate the

---

[39] See Grandguillaume (1995) for a fascinating discussion of the linkages between language and access to resources in Algeria.

constituent dimensions of the national culture – what Clifford Geertz (1973: 234–54), in his provocative discussion of "essentialism" and "epochalism," considers to be indispensable for successful nation-building – Boumedienne nourished the adversarial relationship between them. A fractured national identity persisted, while social frustrations and societal conflicts intensified.[40]

Addressing social conflict

To contain the growing popular dissatisfaction, the state, in 1976, organized a national debate and prepared a new National Charter. The aim was to revitalize the regime's waning legitimacy and ease the burden of the development strategy by institutionalizing some degree of political participation under the aegis of a modestly reinvigorated FLN. After having muzzled dissent and denied real political activity for so long, (the semblance of) popular incorporation would serve a palliative function (Yefsah 1990: 270–7).

Although the national debate was highly controlled by the regime, there were two ominous developments (interview with Algerian sociologist: May 15, 2000). In Tizi Ouzou, the capital of Kabylia, and in Blida, a stronghold of conservatism, the regime was overwhelmed by outbursts of popular discontent. An array of social ills was broached: nepotism, low salaries, poor living conditions, uncertain futures for the youth. Identity concerns were added to the grievances: in Tizi Ouzou, the Berber dimension of Algeria was invoked; in Blida, the acceleration of arabization in schools was demanded, while the regime's secularism was reproached. The outbursts subsided, but these same issues would re-emerge with increasing frequency and volatility.

The new National Charter was indicative of a state that enjoyed some degree of institutional resilience in the face of simmering civil unrest.[41] For one, although there had been a dip in the price of oil and a mini-recession in oil-exporters' economies (Amuzegar 1999: 33), the Algerian state still had funds to distribute from its exports and loans. Second, Boumedienne, in a clever and timely fashion, unveiled a

---

[40] Reflecting on the civil war period from 1992, Ali El-Kenz (1997: 343) echoes Clifford Geertz: "The search for identity drifted into violence. A national culture had failed to integrate its two constituent dimensions, 'an existential experience and a constituted knowledge.' And yet such a synthesis remains the only path to modernity."

[41] See Chaudhry (1997: 269–89) for an illuminating discussion of institutional resilience – so crucial in moments of crisis – in Saudi Arabia in the post-1986 bust period.

new constitution that reiterated the old clichés about the "popular will" and the promotion of the "new Algerian man" (Yefsah 1990: 283). This echoed the persistent effort to paper over deep divisions in society and suppress the resurgence of social conflicts. Third, Boumedienne implemented structural reforms within the bureaucracy and a major re-shuffling of ministerial posts. Most notably, in April 1977, the Ministry of Industry and Energy, Belaid Abdesselam's fiefdom since 1965, was divided into three separate ministries. Abdesselam was cut down: he became Minister of Light Industry.

Was this a return to a "politics of scarcity" after the oil-inspired euphoria? Was it an effort to stunt the stature and maneuverability of Abdesselam and retain all power for the za'im (leader)? Or was it a reaction to the excesses of the development strategy? Indeed, the discourse of egalitarianism, social justice, and inclusion had increasingly come up against a reality of inequality, nepotism, and exclusion. One year later – in December 1978 – Boumedienne died.

Conclusion

In exploring the consolidation of state power in Algeria in the period after independence, we note that at the outset, the leadership enjoyed a very narrow social base. As such, it worked hard to nurture a loyal public, and cement a connection between itself and the people. The shape of institutions created by the regime and the rhetoric that accompanied the institutionalization of power provided the blueprint, and the rationale, for the distribution of resources and privileges in independent Algeria. At the very center was the president himself, initially accompanied by a tiny entourage of wartime companions, and backed by a devoted military. Over time, the tiny entourage would be pushed aside so that the president could rule unconstrained, but in alliance with the military. Personalism, alongside the concentration of power, would characterize rule, and all (potentially) competing power centers would be systematically eliminated.

Apart from the presidency, all state institutions were phantoms or hollow shells. They were de-politicized, virtually from the start. They existed as fiction, to give credence to the socialist ideology and populist rhetoric. Their purpose lay in their symbolic value as conduits for regime ideology and representations of national unity. Figments of state power, they had at their helm loyal subjects who exercised little autonomy, but promised obedience, and filled their positions only as long as the leader deemed fit.

Given the nature of rule and the shape of institutions, all independent voices were silenced – brutally at times – and alternate visions enjoyed no forum. Access to resources and to privilege was determined on the basis of proximity to and discretion of power. In this environment, there was no room for social movements. Constituting a network of inter-personal ties or a collective identity, plus a determination to take action collectively in the face of a common grievance, social movements simply would not be tolerated in Boumedienne's Algeria.

When social movements did threaten to take shape, as in the late 1970s in response to the harsh realities of the regime's social and eco-nomic programs, Boumedienne moved quickly to nullify their *raison d'etre*. Through piecemeal reform, he addressed the very concerns that would have prompted their formation and eventual mobilization. At that moment of leadership challenge, Boumedienne successfully assuaged the rising tide of discontent. Through a combination of more or less trivial structural changes, targetted injections of economic resources, and a generalized, if not superficial, distribution of political resources – in the form of sanctioning some degree of expression – he neutralized the competing cleavage structures that chafed under the distributional arrangements he had put into place.

Recall that in the independent state, as during the war of liberation, no social divisions and no ideological, regional, or linguistic particularisms were admitted to. Ideational and "cultural" concerns were considered at best, distractions from the principal tasks and at worst, threats to the leader's continued domination. Furthermore, the emphasis in official discourse on "the people," the "unity of the people and the party-state," and the denunciation of all social differentiation on the basis of wealth contributed to the production of unanimism, cementing the illusion of uniformity and equality. Thus, it bolstered the legitimacy of the state and its hegemony over society, and heightened the expectations of the population (El-Kenz 1989). This institutional arrangement did away with pluralism, while providing the illusion of popular incorpora-tion. By controlling the extension of participation in this way, it pro-tected elite privileges and Boumedienne's agenda. This was, indeed, an authoritarian regime aimed at radically reshaping Algerian society and economy in the absence of political participation.

Hence, from the inception of oil-based development in the 1960s and through its intensification in the 1970s, key cleavage structures were themselves – and despite the rhetoric – weakly incorporated into the "new Algeria." They routinely competed for, and at times were denied, access to resources. Indeed, the system of redistribution reinforced clientelism, hence the strong collegial, kinship, and regional ties that had persisted from the revolutionary years. Those same social forces that had been denied inclusion in the post-1949 period remained on the margins in the independent state. A politics of exclusion prevailed; it benefited *grosso modo* those who could forge alliances with the regime, either directly or indirectly – because they were related in some manner, or could cultivate a relationship of value. But the politics of exclusion incubated social conflicts that Algerian leaders would be increasingly hard-pressed to manage effectively.

The heart of the problem was the paradox that lay at the core of the construction of the nation. In this highly fragmented and factionalized society, difference and voice were systematically denied. At the same time, the state elaborated an institutional framework that consolidated highly politicized distributional arrangements which themselves invigorated fragmentation and factionalism. Through the selective distribution of rent and other material favors, loyalties were bought, alliances were cemented, and networks were greased. Former members of the *Armée de la frontière* remained the most privileged social category,[42] while the people, in general, were suspect, and Berber nationalists and religious traditionalists were marginalized when they could not be co-opted.

The hydrocarbon sector has been the backbone and principal instrument of state power, while SONATRACH – its representative – has remained above supervision, regulation, and accountability. SONATRACH became the primary vehicle for channeling rents and the principal source for the enrichment of members of the elite. Moreover, it came to epitomize two central features of the system and the related disconnect between the state and society: first, the purposive neglect of the rural sector, where the majority of the population continued to live (until the late 1980s);[43] and second, the preference for francophone, Europeanized elites who could assume positions in the modern sector of the economy and bureaucracy.

The politics of exclusion, concealed behind a rhetoric of inclusion, would promote social conflict from which Algerian regimes would get little relief. As Okruhlik (1999) notes with respect to Saudi Arabia, the state, in effect, had "constructed" its own opposition by reinforcing competing cleavage structures through its spending practices. The polity was fractionalized.

---

[42] For example, on the eve of independence, officers simply established themselves on prime real estate in the highly arable Mitidja plain, southwest of Algiers (Lowi 2005).

[43] See Aissaoui (2001: 10): the rural population represented 68 percent of the total in 1970, 63 percent in 1975, 58 percent in 1980, 53 percent in 1985.

Nonetheless, when faced with domestic challenges in 1976/7, Boumedienne did show resilience and acuity. By responding to popular unrest through gentle manipulation and the provision of "political" resources, he was able to mitigate dissent, impede mobilization, gain acquiescence, and in so doing shore up regime legitimacy. The capacity of leadership to effectively adjudicate distributional conflicts at critical junctures is key to protecting against instability.

5 From boom to bust, and ... verging on breakdown

At the FLN congress of January 1979, Chadli Benjedid was named sole candidate for the presidency.[1] He had been head of *wilaya II* (the second military district) during the War of Independence and was a fairly color-less member of Boumedienne's Council of the Revolution. He was put into power by the military, the most powerful institution in the country. In choosing a former FLN colonel, the preponderance of the military in political life was maintained, while the symbolic role of the party was acknowledged.

Despite some differences in window-dressing, the first three regimes of the independent state were bureaucratic–authoritarian and patrimo-nial in structure. They shared deep ideological affinities that conformed to the foundational myths inherited from the nationalist movement: that of popular sovereignty and national unity. The broad strategies of governance were fundamentally the same as well. The regimes remained wedded to the single party, a prominent state sector, and the national-ization of the economy (Carlier 1995: 335–6). They did so to confront – but at the same time to dismiss – the segmentarity, regional disparities, "ruralism," and underdevelopment that so characterized Algerian society and threatened incumbents. Increasingly, however, a military caste would dominate: it would stand at the helm of what was the FLN–ALN system, and utilize civilian presidents as its "front men" (Roberts 2007: 8).

---

[1] Many Algerians interviewed by this author recounted anecdotes that denigrated Chadli and his capacities. One of his former ministers is quoted as having said the following: "Chadli n'avait ni l'étoffe d'un chef d'Etat, ni les capacités intellectuelles pour diriger un pays" (Aboud 2002: 120) [Chadli had neither the "stuff" of a head of state, nor the intellectual capacities to lead a country (translation my own).] Abdelhamid Brahimi, prime minister from 1984–8, wrote the following of his president: "Ni idéologue, ni stratège, il n'était pas doté d'une ambition particulière à l'égard de son pays ... Il n'avait pas une vision globale et cohérente des exigences de developpement" (Brahimi 2000: 202) [Neither ideologue nor strategist, he did not have a sense of a particular destiny for his country that would inform his efforts ... He did not have a coherent and global vision of what it takes for a country to develop (translation my own)].

Notwithstanding the continuity that so characterized what Algerians came to call *le système*, the latter was constantly fraught with tensions. There were economic conflicts between the public and private sectors, political rivalries between groups and "clans," linguistic tensions between francophones and arabophones, and cultural divergences between secularists and religionists and, somewhat less so, between Arabs and Berbers. The source of these tensions was, at least in part, the imposed integration and the concomitant denial of difference that lay at the core of the myth of national unity.

With the intensification of socio-economic hardships in the 1980s and the failure of the regime to confront them effectively, the state, built as it was on the successful management of both economic rent and foundational myths, was fragilized. The populist formula, and especially the "heroic model of social intervention" (Carlier 1995: 337) of *l'état providence* (the magnanimous state), were laid bare with the precipitous decline in oil prices, the startling increase in the national debt, and the return of shortages and high levels of unemployment. The state was quickly losing the bases of its legitimacy. Social forces, reflecting the deep cleavages within Algerian society, emerged and eventually captured center stage.

In this chapter, I continue the discussion of the historical trajectory of Algeria, from the inception of the Chadli leadership in 1979 through the onset of civil war in 1992. I highlight the challenges that the regime faced, initially in the domain of the economy and then from social forces, and the manner in which it responded. As in previous chapters, I underscore the decisions of leaders regarding the shape of institutions and distributive arrangements. My aim in this chapter is twofold: first, to understand why and how the regime was fragilized, and second, to demonstrate how the combination of leadership choice at a particular historical conjuncture and the organizational capacities of the opposition brought the regime to the brink of breakdown.

I begin this chapter by describing the social and economic policies that President Chadli Benjedid implemented in the early years of his incumbency, coinciding with the second oil boom. I go on to explore societal responses to the new policies and, after 1982, the growing economic constraints. Embryonic social movements – composed of Kabyle Berbers, on the one hand, and religious traditionalists, on the other – emerged to confront persistent issues of exclusion and inequality. I then evaluate Chadli's authoritarian response to the increasing mobilization of discontent. Following that, I describe the cataclysmic oil price downturn of 1985/6 and its profound effects on the Algerian economy and society. I analyze popular responses to the constraints, including the intensification of "parallel" economic activities, the appearance of new social categories such as the *hittistes* and the *trabendistes*, and the striking prominence of "political Islam." Next, I explore government efforts, in the period following the 1988 riots, to address the rising tensions by initiating major reforms. I demonstrate that it was precisely because of the way the leadership responded and the new institutional arrangements it implemented that the country descended into violence. I conclude with an analysis of the period in terms of the principal variables that inform this study, and the linkages between them.

Chadli comes to power

For a two-year period from 1979 to 1981, as Chadli sought to consolidate his power, there was ongoing debate within the state apparatus between the partisans of continued state capitalism and partisans of private capitalism (or economic liberalization) (Hidouci 1995: 90–1). This debate had begun in the final years of the Boumedienne era and reflected a trend occurring elsewhere in the Middle East and North Africa – in Turkey and Egypt especially – and in the developing world more generally. In the context of slow growth and general economic hardship, related, in large measure, to the nature of the country's insertion in the international political economy, third-world elites were progressively renouncing economic nationalist development and state capitalism in favor of liberalization.

Chadli himself sided with those who favored liberalization (Vandewalle 1992: 189–96). In the uncertain political environment of the early years of his tenure, Chadli, lacking any social base whatsoever, aimed to rid the regime of key "Boumediennists," especially among the powerful technocrats, and replace them with members of his "clan." He sought to maintain a consensus within the bureaucracy, and win over those sectors of society which had chafed under his predecessor's leadership. In these ways, he could secure loyalty, neutralize opposition, and legitimize his own rule. As part of his efforts to de-Boumediennize much of the domestic political economy, Chadli subjected the power structure to a major shake-up and re-established the General Staff, which had been abolished by Boumedienne at the end of 1967.[2] He also implemented important policy shifts, very few of which reflected genuine "openness," despite all the talk of the new leader's liberalism (Willis 1996b: 200).[3]

---

[2] This decision would come back to haunt him: he had instigated the growing power and autonomy of the General Staff, and the weakening of his own authority over factionalism within the military (Roberts 2007: 9).

[3] For a detailed discussion of Benjedid's economic liberalization strategy and its different stages, see Vandewalle (1992: 193–200).

Social and economic policies (and their effects)

Under the remarkable slogan *pour une vie meilleure* (*min ajli ḥayaatin aḥsan*: "for a better life"), the first five-year plan of the Benjedid era was unveiled in the summer of 1980, with its recipe for rectifying the errors of the past and leading Algerians to a truly better life (Brahimi 2000: 212–14; El-Kenz 1989: 13–15). The core of the plan was to improve state management of the economy and society. It was thought that this could be achieved by decentralizing and deconcentrating economic decision-making, scaling back the power and autonomy of the huge SOEs that had dominated the economy in the 1970s, encouraging some private-sector activity, and attending to consumption demand of an arguably deprived population (Murphy 1996: 181–7). The stated goals were salutary ones: to protect the non-renewable oil endowment, reduce dependency on the hydrocarbon sector, and reorient development away from heavy industry and toward other, previously neglected sectors such as agriculture, consumer goods, and the social services (Entelis 1988: 49). To assist him, Chadli was fortunate to have significant oil rents at his disposal. Recall that his coming to power coincided with the second oil boom, following the Iranian revolution, when oil prices more than doubled and the regime was awash with capital.[4]

The results of the new economic program, however, were most disturbing. Sub-dividing and restructuring the public enterprises, the brainchild of Abdelhamid Brahimi, Chadli's Minister of Planning and later Prime Minister, and relocating their auxiliary activities were, in principle, positive reforms; they could have curtailed the public enterprises' monopoly status. Nonetheless, the reforms were carried out in a rapid, haphazard fashion.[5] Besides, the many new structures, now called *entreprises publiques économiques* (EPEs) and totaling more than 400, as opposed to the previous 70 SOEs, were headed by loyal clients of the new regime (Abdoun 1990: 40–1). With the proliferation of EPEs,

---

[4] The price of oil had increased from $14 per barrel in 1978 to $32 in 1979 and $37 in 1980. Note that from 1979 until 2003, Algerian exports of liquid natural gas (LNG) were the largest in the Middle East and North Africa region. Its exports of 20 billion cubic meters in 1979 increased to 83 billion cubic meters in 2003, after which it was overtaken by Iran (BP Statistical Review 2008). Since the 1980s, the bulk of Algeria's hydrocarbon revenues derives from natural gas and not crude oil.

[5] According to two high-ranking technocrats of the 1970s and 1990s, who had been with the Plan or with SONATRACH and became government ministers, several of the reforms appeared to have been driven more by the will to destroy the hallmark of Boumedienne's development agenda and the technocrats who had guided it, rather than by sound economic policy (confidential interviews: March 7, 2001; March 9, 2001).

clientelism flourished, as did mismanagement and waste, despite Chadli's touted "cleanup campaign" (Murphy 1996: 181–2).

In effect, Chadli put an end not only to the primacy of developmentalism and the coherence and coordination of industrial strategy, but to investment in industry overall. As for private-sector activity, it increased only slightly. Not only was it wary of the security of its investments after more than a decade of nationalizations and anti-capitalist rhetoric, but it continued to be subjected to an array of government controls. Those engaged in the private sector preferred the security of foreign bank accounts, the quick gains of speculative investment, especially in real estate, or business ventures in conjunction with the state. Productive investment in Algeria, where property rights were uncertain and the rule of law weakly defined, was far too risky for this not terribly entrepreneurial class (Henni nd.; Tlemcani 1986).[6]

While investment in agriculture did increase, from a mere 6 percent of total investments in 1977 to 12 percent in the early to mid-1980s, it was still far too little relative to demographic growth; the latter was only beginning to recede from its high average of 3.2 percent per annum in the 1970s (Goumeziane 1994: 56–61). The need for food imports would continue to grow to alarming levels, reaching 70 percent of consumption demand by the end of the second oil boom (Amuzegar 1999: 117).[7] The importing frenzy that quickly overwhelmed the domestic political economy, as we will see below, discouraged agricultural activity unquestionably. During the initial years of the first five-year plan, overall growth figures for the Algerian economy were disappointing: from a high of 8.5 percent in the 1970s, per capita GDP fell to an average of 2.75 percent between 1979 and 1982 (World Bank). It would continue to fall as the decade unfolded.

What, then, became of the fabulous rents that had accrued to the state with the second oil shock?[8] In fact, during these early boom years, oil rents

---

[6] To be sure, patron–client relations function as a form of protection in environments where the question of property rights has not been satisfactorily resolved.

[7] By the end of the Boumedienne period, external dependence on imports was already quite significant: in 1978, imports of agricultural and industrially produced consumer goods represented 28.4 percent of total imports, while imports of consumer goods represented 45.7 percent of total exports – "almost half the value of hydrocarbon exports" at that time. In fact, hydrocarbon rents (92.3 percent of exports) were used primarily to import consumer goods and service the external debt (25.3 percent of exports) (Abdoun 1990: 29).

[8] In 1980, Algeria's oil export revenues would be $20.2 billion (in constant 1990 billion $), having increased almost five-fold from $4.2 billion in 1972. They would fall back to $4.8 billion in 1986 (Henry and Springborg 2001: 40). Recall that the price of oil was $12/ba at the end of 1978, and then increased to $34/ba in 1980 and $40/ba in 1981.

were used to "liberate" pent-up consumption demand and in that way curry the favors of the middle classes, and the *petit bourgeoisie* especially. Chadli initiated a program – the *programme anti-pénurie* (PAP: Anti-Poverty Program) – to attenuate the shortages of the Boumedienne era which had caused so much frustration. A centerpiece in the regime's *pour une vie meilleure* agenda, the PAP was a variation of Anwar Sadat's *infitah* ("open door" policy) in Egypt. Oil rents plus borrowed funds were expended lavishly to import non-essential consumer goods, which were then made available to the population, or rather, to those who could afford them.[9]

The symbol of the PAP, and of the "better life," was the monument built to honor conspicuous consumption: *Riad al-Feth* (the Gardens of Victory) – a massive, luxurious commercial complex built on 146 hectares of land in the heart of Algiers and containing roughly 200 modern shops, restaurants, and movie theatres. It, along with the *souk al-fellah* (the Peasant's Market), a chain of state-owned department stores, suggested that consumption was not only victorious but also accessible to everyone, even the peasantry.[10] The former obsession with production and reliance on austerity were now replaced by an obsession with consumption – which presupposed material comfort, scorned sobriety, discouraged productivity – and reliance on networking and personal connections. Past practices of personalism, patrimonialism, and clientelism were duly reinforced.

On the surface, the program worked well for a few years. Having fabricated an atmosphere of well-being, it bought social peace. Nonetheless, while the lower middle classes were appeased somewhat, their appetites had been whetted and their expectations blossomed. Within no time, the PAP proved to be a scandalous means of enrichment for those linked to the bureaucracy: while import restrictions had indeed been lifted, distribution remained confined to the "nomenklatura" and their clients. Not only did these "agents of the state" enjoy handsome commissions for services rendered, but also they exploited their privileged positions to exchange state-sector goods amongst themselves.[11] It was at this time that real estate hand-outs – especially of agricultural land in the

---

[9] On the intricacies of the new system of importation and its relationship to the restructuring of the SOEs, see Henni (nd.: 127–36).

[10] When I visited *Riad al-Feth* in 2000, after more than a decade of economic decline, the complex was empty and ghostlike. Most of the shops had been shut down, and the once chic mall was taken over by unsavory characters looking to fade into the shadows.

[11] See Goumeziane (1994) on the commissions system put into place during the Chadli era. As Emma Murphy (2001: 11) points out, the ruling elite became increasingly engaged in private accumulation, thereby blurring the distinction between the public and private sectors.

Mitidja – took off in fantastic proportions (Hadjadj 1999: 42–53, 102).[12] In addition, underground supply networks materialized, and a fairly extensive parallel economy, to mitigate the failings of the public and private sectors, was launched (Henni nd.: 52–3).

The way in which oil rents were utilized, in the new context of controlled liberalization, favored the proliferation of rent-seeking opportunities, the institutionalization of patronage, and the consolidation of bureaucratic–authoritarianism. Overall, rents had become a means to satisfy appetites and maintain *le système*; they were no longer a source for productive investment, as they had been, for the most part, during the Boumedienne era (Hidouci 1995: 91). Furthermore, soon after adopting the PAP, the government had to start paying back its substantial loans, and this coincided with the sharp decline in oil revenues after 1982. The PAP came to a bitter end. It had fostered corruption and intensified inequalities; it contributed indirectly to the renewed scarcities which it had been meant to offset.

Society responds; the regime backpedals

In the early years of his tenure and in the absence of genuine reform, Chadli's encouragement, through loose, "liberal" talk, of a more politically permissive atmosphere, seemed to backfire. Rather than elicit widespread support for his regime, it inspired the emergence of "autonomous movements of social protest" which would eventually overwhelm the public space (Roberts 1984: 33). Reflecting deep social cleavages that were integral to the Algerian landscape and the persistent refusal of the leadership to address them, the *mouvement culturel berbère* (MCB – Berber culturalist movement) emerged for the first time as a powerful force, as did a number of Islamist formations and figures – among them, the future founders of the *Front Islamique du Salut* (FIS – Islamic Salvation Front), as well as precursors of the Islamist *maquis* (guerilla resistance) of the 1990s. In the ensuing years, both Berberists and Islamists would rally increasing numbers of adherents from among the disillusioned and excluded.

Based in the mountainous Kabyle region some fifty miles east of Algiers, the MCB, as its name suggests, sought to promote and defend the distinct cultural and linguistic identity of the Kabyle Berbers, the most culturally assertive of the four Berber groups in Algeria. Recall that Kabyle Berbers had been among the initiators and leading figures of Algerian

---

[12] Recall that this practice had begun with independence (above, chapter 4).

nationalism, and that the question of the Berber identity of the Algerian nation had been raised during the nationalist period.[13] This movement came dramatically and spontaneously to the fore in the spring of 1980 when Tizi Ouzou, the capital of Kabylia, became the scene of a series of anti-government demonstrations, including a general strike. The events were sparked by the refusal of the local authorities to allow Mouloud Mammeri, a prominent Kabyle writer and cultural figure, to give a public lecture in Tamazight on Berber poetry.[14] The government responded to the unrest – what came to be called the "Berber Spring," evoking the Prague Spring of 1968 in then Czechoslovakia – with a harsh crackdown and severe repression (Chaker 1987; Roberts 1982). In responding thus, it paved the way for mounting indignation and determined resistance toward the arabophile, exclusionary, anti-democratic state.

Chadli stepped up the arabization of the educational system as soon as he took office. Recall that as of the end of the Boumedienne era, there was unrest at the universities, as students of arabized disciplines protested against the favoritism shown to francophone students and the superior career opportunities available to them.[15] Ironically, this provided Chadli with what he considered an opportunity: as noted above, he was determined to fight the technocratic elite that had guided Boumedienne's development strategy. They opposed Chadli's economic reforms, and Chadli accused them of francophilia. He proceeded to dismiss key figures from important government positions, replacing them with *cadres* who had been marginalized in the past and therefore would happily endorse a change of direction.[16] At the same time, he accelerated the process of

---

[13] Above, chapter 3.

[14] Hugh Roberts (1993, reprinted in 2003: 14) notes that the MCB was concerned largely with language and culture. It was only with the founding, in 1989, of the *Rassemblement pour la culture et la démocratie* (RCD), the "Berberist" party of Saad Saadi that grew out of the MCB, that secularism was embraced as well.

[15] See chapter 4, p. 96.

[16] Among Chadli "loyalists" at this time, two in particular stand out as reflecting the regime's direction. Abdelhamid Brahimi, prime minister from 1984–8, was the son of a founding member of the pre-independence *Association des 'Ulama*. He himself militated first in the MTLD and then, with military training acquired in the Middle East, commanded a division during the war of liberation. During the Ben Bella period, he was *wali* (governor) of Annaba, and then spent the Boumedienne years on the sidelines and/or out of the country. Trained as an economist, he was brought back by Chadli Benjedid in 1979 to head the newly created *Ministère de la Planification et de l'Aménagement du Territoire*. Brahimi was the architect of the economic "restructuring" policies of the Chadli period. With the October 1988 riots, he was dismissed from his position; he subsequently left the country, in disgrace. From exile, he charged the regimes of Boumedienne and Benjedid with rampant corruption and embezzlement, and advocated an Islamist alternative.

Belkacem Nabi, Minister of Chemical and Petrochemical Industries from 1979–88, was an engineer who had been active in the *Fédération de France du FLN* during the war

arabization in high schools, at the university, and within the justice system. Staunch proponents of arabization quickly populated the related ministries (Ruedy 1992: 240).

Chadli believed that such measures would appease Islamists who, throughout the 1970s, had become increasingly visible, despite remaining quite restrained in their actions (Entelis 1988: 56). He expected that they, in return, would support him in his efforts to right the wrongs of the past and neutralize the "francophile" elite. Instead, his reforms, not unlike Anwar Sadat's, played directly into the hands of the Islamist opposition and galvanized Islamist activism of considerable proportions (Willis 1996a: 70–2).

The choice of Arabo–Islamism emboldened Algerian Islamists. Within no time, large-scale demonstrations spearheaded by Islamists were demanding compulsory nation-wide religious instruction, respect of Islamic dress codes, prohibition of alcohol, and limitations on the education of females. Chadli responded with a severe crackdown: he had several hundred Islamists and their supporters arrested (Willis 1996a: 72–4). It was at this time, the fall of 1982, that Abassi Madani surfaced alongside two other, soon to become prominent leaders of Algeria's Islamist movement: Sheikhs Abdellatif Soltani and Ahmed Sahnoun (Al-Ahnaf et al. 1991). The Islamist opposition had become a distinctive feature of the social and political landscape: one that would be increasingly difficult for the state to contain.

Chadli's early years witnessed the growth of a new type of Islamist activism that would eventually overwhelm the domestic political economy. In 1982, the first guerilla movement in the history of the independent state emerged, calling itself the *Mouvement algérien islamique armée* (MAIA: Armed Algerian Islamic Movement). Its leader, Mustafa Bouyali, was an FLN veteran of the Algerian War of Liberation. At the end of the 1970s, he founded a clandestine organization, the Group for Defence against the Illicit, to campaign for a "return to Islamic values in social and political life" and the eventual implementation of the *shari'a* (Moussaoui 1994: 1324–5; Willis 1996a: 71–2). When the efforts of the organization went unheeded, Bouyali concluded that armed struggle was the only way to achieve his goals. He created the MAIA, which was

years, before working in the energy and petroleum sector in the early years of the independent state. Removed from this sector in the Boumedienne period – when Belaid Abdesselam and Sid Ahmed Ghozali became prominent – he worked first as *wali* of Tlemçen and then as advisor at the Presidency. With Chadli's accession to power, he was named member of the Political Bureau of the FLN and then Minister of Energy. His management of the hydrocarbon sector was virulently criticized by his predecessors, and Belaid Abdesselam especially.

organized along the lines of the *wilaya* system – a network of regionally
dispersed clandestine cells, reminiscent of the wartime FLN strategy –
and was equipped with weapons seized from military outposts.

Between 1982 and 1987, when Bouyali himself was gunned down and
most of his followers were either dead or imprisoned, the MAIA was a
source of humiliation for the regime. Although it was only several hundred
strong, it managed to launch spectacular operations that targetted
the state and "looted" its resources, and evade capture (Roberts 1988,
reprinted in 2003a: 23–4).[17] Bouyali, because of his courage, defiance,
and the originality of his tactics, became something of a mythic hero; he
would inspire *maquisards* of the 1990s.[18] Besides, he and his supporters
reflected a sentiment that was growing among the populace: disillusion-
ment with the regime and the status quo. The view that a "return to Islam"
was the antidote to the Algerian predicament was gaining adherents.

The particularistic challenges that emerged at the beginning of the
1980s were by no means new. Nonetheless, they had been more or less
dormant until they were rekindled by the new leadership's disingenuous
liberalism and reckless economic policies, and their profound socio-
economic effects. Taken aback by the audacity and mobilizational
capacity of these newly emergent social forces, and desperate to regain
control, Chadli responded with a prompt return to authoritarianism and
stepped up centralization of decision-making. He pushed aside many key
members of the political elite, neutralizing powerful liberals and advocates
of state capitalism alike, appointed sympathetic army commanders to
sensitive posts, and surrounded himself with a handful of his closest allies
from his immediate entourage. Alone and unencumbered for some time,
they would be responsible for the formulation and implementation of
policy (Brahimi 2000: 197–203).

So as to capture the reconfigured social forces, Chadli sought to revive
the FLN which, although still "the single party," had served little more
than a symbolic role for nearly two decades. As if to reconnect the regime
with the people, Chadli, via the *article 120* of 1982, imposed membership in the FLN as the condition for both membership in any mass
organization and employment within the state sector (Yefsah 1990:

[17] See the colorful descriptions of MAIA operations in Moussaoui (1994: 1324–5) and in
Merah (1998). They included such things as stealing 160 kilograms of TNT from an
SOE, plans to seal public buildings with plastic, etc.
[18] Several high-ranking members of the FIS, including its co-founder, Ali Belhaj, had been
associated with Bouyali and his MAIA. Another source for Islamists in the 1990s were
those Algerians who, encouraged by Chadli and supported by Western powers, had
fought in Afghanistan in the 1980s against the Soviet Union. On the "Afghans," see
Mokeddem (2002).

445). While suggesting a tripartite alliance among the people, the party, and the state, this new law, coupled with Chadli's decision to decrease the size of the FLN Political Bureau and assume some of its functions for himself, provided the state with a powerful means for reinforcing its control and removing hundreds of *cadres* from positions of responsibility in the public domain (El-Kenz 1989b: 15).

Albeit a prop of the regime, the renascent FLN became – not unlike the Chinese Communist Party – the sole, licit, acknowledged means of social promotion. At the same time, it imposed conformity on its membership, and provided a cover for the greatly enhanced powers of the presidency and the overwhelming importance of social capital in the form of personalized linkages (Carlier 1995: 333; Henni nd.: 27–8). Until 1989 and the introduction of multipartism, a hollowed-out FLN would exercise a legal monopoly over political life, while the regime – indeed, a small number of *décideurs*, most of whom had military backgrounds – tightened the reins of control and nourished patrimonial structures.[19]

Chadli's response to the reinvigorated social cleavages was fraught with confusion. On the one hand, he became increasingly dictatorial and reclusive, conferring only with his innermost circle of advisors (Brahimi 2000). On the other hand, he seemed terrified by the growing Islamist opposition: when he could not repress it, he yielded to it. In 1984, for example, his government enacted a new and highly regressive family code which profoundly constrained the rights and freedoms of Algerian women.[20] Furthermore, government funding for Islamic education and the building of mosques and other Islamic institutions increased dramatically (Ruedy 1992: 243). As for the Berbers, they gained a very slight concession insofar as the National Charter of 1986 acknowledged, for the first time, the Berber dimension of the Algerian nation.

1985–6: oil prices plummet

On the surface, all was more or less under control through Chadli's first term in office. By the end of 1983, he seemed to have consolidated his power and purchased some degree of social peace. After that, the price of

---

[19] As Willis (1996b: 200) writes: "Chadli in the early 1980s seemed no more willing than his predecessors to alter the 'iron triangle' of state, party, and army that made up the political structure of Algeria."

[20] According to the new family code, a woman was the ward of her father, and then her husband. She could not marry a non-Muslim, nor could she request a divorce; and she could work outside the home only with the permission of her male guardian. This legislation, repressive as it was, is even more disturbing when one reflects on the key role played by Algerian women in the struggle against French colonialism. See Slyomovics (1995) and Gillo Pontecorvo, La Battaglia di Algeri (*The Battle of Algiers*, 1965).

oil, which had been hovering around $30 per barrel for a few years, began to fall. By the summer of 1986, it had plummeted to an all-time low of $10.[21] Government receipts from the sale of oil were halved; they declined from $14.2 billion in 1981 to only $7.3 billion five years later, while the proportion of hydrocarbon revenues in total government revenues fell from 44 percent to 24 percent (Joffe 2002: 8).

Chadli's initial response was classic. Rather than devalue the currency, fearing its inflationary effects, he chose to step up foreign borrowing to cover the shortfall in revenues. This worked for a very short time, but then Algeria fell victim once again to international structural forces, and to its own short-sighted economic policies that had intensified its dependence upon the external environment.

With the return to monetary policy in the US as of the early 1980s, and the catastrophic Mexican peso crisis of 1982, foreign lending to developing countries like Algeria decreased considerably, and borrowing conditions became more stringent. No longer were private banks lending at less than 10 percent interest, as they had been in the 1970s (Goumeziane 1994: 91–2). Besides, the limits of oil-based, heavy industrial development programs – their limited productivity and tremendous waste – were coming to light, while the degree of indebtedness of oil-exporting LDCs began to give creditors cause for concern. The earlier view that oil exporters were infinitely reliable clients of international financial institutions, as a result of what were assumed to be limitless supplies of oil, quickly vanished. Indeed, with the intensifying debt crisis, aggravated by the decline in receipts from hydrocarbon exports especially after 1986, international financial markets were closed to Algeria and other LDCs (Tables 5.1 and 5.2).

Unable to borrow, the Benjedid government cut back drastically on imports. While in 1985 imports were cut only 5 percent by value over 1984 levels, one year later they were cut 15 percent, and by 1987 as much as 28 percent (EIU 1989–90: 45). Luxury goods in the form of consumer durables and non-essential food items were the hardest hit, while capital goods became increasingly rare as well. Within no time, shortages of some of the most basic commodities became routine (Goumeziane 1994: 117–21). GDP growth slowed considerably, and by 1987 turned negative.[22] The economy had undergone a growth collapse (Table 5.3).

---

[21] Around the same time, the US dollar lost about 40 percent of its value relative to European currencies. "It was these currencies that Algeria depended upon for the roughly two-thirds of its imports ... from the Common Market" (Ruedy 1992: 246). The price of oil was $12/barrel at the end of 1978, $34 in 1980, $40 in 1981, $30 at the end of 1985, and $10 in July 1986.

[22] In fact, real GNP declined every year between 1985 and 1995 at an average rate of 0.1 percent (ICG 2001c: 7).

Table 5.1 *Algeria: evolution of hydrocarbon rent*

	1981	1986	1994	1999
Hydrocarbon export earnings	$14.2 bn	$7.3 bn	$8.6 bn	$11.9 bn
p.c. hydrocarbon rents	$1200	$875	$250	$400*

*They would fluctuate between $200 and $450 through the 1990s.
Sources: Aissaoui 2001: 30; IMF 2000

Table 5.2 *Algeria: debt service ratio*

1982	1986	1988	1992	1993	1994	2000
33%	68%	86%	72%	82%	49%*	21%

*They would fluctuate between 29% and 45% for the remainder of the decade.
Sources: IMF: September 1998; IMF: August 2000; ICG October 26, 2001: 7

Table 5.3 *Algeria: GDP growth rate (%)*

1984	1985	1986	1987	1988
5.2	2.7	0.6	−1.4	−2.7

Source: IMF (1989), in Ruedy (1992: 247)

The country's financial woes coincided with enormous demographic pressures.[23] By 1980, the population of Algeria had reached 20 million, having doubled in less than two decades. In the 1970s, the population growth rate was 3.2 percent, among the highest in the world, and the labor force was growing at 3.4 percent. Population growth fell to roughly 2.9 percent in the 1980s; however, because of a "youth bulge" – a disproportionately large young population – the labor force was, in fact, growing at 3.8 percent. Since 1980, over 70 percent of the Algerian population has been under thirty years old, and according to the census of March 1987, as much as 54.8 percent of the population was younger than twenty at that time (Carlier 1995: 341).

---

[23] For the conditions under which rapid population growth is problematic, see Goldstone (1999).

Table 5.4 *Algeria: select social and economic indicators*

	1970	1975	1980	1985	1990	1995	2000
Unemployment rate (%)	28.5	22.7	16.2	16.5	19.8	27.9	30.2
5-year real GDP growth (%)	4.9	7.5	8.7	3.9	−1.2	0.7	3.4
p.c. GDP (current $)	324	930	2268	2654	2479	1410	1600
5-year inflation rate (%)	5.0	6.3	11.0	9.2	11.6	27.5	6.0

Source: Aissaoui 2001: 10

Masses of young people – most of them the products of Boumedienne's educational system – were entering the workforce (and the housing market) precisely when the economy was shrinking dramatically. These demographic features had severe distributional effects that would plague social peace.[24] To be sure, educated generations were condemned to joblessness, inadequate lodging, and frustration. The unemployment rate, which had improved from 22 percent in 1971 to 17 percent in 1982, increased steadily from then on, reaching close to 20 percent in 1988, at the time of the riots. By the turn of the century, it would reach a staggering 30 percent, almost double what it had been at the end of the Boumedienne presidency (ICG 2001c: 7) (Table 5.4).

Popular response

Indeed, the decline in the financial means of the state, the growing debt burden, and the return of shortages followed on the heels of an industrial disinvestment strategy and the stimulation of domestic consumption. These economic constraints coincided with the eruption on the labor and housing markets of hundreds of thousands of energetic and educated young people. Having been nurtured on Chadli's rhetoric of "a better life," and seduced for some years by the abundance of consumer goods, those entering the saturated job market were thrown into disarray. At the same

---

[24] Albeit structural, the demographic condition could have been mitigated through sound policy. Liberal technocrats in Boumedienne's government had cautioned that the high growth was problematic. Not only did Boumedienne refuse to implement policies to slow down population growth, but he even launched a counter-campaign to birth control. According to one of Algeria's most prominent diplomats, he retorted, on one occasion, something like the following: "What is the population of Egypt? If they can have tens of millions, why can't we?" (interview: March 6, 2001). On other occasions, he insisted that "our pill is development" and suggested that limiting the population of the Third World was a ploy of imperialism to clear the anti-imperialist ranks (Fargues 1994: 165).

time, a small but growing and increasingly visible minority – closely allied with the regime and enjoying the protection of the military – amassed spectacular fortunes; they had successfully manipulated the opening up of supply and distribution networks during Chadli's first term (El-Kenz 1989: 21–5; Henry and Springborg 2001: 109–11). The coalescence of these factors created an explosive social situation.

In a system that for decades had extolled social justice, insisted on the principle of equality, and denied personal enrichment, the increasing pervasiveness of corruption and inequalities became intolerable.[25] The populist rhetoric and sloppy pronouncements of the Benjedid regime gave way to an attitude of "catch as catch can" among those segments of the population which had been excluded from official routes to enrichment.

As of the mid-1980s, two new social categories – the "*hittistes*" (those who are "of the walls," standing on street corners because they have nothing else to do) and the "*trabendistes*" (those who engage in contraband, "black-market" activities) – came into view.[26] Excluded from the official routes, the *hittistes* and *trabendistes* would be captured by the parallel economy that had been stimulated by scarcity and poor productivity. Connecting up with the parallel economy was an effective means to soften the blow of idleness and economic depression.

Recall that Chadli's earlier measures to free up import activity and extend distribution networks had spawned a burgeoning private trading sector. Egged on by state patronage, the sector saddled itself to the increasingly lucrative parallel economy in which goods were acquired primarily through smuggling networks and corruption (ICG, 2001c; Henni 1991; Talahite 2000). By the end of the 1980s, as inequalities and unemployment worsened, contraband trade – or *trabendo*, as it is called in Algeria – was flourishing. To reiterate, it engaged the unemployed, disillusioned, and marginalized of Algerian society in its smuggling and distribution networks, and quickly became linked to the private trading sector. Together, they nourished the parallel economy, the extent of which has been thought to account for anywhere from 30 to

---

[25] As for the pervasiveness of corruption in Chadli's Algeria, consider the allegation presented by Abdelhamid Brahimi when he was pushed out of office at the end of 1988: that money laundering and embezzlement (by the state) over the previous twenty years totaled some $26 billion – roughly equivalent to the country's foreign debt at that time (Brahimi 2000; Hadjadj 1999: 75).

[26] *Hittistes* comes from colloquial Arabic – *ḥit* means "wall"; it includes the French ending *–iste* that denotes "the appropriation of" by a person (or ideology). *Trabendistes* derives from the French word "*contrebande*;" again, it includes the French ending that denotes "the appropriation of."

70 percent of economic activity (ICG 2001c; Henni 1991; Talahite 2000).[27]

By 1986, anti-state violence of various forms colored the landscape. In Algiers, Oran, Constantine, Skikda, and Sétif, demonstrations, strikes, and riots, often starting out from the universities or high schools, rocked *le système* (Entelis 1988: 53).[28] Symbols of the state, such as offices of the FLN and Air Algérie, and of its bankrupt development programs – the *souks al-fellah*, for example – were targetted systematically (Carlier 1995: 348). In this climate, it was virtually impossible to purchase social peace, absent far-reaching political reforms. Chadli, however, responded to the challenges with severe repression. In that way, he intensified the opposition.

In this impoverished environment, where political expression and participation had been methodically circumscribed for decades, there existed no institutional space for debate about political, economic, or social matters.[29] Social or political formations that could have channeled the energies of the disenchanted were in woefully short supply. For one, the former leftist oppositions, that could have directed the frustrations of the popular classes especially, had long been co-opted, weakened, or had disappeared altogether.[30]

"Political Islam," that had functioned more or less on the sidelines until the early 1980s, quickly emerged to fill the void. By the end of 1982, when Abassi Madani, who would later co-found the FIS, surfaced for the first time at the head of anti-state demonstrations, the Islamist opposition had become a distinctive feature of the social and political landscape. From the mosque that served as their podium and through welfare activities that consolidated their social networks, Islamists embraced the unrest:

---

[27] According to a study conducted by the Algerian *Office Nationale des Statistiques* (ONS), 40 percent of GDP in 2003 derived from informal economic activity.

[28] According to Hadjadj (1999: 73), the very first demonstrations of the tumultuous 1985/6 period began in the depressed Casbah of Algiers in April (1985). The principal demands of the demonstrators were better housing, regular water supply, and an end to corruption.

[29] The only forum for "debate" remained the FLN party and its various appendages – such as the Rassemblement Nationale Democratique (RND), the Organization of Mudjahidins – and in which the different currents within the army participated actively. Debate about how to organize society was virtually nonexistent (confidential interview April 14, 2003).

[30] On the vagaries of the Algerian left, see Roberts (1988, reprinted in 2003a: 13–15). The *Ettaḥaddi* ("Challenge" or "Defiance") party, led by El-Hachemi Cherif, was created in 1989 as an offshoot of the PAGS, itself a derivation of the pre-Independence *Parti Communiste Algérien*. By 1992, the PAGS had dissolved itself; some of its members joined *Ettaḥaddi*. The Trotskyist *Parti des Travailleurs* (PT) was co-founded by Louisa Hanoune in 1990. While for many years it had a weak following, by 2002 it had become the leading secular democratic party in parliament (Roberts 1995, reprinted in 2003: 165).

they grafted themselves upon it and appropriated it for themselves (Carlier 1995: 348). They were able to do so successfully because they could provide what many craved: a means for channeling frustrations, an "ideology" to believe in, a community to feel a part of, and a recipe for a better life. By the mid-1980s, an important portion of Algerian society was primed to receive a new type of discourse, identify with it, and rally behind it. The view that a "return to Islam" may be the antidote to the Algerian predicament was gaining adherents. It was, alas, the only articulated alternative.

Algeria from 1988, or the uncertain descent into the abyss

"Political Islam" would successfully play its hand in the fall of 1988. By no means did Islamists initiate the events of October – a watershed in Algeria's political development – yet they had the capacity to react quickly and effectively to a movement that had begun without them, and take it over. The massive demonstrations that started out either from the Rouiba industrial zone on the outskirts of Algiers, according to some, or on the streets of Bab el-Oued, a poor neighborhood of Algiers, according to others, were of uncertain origin: some maintain they were a spontaneous response to the dire socio-economic circumstances (Mortimer 1990: 163–4; interview with a former prime minister: March 2, 2002); others suggest that they were purposefully organized by the state for its own self-interest (Brahimi 2000: 230–3; Hadjadj 1999: 73–4).

Whatever the truth of the matter, several details are irrefutable. First, the targets of the demonstrators were symbols of state authority – Chadli and the FLN especially – and of wealth. Second, Chadli, overwhelmed by the popular explosion, declared a state of emergency; this devolved responsibility onto the military and unleashed much bloodshed. Following that, Ali Belhadj, the fiery Imam from the Sunna mosque in Bab el-Oued, and his followers were somehow encouraged by the regime to try to de-mobilize the crowds and restore order. Third, in the first week of October, Islamists, in assuming control over the fairly disparate groups, led a cortège of daunting proportions – some 20,000 of their followers. Fourth, the army, face to face with a crowd of this magnitude, opened fire.[31] Hundreds were killed.

Whether or not the regime had played a key role in drawing the crowds into the streets in the first place was beside the point: its reaction – that of

---

[31] For different descriptions of the events of October 5–10, see, among others, Aboud (2002: 124–33); Hidouci (1995: 160–2); Moussaoui (1994); Willis (1996a: 107–12).

alienated, fragile, yet arrogant, power – deprived it of its already tenuous legitimacy. "Political Islam" had won the day ... for some time, at least. Within less than one year, it had developed into a formidable political force that spread throughout the country. In the absence of any other political formation with a powerful message, an organizational structure, and a broad-based social network, it recruited actively from among the excluded and disenchanted.[32] Tens, if not hundreds, of thousands of new "converts" found solace and hope in the Islamists' project for righting the wrongs of the past, healing the fractured society, and building, at long last, the Algerian nation.

Following the events of October 1988, Chadli tried desperately to regain control and support. He sacked some of his key ministers – among them, Abdelhamid Brahimi – and promulgated a new constitution. Adopted in February of 1989, the constitution removed reference to Algeria as a "socialist" state, made no mention of the FLN, protected the powers of the presidency, and referred to the armed forces as a strictly military institution. Moreover, it guaranteed some democratic freedoms and extended a transition to multipartyism (Ruedy 1992: 250–1). For the first time, groups of fifteen or more Algerians were granted the legal right to form, not political parties – no, that term was reserved for the FLN – but rather *"associations à caractère politique"* (associations of a political character). The way was paved for multi party elections that would take place in June 1990.

The combination of what appeared as a democratic transition and the investiture in September 1989 of a reform-oriented government under the prime ministership of Mouloud Hamrouche left the impression that a veritable system change was under way and that political resources were finally being (re-)distributed. For a brief moment in the history of the independent state, and after the bloody October riots, Algeria would have its own "Hundred Flowers Movement."[33] Issues that had been occulted for so long – language, religion, the Berber question, regionalism, and

---

[32] On FIS strategies for garnering support, see Willis (1996a: 121–4). For its program, see *Projet de Programme du Front Islamique du Salut*, March 9, 1989, reproduced in part in Al-Ahnaf (1991: 179–87).

[33] The Hundred Flowers Movement was a brief period (1956–7) in the People's Republic of China during which Chairman Mao and the Chinese Communist Party (CCP) authorities encouraged the population to openly express their views about and offer solutions to ongoing problems. Overwhelmed by the outpouring of criticism, Mao responded with severe repression and the initiation of an ideological crackdown, referred to as the Anti-Rightist Campaign.

their place in the Algerian nation – were back in the public realm. And the pressing socio-economic problems related to joblessness, corruption, and non-existent or ineffectual regulatory mechanisms were given much attention.[34] Furthermore, political tendencies of various colors organized themselves as alternatives to, or saviors of, the discredited FLN and the regime associated with it.[35]

Recall that in this still quite impoverished institutional environment, cleavages remained profound and social conflicts scratched the surface, on the verge of erupting. Virtually all the new parties were region-, clan-, or ethnicity-based, if they were not, themselves, variants of the FLN or tribunes erected to the glory of an individual. Apart from the religious formations, and especially the newly created FIS, there was no party which carried a message that echoed throughout the country and with which Algerians as a community could identify.[36]

For some years, in the ante-chambers of the presidency where he had assisted Chadli Benjedid, Mouloud Hamrouche conferred with Ghazi Hidouci, then economic advisor to the president. The two brought together groups composed of young, highly trained economists and engineers to discuss a variety of topics related to Algeria's development, and to propose changes. Eventually, the discussion groups formulated a set of reforms which was presented to and accepted by the government in 1987, and published as Les Cahiers de la Réforme (Hadj Nacer 1989). Aiming to impose the rules of a market economy, separate the economy from politics, and abandon "bureaucratic and patrimonial management," the program included reforms regarding economic decision-making and the supervision of economic activities, regulatory mechanisms in the banking and public sectors, pricing and commercial activities, and so forth (interviews with members of the Hamrouche government: June 29, 2000; March 16, 2001). From September 1989 until June 1991, when Chadli Benjedid evicted the reform team from

---

[34] For well-informed analyses of the efforts of the Hamrouche government (1989–91), see especially Corm (1993), Goumeziane (1994), Hidouci (1995), and Henry and Springborg (2001: 112–15).

[35] By early 1991, as many as thirty-three parties had received official recognition (Ruedy 1992: 252).

[36] On the peculiarities of parties in Algeria, see Roberts (2003a: 232–6). For example, Ben Bella's Mouvement pour la Démocratie en Algérie (MDA), founded in 1984 but legalized in 1989, was essentially a "splinter group" of the old FLN, organized on the basis of the personal following of a historic leader, and expressing a broadly Islamic outlook. Although the FFS sought broad appeal by promoting cultural pluralism, it attracted Kabyle Berbers primarily, and remained intimately linked to the persona of its founder and leader, Hocine Ait Ahmed, another chef historique.

government, the latter's blueprint promised fundamental changes to access to power and resources.

The democratic – or shall I say, reformist – experiment would be short-lived. In the first round of multiparty legislative elections in December 1991, the FIS won 47 percent of the popular vote. Threatened with losing its monopoly of power – a monopoly that it had jealously guarded since 1956 – the military stepped in, out of the shadows, not unlike the militarized core had done in the aftermath of the Soummam Congress thirty-five years earlier. It annulled the election results, cancelled the second round of elections and with it the constitutionally approved transition to a multiparty system.

On January 11, 1992, the military staged a symbolic coup d'état, removed Chadli Benjedid from the presidency, and replaced him with a five-man *Haut Comité d'Etat* (High Council of State).[37] A state of emergency was declared, the legally constituted FIS was outlawed, while its leadership and thousands of its members and supporters were arrested and imprisoned – many in detention centers in the desert (Willis 1996a: 256–7). By late spring, Algeria exploded. The army and an array of Islamicist groups would compete in a struggle to capture the state and (re-)define the nation.

Conclusions

Two critical junctures marked the Chadli era, presenting distinct challenges and the opportunity for significant change: the oil boom of 1979/80, when the price of oil increased to $40/barrel, and then the oil bust of 1986, when the price plummetted to $10/barrel. Shocks to the system, exacerbated by the regime's response at each juncture, reverberated in 1982 and then again in October 1988, culminating in the cancellation of elections in December 1991 and the onset, in the spring of 1992, of protracted political violence. At each one of these moments of leadership

---

[37] Members of the *Haut Comité d'Etat* (HCE) either belonged to the *janvieristes*, those thirty or so officers within the military's high command who made the decision to stage the coup, or were chosen by them. It was composed of two generals and three prominent "revolutionaries," one of whom – Mohamad Boudiaf – was named chairman (Werenfels 2007: 44–5). Boudiaf was assassinated in June 1992 – most likely by one or another faction within the regime; his insistence on addressing corruption, among other things, threatened the power and privileges of the military. He was replaced by Ali Kafi, another prominent revolutionary. When the HCE was dissolved in 1994, General Liamine Zeroual, who had been Minister of Defense, was named president.

challenge, as in the past, pluralism and difference were denied, the interests of the regime and its clients were safeguarded, and institutional mechanisms of conflict management proved woefully inadequate. This type of response would have grave consequences, especially in light of the growth collapse Algeria experienced post-1985/6.

Given that economic resources were scarce, the salutary response to the shocks would have been to open up the system, encourage participation, and distribute political resources as widely as possible so as to tap the capacities of whatever domestic forces could have contributed to easing the crisis (Rodrik 1999). Recall that this was a crisis that had been provoked, in large measure, by short-sighted economic policy decisions, linked to a perhaps overzealous social project that came up against unanticipated international structural forces well beyond the control of any one state. But that was the road not taken.

Whatever economic and political liberalization was initiated, either by Chadli Benjedid in the pre-1988 period or by the reformist government of Mouloud Hamrouche (1989–91), was ultimately straitjacketed by the rigidities of a militarized authoritarian system and its deep, well-greased patrimonial structures. Furthermore, conflicts in the social, political, and economic spheres would continue to be resolved in a demagogic fashion, relying on both force and co-optation.

The second oil shock (1979/80) had provided the new president of Algeria with the means to spend generously on welfare and line the pockets of the new middle class. Chadli's hope was that some liberalization, plus lavish payoffs, would shore up his legitimacy and hold on power. His efforts would have the opposite effect. Short-sighted economic reasoning would come up against international structural forces. That, combined with the inattention to social cleavages, resulted in the new measures exacerbating socio-economic hardship and stimulating an already brewing opposition to the regime and the system it protected.

In effect, Chadli's politically driven changes to the domestic political economy and to the utilization and distribution of the oil rent transformed domestic alliances and institutional relationships in an incontrovertible fashion. Executive powers were enhanced, with the president being informally accountable to the all-powerful but seemingly invisible military, while patronage and informal economic activities blossomed. They engaged a growing number of people in the public and private sectors, and among the unemployed. Soon after 1986 and the plummetting of oil prices, the economy fell apart and large segments of the population were impoverished, while a small but important minority amassed spectacular fortunes. They did so by organizing consumption, scarcity, and parasitic activities, often in alliance with the state and a reinvigorated "class" of intermediaries – a vibrant parallel economy (Brahimi 1990).[38]

This combination of factors arose in a very particular type of authoritarian environment. As in other resource-rich patrimonial systems, the legitimacy of rule is built squarely upon the uninterrupted distribution of favors, while foundational myths – of unity, equality, social justice, and the magnanimous state – are reaffirmed to make up for the frailty of the institutional framework and the poverty of politics (Linz 2000: 151–5). Such an environment requires that difference is denied: social cleavages are addressed only insofar as they may bolster the leader's monopoly of power.

Chadli showed favor to the "traditionalists" by completing the arabization of the educational system. He aimed, thereby, to undermine the influence of the "modernists" whose technocratic skills and leadership capacities he feared. When forced, Chadli would acknowledge the Berber dimension of Algeria, but only when all else failed and only to the extent that he deemed necessary so that threats to his leadership would recede.

Despite the rhetoric, there was, at the heart of the militarism that dominated Algerian political life, a visceral distrust of the people (Roberts 1984). This stemmed, in part, from the leadership's detachment from the people – conceived with the hijacking of power in the 1950s and consolidated over time. It reflected, as well, an implicit recognition that the success of the revolution had been the result of mass mobilization. The people could turn against those who had seized power, just as they had successfully turned against their former colonizers. Nonetheless, because of the fractionalized and weakly constituted opposition, derivative of a fragilized institutional framework, cultivated by the decisions of leaders and nurtured for decades, it was very difficult for most emergent social forces to effectively confront the militarized core that so dominated the political–economic system.

Much of what went awry in the 1989–91 transition period had to do with two inherent features of *le système*: first, that the Hamrouche government *réformateurs* (reformers), while given a mandate to resuscitate the economy and prepare the transition to democracy, were not given a free hand to implement the reforms they had elaborated.[39] The

---

[38] Already during the Boumedienne era, austerity measures and related constraints on consumption had spawned a small parallel market and a "class" of intermediaries (Henni, n.d.).

[39] This allegation was repeated to this author in interviews with members of the reform team: July 7, 1999, June 27, 2000, June 29, 2000, March 7, 2001.

reformers sought to create a dynamic of rupture with the political system that had been in place since 1965, by permitting those currents that accepted the democratic process to express themselves openly outside the traditional networks. However, the military, and the various client networks associated with the regime, could not envisage a formal modification of the rules of the exercise of power that did not include the preservation of their own hegemonic control over society. As soon as the reforms began to threaten the opaque interests of power holders, they were vigorously interrupted and the reformist agenda was terminated. For example, the effort to impede pervasive rent-seeking by abolishing many of the very lucrative state monopolies and imposing transparency and open markets was sure to impact many in the higher echelons of the state.

Second, both regime dynamics and the poverty of politics prevent the emergence in Algeria of effective, nation-wide political parties with agendas that could bridge the many cleavages, and embrace the interests and concerns of a broad cross-section of Algerian society. Except for the FIS, virtually all the parties that emerged in the 1989–91 period (and that exist today) are built around a single individual, the party founder, and promote the interests of a single, relatively narrow community.[40] They have neither broad appeal nor a truly "national" agenda. Rather, they both reflect and deepen the factionalism that plagues Algerian politics and society, and the centrality in political structures of authoritarianism, personalism, and patron–client relations.[41]

The FIS, however, could not be allowed to win power. Despite being mass-based, a FIS-led government would have excluded the military from power. Moreover, the FIS economic program, like that of the *réformateurs*, threatened the interests of the politico–military oligarchy and those closest to it: it advocated economic liberalization, including lower taxes and incentives for private-sector development, plus the investment of oil revenues in local economic projects (Al-Ahnaf *et al.* 1991: 179–87). It opposed industrial and commercial monopolies, and favored limitations on state intervention in the industrial sector (Henry and Springborg 2001: 115–16). It demanded not only that the economy be privatized, but also that public-sector privileges be reduced to a minimum (Benderra 2002: 20–1). Because of the persistent domination of the political and economic landscape by the military-backed

---

[40] To be sure, clan-, region-, and personality-based parties are unsuited for engaging effectively in democratic politics, even if a genuine democratic transition had been the agenda in the 1989–91 period in Algeria.

[41] For a thoughtful model of authoritarianism in the Arab world, see Hammoudi (2001).

regime, whatever reform measures have been implemented to date have precluded real transformation of *le système* (Lowi 2007).

Finally, it is crucial to remember that in Algeria, ideology has enjoyed a social presence; political–ideological discourse is pervasive and banal. Furthermore, the dominant discourse has consistently upheld traditional values of egalitarianism, while never addressing the issue of whether that means that all Algerians are identical – in which case there is no acceptance of difference – or whether they are all subject to equitable treatment. In fact, there has been neither equitable treatment nor acceptance of difference. This was tolerable as long as abounding oil rents promoted an old-style distributive state, in which goods and services were exchanged for loyalty and acceptance of the social project, and there was a general feeling of well-being (Henni n.d.; Lowi 2004). But when that contract was broken, with a decline in the distribution of material resources and a failure to redistribute political resources, the system lost its efficacy and legitimacy, and was severely destabilized. Violence erupted. In the hands of the marginalized and excluded, it was an expression of contestation and a means of self-affirmation. In the hands of incumbents, it was, as we will see below, a means of self-preservation and system re-equilibration.

The violence in Algeria between 1992 and 2002 was, as in other cases characterized by what Pierre Hassner (1997) refers to as "a deficit of politics," a form of (political) expression. It is what remains when all other avenues are closed. Violence serves to fill the void left by failing social and political relations. In this context, violence functions as a type of social institution: one that assumes the responsibility for punishing mistreatment and repairing or overcoming the condition of exclusion, marginality, having been dishonored or humiliated. Violence, in this sense, is a phenomenon of pure affirmation of the subject: it is "the voice of the subject when he is not recognized, but rather rejected" (Wieviorka 1997: 55–6; translation my own).

6   The persistence of violence and the process of re-equilibration

In the ten years of civil war that followed the military coup, more than 100,000 Algerians died and several thousand remain unaccounted for. During this period, there were four different presidents and eight prime ministers.[1] An International Monetary Fund (IMF)-backed structural adjustment program, furthering efforts at economic liberalization, was also implemented.

In its early stages, the violence pitted the state against members and supporters of the FIS, and then an array of Islamist groups.[2] It went through at least three different phases. In the first phase (1992–4), the violence took the form of urban civil war, characterized by targetted killings by insurgents and fierce repression of Islamists in and around Algiers. The second phase (1994–8) witnessed the collapse of the state's monopoly over violence and its almost total loss of control over the domestic political economy; this combined with the "privatization" of violence in the hands of not only Islamist insurgents, but government-backed militia forces as well. Mass terror, generalized insecurity, and a high death toll characterized this period.

Writing in the winter of 1995, Hugh Roberts, one of the more astute analysts of Algerian affairs, described the situation thus:

---

[1] Since the October 1988 riots, Algerian governments have undergone rapid, practically constant, changes. From 1988 through 2004, Algeria had twenty-two governments. In President Bouteflika's first term (1999–2004), a period that produced four prime ministers, there were as many as six governments. Of the eleven prime ministers since the end of the single-party state in 1989, Ali Benflis, in office for almost three years, was the longest serving. Several cabinet ministers have occupied their posts for as little as 2–3 months, such that from 1989 and the advent of the Hamrouche government to 2003 and the firing of Benflis, there was a total of 217 ministers (Werenfels 2007: 63).

[2] Despite differences of opinion on whether or not the protracted violence from 1992–2002 was a civil war, I employ the definition in Sambanis (2004): that of large-scale armed conflict within the boundaries of a sovereign state, pitting the government against one or more groups that challenge the government's sovereignty and are able to mount some resistance, and in which the violence results in at least 1,000 deaths.

The Algerian state is weaker than at any moment in its history since 1962. It has lost such legitimacy as the old one-party system procured for it until 1988 ... [i]t is still unable to offer most of its citizens the prospect of substantial relief from economic distress, and cannot even guarantee elementary security for their lives and property, since the Algerian army has clearly long since lost its monopoly of the use of physical force and has been failing quite spectacularly in its elementary duty of restoring order. In short, *the Algerian state is on its knees, if it is possible to speak of it in the present tense at all.* (Reprinted 2003: 160–1; emphasis, my own)

In the third phase (1998–2002), however, the violence was winding down. The death rate dropped considerably and the civil war took on the form of low-intensity conflict characterized, primarily, by random violence (Table 6.1). How was the regime, that had appeared in the mid-1990s to be on the verge of collapse, able to reassert its power and authority, and bring the insurgency to heel? What changes (or continuities) did the country undergo that may shed light on this outcome?

From 1992 through 1997, oil prices fluctuated between $15 and $21 per barrel; they fell to just over $12 in 1998/9. Since 2000, however, they have witnessed important increases, reaching $40 per barrel in 2004, $65 per barrel in 2006, and as much as $140 per barrel in 2008 (BP Statistical Review 2008). In recent years, explorations in Algeria have identified new, rich hydrocarbon deposits. The country's natural resource endowment, as well as the regime's revenue base, are relatively impressive once again.

Nonetheless, and despite what has been described as the most radical democratization process that the Middle East and North Africa have known, there have not been significant changes to the distribution of power and resources in Algeria. What persists is a patrimonial system of clan politics, elaborated by a military–bureaucratic oligarchy, that, along with its clients, are the principal beneficiaries. It is a vertically fashioned system, composed of intricate and overlapping networks of interests, where the principal objective of all players is to increase their access to the rent and to power.[3]

Not only has the military regained its position as the decisive force, constraining the maneuverability of the political leadership, but the highest echelons of the military-backed political leadership continue to be as removed from the population and insouciant to its needs and interests as Chadli Benjedid, for example, had been. President Abdelaziz Bouteflika, in power since 1999, had been living outside the

---

[3] See Werenfels (2007) for a detailed analysis of the networks.

Table 6.1 *Algeria: phases of violence*

	Years	Protagonists	Goals	Type	Location	Tactics	Death rate	Outcomes
PHASE 1	1992–4	FIS/MIA vs. government	reinstatement of 1992 election results and capture state for Islamists vs. retention of status quo ante and hegemony of military-backed regime	Hegemonic-counter-hegemonic war	district of Algiers	targetted killings vs. fierce repression of Islamists	<1200/mo.	growth and radicalization of insurgency; weakening of state
PHASE 2	1994–8	AIS/GIA/MEI/ LIDD vs. gov't and allies (civilian militias)	capture/replace state vs. "total war" against insurgents	Privatization of violence; collapse of state monopoly over violence	south-west of capital; Mitidja plain; mountainous zones	mass terror; massacres; thuggery and criminality; counter-mobilization of pop.	1200/mo.	AIS/LIDD sign truce; GIA/ GSPC continue struggle
PHASE 3	1999– 2002	GIA/GSPC vs. gov't and allies	self-enrichment; political survival; maintain status quo	low-intensity conflict	west and east of capital; mountainous zones	random violence and criminality; cooptation, manipulation, repression	200/mo. (1998–9) 400/mo. (2000–)	regime reequilibration

country for much of the 1980s and 1990s.[4] A member of the war-time "Oujda clan" and foreign minister under Boumedienne for more than a decade, he was closely associated with the creation of the independent state and its mythology. His re-emergence in the 1990s, after a long period of hibernation, and the re-integration of other "old guard" nationalists into the highest echelons of government, testifies to a pattern of recycling the "dinosaurs:" this is a political system that consistently reproduces itself while skillfully resisting reform (Werenfels 2007: 81, 95).

Despite some new injections, the regime remains largely unchanged in its makeup and strategy. Nonetheless, it has redoubled its efforts to integrate both real and potential oppositional forces into le système. Indeed, co-optation has become a principal survival strategy; it was the primary means for the regime to recapture its hold on power after years of acute instability and protracted violence. The effects of regime strategy are incontrovertible: by 2002, the ten-year civil war was on the wane.[5] Severely weakened, the insurgency comprised less than 1,000 men and managed to carry out only sporadic operations (Lowi 2005).

In this final chapter on the Algerian experience, I return to the key question: how was the regime able to win back its hegemony and control of the political landscape, despite several years of acute instability and horrendous violence, and an insurgency that appeared to enjoy significant power resources, including a fairly rich field for recruitment, until well into the mid-1990s? I note that by successfully playing its hand during the civil war years, the politico–military oligarchy averted state breakdown and system change. It was largely leadership efforts to weaken the forces of opposition, revitalize traditional mechanisms for distributing power and

---

[4] Two of Bouteflika's key ministers, Abdelhamid Temmar and Chakib Khalil, had lived outside the country for long periods as well. Temmar had been with the United Nations from 1981–95, and Khalil was an economist at the World Bank from 1980–99.

The choice of Abdelaziz Bouteflika as president of Algeria after Liamine Zeroual's resignation was significant: he was reputed to have considerable skills in diplomacy and good relations in the international arena. He was, therefore, well suited for improving Algeria's image abroad (Mortimer 2006: 156).

At the end of the 1990s, the principle decision-makers – le pouvoir réel – included President Bouteflika and roughly five Generals: Mohamad Lamari, Mohamad "Tewfik" Mediène, Smaïl Lamari, Mohamad Touati, and Larbi Belkheir. Khaled Nezzar may or may not have been among them at that time (Werenfels 2007: 56). For an excellent discussion of the role of the military in Algerian politics, see Roberts (2007).

[5] Note, however, the recent resurgence of insurgent activity. The Groupe Salafiste pour la Prédiction et le Combat (GSPC), renamed al-Qa'ida in the Maghreb, has claimed responsibility for several, fairly spectacular incidents since 2006, including a triple bombing in and around Algiers on April 11, 2007, and the bombing of United Nations offices in Algiers on December 11, 2007.

privileges within the country, and enhance the country's international stature that have been at the heart of the process of re-equilibration. Toward the end of the civil war years, (international) structural forces – the notable increase in oil prices and the discovery of new oil fields, plus a budding relationship with the United States in the post-9/11 context – have contributed to the process as well.

I begin the chapter by describing the principal forces of opposition that the regime has faced since the early 1990s, comprised of Islamists on the one hand, and Kabyle Berbers on the other. Second, I explore the regime's strategy for weakening its opposition. The strategy has included repression, co-optation, and manipulation, and has targetted moderate, radical, and "official" Islamists, as well as Kabyle Berbers. Third, I demonstrate how international structural forces in recent years have favored regime interests, and how the regime has managed to manipulate those forces for precious political capital. I conclude by summarizing how the combination of the above factors has allowed the regime to re-equilibrate after an acute political crisis on the heels of an economic shock.

Forces of opposition

During the ten or so years of civil war, there were at least as many insurgency groups; between two and five operated at any one time.[6] Armed Islamist formations, embracing the marginalized and excluded, have been the principal adversaries of government forces. The groups emerged from four main sources. First, former "Bouyalists" were among the first members of both the MIA and the GIA (Labat 1995:

---

[6] They are the: AIS (*Armée Islamique du Salut*), FIDA (*Front Islamique du Djihad en Algérie*), GSC (*Groupe Salafiste Combattant*), GIA (*Groupe(s) Islamique Armée(s)*), GSPC (*Groupe Salafiste pour la Prédication et le Combat*), GSPD (*Groupe Salafiste pour le Djihad*), HES (*Houmat Eddaoua Salafia*), LIDD (*Ligue Islamique de la Da'wa et du Djihad*), MEI (*Mouvement pour l'Etat Islamique*), and MIA (*Mouvement Islamique Armée*). Of these groups, the AIS and the GIA were the most important from 1994–7 – the most difficult of the war years – in terms of visibility, engagement in armed activity, and membership (Ait-Larbi 1999). The MIA was dismantled in 1994, and the AIS and LIDD called a truce and disarmed in 1997. From 1998 until 2003, only the GIA and the GSPC (and the related GSC, GSPD, and HES), representing an estimated 600–700 men, remained active (Maiza 2002; Zerouk 2002). The GIA disbanded in 2004. As for the GSPC, it claimed affiliation with al-Qa'ida in 2006, and changed its name in the winter of 2007 to al-Qa'ida in the Maghreb. It was thought to have 300–500 fighters in Algeria in 2006, but it has been recruiting actively in neighboring countries as well. "Profile: Al-Qaeda in North Africa," April 27, 2009, http://news.bbc.co.uk; David Cutler, "Factbox: Key Facts on Algerian Islamist Group," December 12, 2007, www.reuters.com

89–90; Moussaoui 1994: 1324–6). Second, *Afghans* – those Algerians who had fought alongside the Afghans in their war with the Soviets during the 1980s – figured prominently in the insurgency. Some had played important roles in the FIS, while others had been among the leaders of the first armed groups; and they comprised some portion of the rank and file, as well, at least in the early years of the insurgency.[7] Note that from 1986 to 1989, between 2,000 and 3,000 Algerians joined the Afghan struggle and were trained in Afghanistan (Mokeddem 2002; Bouzghaia 2002: 17). They were recruited in poor neighborhoods and through local mosques in Algeria, or while on pilgrimage in Saudi Arabia (confidential interviews: February 26, 2002; March 4, 2002).

Third, members and supporters of the banned FIS, who had been victims of government repression, constituted an important base for these movements. Upon their release from detention, hundreds, if not thousands, of radicalized young men would join the resistance. Both the AIS and the GIA recruited heavily from among former internees (Martinez 1998: 306–13). Fourth, migrants from the Algerian country-side formed the core of the rank-and-file of the insurgency. Recall that in Algeria, rural exodus throughout the 1970s and 1980s overwhelmed the urban fabric. The cities could not successfully absorb the increased numbers.[8] Hence, with the intensification of socio-economic dislocation and marginalization, the pool of potential insurgents grew significantly. The depressed peripheries of urban areas, and especially the overpopulated and less urbanized suburbs of Algiers – Baraki, Les Eucalyptus, El Harrach – as well as the smaller towns of the neighboring Mitidja plain – Boufarik, Larbaa, Meftah – provided the bulk of recruits (Labat 1995: 92; Martinez 2000).[9] Finally, membership in these armed groups has been filled primarily by young, unemployed men, many of whom had

[7] Recall that Ali Benhadj, co-founder of the FIS, had himself been involved with Bouyali and his MAIA (Willis 1996a: 143–4). While there are rumors that the first cells of the Algerian Islamist resistance were created in Peshawar (Pakistan) in the late 1980s, it is confirmed that Said Mekhloufi, a dissident member of the FIS and founder of the MEI, Aissa Messaoudi of the *al-Takfir w'al Hijra* group, and Kameredine Kherbane and Abdallah Anas, two of the leaders of the four-man "Executive Authority of the FIS Abroad," were all veterans of the Afghan war (Martinez 1998: 304; Mokeddem 2002; Willis 1996a: 221–9, 268–70).

[8] The same phenomenon has been noted in Turkey and Sierra Leone on the eve of their civil wars in the 1970s and 1990s respectively (Bozarslan 2001: 9–10; Davies and Fofana 2002: 6). In fact, Bozarslan (2001: 17) notes that roughly two-thirds of militia members in the Turkish insurgency issued from the rural exodus.

[9] An important effect of demographic growth and economic development, rural exodus became a principal venue for politicization as well.

been *hittistes* and/or *trabendistes*, who could be easily seduced by what the insurgency offered.[10]

At the same time, a "legal" Islamist opposition, composed of the HAMAS and Ennahda parties, emerged on the back of the FIS. Led by Mahfoud Nahnah (until 2003) and Abdallah Djaballah respectively, both of whom had been influential figures in the Islamist movement since the 1970s, the parties aimed to distinguish themselves from the FIS and, after 1992, from the insurgents. They tried to promote their ideas of Islamic values from within the political system, and gain adherents from among the disillusioned former supporters of the FIS and of an Islamic alternative more generally. While in the early years, Nahnah and his HAMAS party sought to appear more moderate than the FIS – advocating negotiation, denouncing violence, and accepting the basic principles of democratic practice – Djaballah and Ennahda had greater affinities with the FIS, even though it opposed the reformist economic policies of the Hamrouche government (Roberts 2003: 130–6; Willis 1996a: 165–7). The success at the polls of these two parties and their successors, the *Mouvement de la Société pour la Paix* (MSP) and the *Mouvement pour la Réforme Nationale – El Islah* (MRN-I), waxed and waned over the course of the 1990s and into the new millennium.[11]

In addition, a Kabyle opposition rapidly gained momentum from the spring of 2001 when Kabylia was the scene of repeated confrontations between the state and the Berber population. Demonstrations of anti-state sentiment, and riots that targetted symbols of state power and authority, persisted for some time (ICG 2003b). While the ill-treatment and neglect of this ethnic community were what incited the unrest in the region in the first place, the latter quickly assumed an important socio-economic dimension. Demonstrators qua insurgents and their supporters were demanding not only cultural and linguistic rights, as in the past, but also social justice with national appeal: improved living conditions and life chances, and an end to the glaring inequalities, social marginalization, and false promises (Algeria Watch; Yacine 2001).

Two legally constituted secularist parties, the RCD led by Saad Saadi and the FFS led by Hocine Ait Ahmed, have consistently promoted Berber demands through government channels. Although the FFS has flaunted a much broader, multi-culturalist and socialist

---

[10] One analysis of *repentis*, those who surrendered to government authorities after the presidential elections of November 16, 1995, indicated that 70 percent were between the ages of twenty and thirty-five, and 80 percent were unemployed (Willis 1996a: 374). On the attraction of the insurgency, see Lowi (2005: 234).

[11] For details, consult the very rich documentation on www.algeria-watch.de.

agenda, both parties draw their support largely from the Kabyle population.

Both the Kabyle protest movement and the various opposition parties – Islamist and berberophile – that entered electoral politics and, in some cases, gained seats in parliament, do indeed exert influence on the system (Werenfels 2007: 70–3).[12] Nonetheless, several of these forces have been co-opted: they have been fractionalized through the machinations of the regime and/or seduced by various government "rewards." The regime has proven adept at exploiting structural weaknesses of the opposition.

Regime strategy for weakening the opposition

Regime strategy for weakening the opposition and reasserting its hegemony over the political landscape has included repression, co-optation, and manipulation. Severe repression had been a preferred tactic. In the early years of the insurgency, however, the policy of repression backfired. While the FIS had been a fairly moderate force during the transition period of 1989–91,[13] attracting a large following from a cross-section of Algerian society, the decision to round up its members, confine them to camps in the desert, and submit them to brutal treatment radicalized many.[14] Upon their release from confinement, and denied their leadership – which remained imprisoned or under house arrest in Algeria, or living in exile abroad – numerous of the formerly moderate Islamists would create and join far more radical splinter groups that adopted maximalist strategies.[15]

Indeed, the fractionalization and radicalization of the Islamist opposition resulted, in the first instance, from the decimation of the FIS by the security forces in the aftermath of the 1992 coup d'état and during the initial phase of violence (1992–4) (Lowi 2005). First the charismatic leaders, and then hundreds, perhaps thousands, of members and supporters of the Front were targetted by the security services. The arrest of the FIS leadership left militants without elaborated directives and with hardly any clear strategies apart from a few simple slogans. In this context,

---

[12] The Trotskyist PT, led by Louisa Hanoune, was another prominent opposition party, in addition to those mentioned above.

[13] On the FIS program and platform, see Al-Ahnaf et al. (1991: 179–87); Willis (1996a: 138–49).

[14] See Wickham-Crowley (1990: 234) for a similar phenomenon in Latin America. There, too, radicalized guerilla movements formed in the aftermath of severe repression of oppositional forces.

[15] The first members of the MIA and the GIA were former Bouyalists (Maiza 2002: 3; Willis 1996a: 269, 279–81). In fact, the MIA seems to have been (re-)created in 1991 from the remnants of Bouyali's MAIA (Labat 1995: 89–90; Moussaoui 1994: 1324–6).

the temptation toward extremism was strong (CHEAr 1992–7).[16] Besides, the absent leaders of the FIS had lost control of the situation on the ground, as well as access to information.

The deficit of political and moral authority over a clientele that had no affinities to other local political forces led to the proliferation of very small, dispersed, and heterogeneous opposition groups which were poorly coordinated and uncontrollable. In the absence of a sophisticated political discourse and the means to express one, the only way these groups could gain recognition, or gauge their importance and their impact on the environment, was by demonstrating and exercising a capacity for maximum disruptiveness, especially relative to their rivals. Hence, maximalist strategies of outdoing one another through violence became the order of the day (CHEAr 1992–97).

Profitting from the void left by the massive arrests of leaders of the FIS in 1992 and 1993, the new chiefs of these small bands engaged in desperate, gratuitous violence. Through threats and seduction, they won over many of the former clients of the FIS who had originally been attracted to Islamism by the populist rhetoric of the traditional Islamist opposition. The differences among these groups were more apparent than real. For one, there is no evidence of real ideological or tactical distinctions, apart from the suggestion that the AIS and the GSPC did not target civilians. There are, however, strong indications that splits derived largely from personality conflicts, and related struggles for power and access to resources (confidential interviews: March 4, 2002; March 6, 2002).[17]

In response to the repression, armed Islamist groups grew from 2,000–4,000 fighters in 1993 to perhaps as many as 27,000 in 1995. During the second phase of violence (1994–8), the government was deeply engaged in encouraging, supporting, and funding anti-Islamist civilian militias.[18]

---

[16] Note that the FIS was a confederation of local groups organized around individuals who were responsible for strategic matters. At times, local group leaders had rival ambitions which were teased by hopes of acceding to power.

[17] The GSPC, for example, originated in a rift within the GIA leadership and was composed, at least initially, of former GIA fighters. The movement was founded in 1998 by Hassan Hattab, who had begun his career in the FIS before adhering to the short-lived MEI, and then, in 1994, to the GIA (Salgon 2001; Zerouk 2002). An earlier rift within the GIA was responsible for the creation of the LIDD in 1995 or 1996. Composed primarily of those who had seceded from the GIA, it then allied with the AIS against the GIA (Amnesty International 2000; ICG 2000).

[18] For further information on the civilian militias – the *Groupes de Légitime Défense* and the *Patriotes* – see Ait-Larbi *et al.* (1999: 74, 119–20); Bedjaoui (1999: 318); Garcon (1998). There is no reliable information regarding the size of the militias, although estimates vary from a total of between 100,000 and 300,000 men (Amnesty International 2000). Apparently, the militias were financed through a special fund from the president's office (CHEAr 9/97).

Alongside the rapid growth and fragmentation of the insurgency, this period witnessed the greatest mass terror and highest degree of victimization of the civil war years (Ait-Larbi *et al.* 1999: 24–5).

In contrast to repression, co-optation of the opposition – both Islamist (insurgent and "official") and Berberist – has proven to be a far more effective strategy for the regime. Over time, the regime has hijacked and more or less neutralized the political agendas of these two prominent forces. It has capitalized on the persistence, within the Islamist insurgency, of group fractionalization (with internecine battles), weak leadership, and the cult of personality.[19] By exploiting these tendencies, the Algerian leadership has prevented Islamists and Berberists from functioning as effective agents of reform. It has managed to transform (some of) them into conservative forces or even, in some cases, props of the regime.

The two "official" Islamist parties, created one year after the FIS was established in 1989, have enjoyed direct support from the regime. Both Mahfoud Nahnah and Abdallah Djaballah, feeling marginalized by the FIS success and anxious to remain influential in the broader Islamic movement, were encouraged by the regime to enter party politics. Some say that the regime went so far as to finance the two new parties, HAMAS and Ennahda, and generously so as well (Willis 1996a: 168). From the point of view of the regime, there was political capital to draw. First, creating and supporting these parties was a way to divide and fragment the Islamist movement and its constituency, which had been monopolized by the FIS. Second, "official" Islamist parties in government would attract the support of those who may have otherwise favored the FIS, had it continued to exist. In later years, they would garner the support of those who defended a role for religion in governance, but had become disillusioned by the seemingly gratuitous violence of the insurgents. Third, the existence of Islamist political parties demonstrated to the Algerian public that the concerns of those who defend an "Islamist" agenda were being acknowledged by the regime. Thus, sponsoring Islamist parties would enhance the regime's popularity and legitimacy at the expense of insurgents. To be sure, it was late in the day before the regime recognized that Algerian Islamism, that had been integral to the nationalist tradition, had to be reintegrated into domestic politics; only by doing so could Islam be "domesticized" and the system restabilized.

---

[19] Indeed, as we will see below, it was the combination of these three factors, teased by the regime, that accounts for the failure of the Islamist opposition to organize and institutionalize itself. Interestingly, these same three factors account, in large measure, for the factionalism that characterizes Algerian politics more generally.

The official Islamist parties, however, would remain more or less co-opted forces. HAMAS – and its later incarnation, the MSP – has rarely criticized the regime vehemently, wary of endangering its privileged position. In fact, it often sided with the regime against the FIS. Its first leader, Mahfoud Nahnah, enjoyed good relations with the regime until his death in 2003 (Willis 1996a: 168–9). In contrast, Ennahda was closer to the FIS in the early years and far more radical in its program than HAMAS/MSP has been. However, once it began to do very well at the polls, it was immediately destabilized, most likely via regime interference (Roberts 1993, reprinted in 2003c: 264).[20] Following the October 1997 elections, the party split and Abdallah Djaballah was forced out by pro-regime elements within Ennahda. In 1999, he started his own party, the *Mouvement pour la Réforme Nationale – El Islah* (MRN-I), which remained seriously weakened until its spectacular comeback as the third most influential political force in the 2002 parliamentary elections.[21]

The fate of the Wafa party is especially noteworthy for understanding regime tactics. Headed by Ahmed Taleb Ibrahimi, a former revolutionary figure and member of the prominent family of Sheikh Bashir al-Ibrahimi of the AUMA, Wafa was refused official recognition. Accused by the regime of a variety of misdemeanors, Ibrahimi was prevented from running in the 1999 and 2004 elections (Werenfels 2007: 70). Presumably, his stature and popularity aroused grave concerns within the leadership structure, at the same time as the latter recognized that he could not be easily co-opted.

As for the outlawed FIS, its representatives seem to have conservatized themselves over time, if only for the sake of maintaining some degree of relevance once they had lost the political battle (Werenfels 2007: 71). Both Abassi Madani and Ali Belhadj, who were in prison from June 1991 to July 2003, endorsed the 1999 government-sponsored *Concorde Civile*, or legal amnesty provisions for insurgents – a quintessential co-optation strategy.[22] A third FIS leader, Rabah Kebir, who was living in exile, endorsed the 2004 re-election of Bouteflika. These gestures were highly

---

[20] Hugh Roberts suggests that the results of the October 1997 elections provide a fairly clear indication of how the system restabilizes itself: via a "return to the *status quo ante* 1989 with pluralist trimmings" (1998: 196). Through considerable rigging, the two regime-sponsored parties, the FLN and the RND, secured a monopoly of power, while the two legally sanctioned Islamist parties, the MSP and the MRN-I, became the official opposition. Hence, the electors had a sense of some degree of choice and voice.

[21] On the significance of the results of the 2002 elections, see Roberts (2003a: 347–61); www.algeria-watch.org. However, in the 2004 presidential elections, Djaballah did quite poorly, attaining only 5.02 percent of the vote.

[22] On the *Concorde Civile*, see ICG 2001a.

publicized by the regime; they were, no doubt, valuable sources of political capital.

Amnesty has proven to be an important co-optation strategy as well. The *Concorde Civile* law, ratified by an overwhelming majority of the population through a referendum, formalized the truce that had been arrived at in 1997 between the army and the AIS – the military wing of the FIS. The violence decreased substantially from that time on. A second amnesty, for Islamists who had not committed rape or murder, was promulgated through a referendum, held on September 29, 2005, on President Bouteflika's Charter for Peace and National Reconciliation. Included in the Charter was monetary compensation for the families of victims of violence and of the disappeared, plus exoneration of the military and security forces for their, at times, dubious activities related to combatting the insurgency (Slackman 2005: A3; Werenfels 2005). The overall message was one of co-optation: the state was providing the resources to encourage Algerians to "forgive and forget," and desist from demanding explanations or accountability. Separate from but not dissimilar to these amnesties in the anticipated effect is the recent decision of the regime to indemnify former *patriotes* for their work during the civil war years. Indeed, providing them with a regular stipend is a means to guarantee both their loyalty and their silence.[23]

As with the Islamist opposition, the Kabyle protest movement, which grew out of the spontaneous uprising in Kabylia in April 2001, would also be coopted by the regime.[24] Furthermore, the movement's demands would be systematically and purposefully distorted so that the regime could exert control over it more effectively. Interestingly, the demands enunciated in the *El Kseur* platform of June 2001 included socio-economic grievances shared by a broad cross-section of Algerian society; for the most part, they did not reflect the particularistic concerns of a single ethnic community (ICG 2003b). Because of its national appeal, the movement quickly gained support throughout the country, and spearheaded what appeared to be the beginnings of a mass movement aimed at promoting social justice.

In an effort to delegitimize and dominate the movement, the regime ethnicized it from the start, insisting that it reflected nothing more than a

---

[23] It is likely that many of them would have highly incriminating information regarding government-supported activities. See Tigha (2006).

[24] The killing of a young Kabyle in a *gendarmerie* in Kabylia sparked riots throughout the region. The security forces responded with live ammunition, killing more than 100 Kabyle youth. The protest movement which emerged organized itself around a coherent set of political demands, and into various smaller groups, or *coordinations*, each with a collective leadership.

"Berber problem." To prevent it from spreading further, the regime quarantined the movement, while exploiting its internal divisions so as to encourage its fragmentation. At the same time, President Bouteflika, anxious to get away with ceding very little, agreed that Tamazight should be recognized as a "national" language, but not an "official" language. The constitution was revised accordingly in April 2002.

Manipulation was another key strategy of the regime in its efforts to reclaim its authority and control. It sought to win over the Algerian public, but also the international community. To win over the population, the state may have used violence as a source of political capital, employing it against civilians and then attributing that violence to insurgents. The massacres in the Mitidja plain in 1997/8, for example, have been the subject of much controversy. There have been repeated allegations that government forces either perpetrated or facilitated the killing of civilians (Aboud 2002; Charef 1998; Souaidia 2001; Yous 2000).[25] Either the state acted directly, disguised as Islamist guerillas, or it arranged for an infiltrated group to do the job. Whatever the logistics, it is thought that on a number of occasions, military-backed assailants terrorized target populations so that they would condemn the insurgents and transfer their loyalties to incumbents (Bedjaoui 1999: 312–18). In this way, government-perpetrated terror that was blamed on insurgents delegitimized the latter and won support for incumbents (ICG 2001a: 5). Similarly with the operation of protection rackets and the preying on passing traffic: in part through manipulation by Algerian intelligence services, the GIA, especially, appeared over time to be far less motivated by political objectives, as its activities became reoriented toward banditry (Lowi 2005; Roberts 2003c: 269).[26]

As the numbers of Islamist fighters grew in the second phase of violence, the financial needs of the insurgency soared. Meeting those needs in an environment of persistent economic crisis and little or no (material) support from the exile community was difficult. Over time, the apparent loss of clear political goals on the part of some of the insurgency groups, within the context of a flourishing informal sector and woefully

---

[25] Witness the prolific *Qui Tue Qui* debate in the Algerian press, as documented on the Algeria Watch website: www.algeria-watch.org.

[26] From 1962, the Algerian intelligence services, successor to the pre-independence MALG, were referred to as the Sécurité Militaire (SM). Since 1990, they have been called the *Département du Renseignement et de la Sécurité* (DRS). Headed by General Mohamed (Tewfik) Mediène since 1990, the DRS is, most likely, the most powerful institution in the country. It supervises a very important sub-division, the *Direction du Contre-Espionnage et de la Sécurité Interne* (DCE), which was headed by General Smaïl Lamari until his death in August 2007 (Roberts 2007: 12). Werenfels (2007: 56) notes that both Mediène and Lamari were members of the *décideurs* – the *pouvoir* (*réel*) – of Algeria in 1999.

inadequate regulatory institutions, contributed to transforming the means of financing the insurgency from raids and armed robberies, especially of military outposts and financial or commercial institutions, to extortion and looting of various forms: pillaging commercial traffic, "taxing" local populations, seizing property (Hadjadj 1999: 240–54). It was not long before insurgents got involved in the parallel economy and contraband trade as well.[27] These activities became increasingly common and increasingly competitive insofar as groups fought regularly over "turf." Controlling roads, for example, became a major objective of guerilla strategy and a major source of rivalry among insurgency groups, particularly between the AIS and the GIA in the mid-1990s.

To be sure, the IMF-backed structural adjustment program, accepted by the regime in 1994, contributed to the proliferation of private economic activities of insurgents as well. The measures that were part of the reform package – especially the abolition of price controls and liberalization of access to foreign exchange – enhanced guerillas' access to financial resources, and allowed them to get involved in business and trade (Hadjadj 1999: 92–4; Martinez 1998: 282–92).

As the violence became increasingly articulated with the micro-economy and new networks of political banditry were created, the regime intimated repeatedly that the insurgents were not genuinely interested in transforming the system; rather, they were focussed, single-mindedly, on looting the state and bleeding the population.[28] In this way, the regime managed successfully to turn attention away from its own dubious economic activities – in which, for example, high-ranking generals enjoyed personal monopolies over the import of essential goods – and at the same time, discredit the insurgents.[29]

---

[27] The GSPC, for example, is said to have controlled an important portion of the contraband traffic operating between Tunisia and Algeria. In doing so, it forged a commercial alliance with the traditional mafia, reaping fantastic profits from the illicit trade in hashish, vehicles, and food products (Salgon 2001: 68).

[28] There have been suggestions that when he was gunned down, Zouabri, then head of the GIA, was in possession of a considerable amount of gold. See Florence Beaugé, "Antar Zouabri, chef du GIA algérien, a été tué par les forces de sécurité, vendredi, à Boufarik," Le Monde February 2, 2002, p. 5. There is little doubt, however, that the GIA at least, and perhaps other groups as well, were infiltrated by the security services (Roberts 2003: 269). For example, there exists some evidence that Djamal Zitouni, leader of the GIA from October 1994 to July 1996, was an agent of the Algerian security services, and in that capacity carried out the GIA-attributed attacks in the Paris subway in 1995. See the powerful documentary "Attentat de Paris: Enquête sur les Commanditaires," by Jean-Baptiste Rivoire and Romain Icard, produced by Canal Plus, France, November 4, 2002.

[29] The DRS apparently became increasingly involved in economic activities during the 1990s, overseeing the business of imports especially (ICG 2001c; Werenfels 2007: 50, 88).

By manipulating the Algerian public and insurgents thus, a divisive struggle at the national level over political issues was averted. Furthermore, the insurgency, via gratuitous violence and terror, was deprived, with the passage of time, of a sympathetic public, a voluntary support network, and whatever legitimacy it had initially enjoyed. This, combined with group fractionalization and personalistic politics, accounts for the failure of the Islamist opposition to organize and institutionalize itself. The insurgency proved unable to assume the longer-term function of an effective movement of opposition to the Algerian state.

The regime's manipulation of conjunctural forces within the international environment has been quite successful as well. By cleverly equating Islamism and terrorism, the military-backed regime has received much support from Western governments and international institutions, as well as much indulgence relative to corruption and human rights violations. First, despite its initial isolation, the Algerian regime eventually received tacit support from Western powers for the coup that brought the democratic transition to an end (Bedjaoui et al.1999: 695–965).[30] Second, in the midst of the civil war, the international community, via IMF intervention, saved the Algerian state from bankruptcy. Two agreements for debt rescheduling, in 1994 and 1995, gave the state about $20 billion that included deferred payments, IMF credits, as well as credits made available by the European Union and the European Investment Bank (Benderra 2003; Talahite 2000). Bailed out, incumbents could retain power, as well as the ability to nourish their networks and pursue the costly repression of insurgents (Lowi 2005).

The West's fear of Islamism, coupled with the Algerian regime's dogged insistence on an "Islamist threat," have promised uninterrupted external support for incumbents, especially in the post-9/11 environment. Moreover, by transforming the oilfields in the south into heavily guarded zones of exclusion, the regime has convinced foreign oil companies that it is safe to continue to invest in the Algerian hydrocarbon sector: the only sector of the economy that attracts foreign capital and is the most important source of large-scale corruption (CHEAr 1995).

International structural forces

By the late 1990s, the military-backed regime's grip on power had been restored. The AIS had laid down its arms and other groups disbanded,

---

[30] The solidarity of foreign governments was especially forthcoming once terrorism was exported to Europe in 1995, and attributed to the GIA (interviews with members of the Algerian military: October 28–29, 2002).

having been seduced by the government-backed amnesty, coopted or infiltrated via the skillful maneuvering of the regime. At the same time, scant material resources available to insurgency groups combined with growing popular disgust with the violence and predation to frustrate the efforts of most of the remaining insurgents.

Favorable international structural forces coincided with auspicious regime efforts to neutralize its opposition and reassert its power and hegemony. For one, the price of oil, that had registered just under $13/barrel in 1998, began to surge. By 2000, one year after the promulgation of the *Concorde Civile*, which had contributed significantly to the decrease in violence, it reached $28.5/barrel. Apart from the brief spike in 1991 at the time of the first Gulf War, this represented the highest it had been by far since 1985.[31]

In 2001, the government's total budget revenue and grants reached approximately $21 billion, or double what they had been in 1998 (ACC 2002).[32] The current account increased from a deficit of −1.9 percent of GDP in 1998 to a massive surplus of 16.8 percent in 2000 and 12 percent in 2001. Gross official reserves rose from $6.8 billion to $17.9 billion, while total debt as a percentage of GDP dropped from 64.3 percent to around 40 percent. While economic growth as a whole remained sluggish, hovering between 2.4 percent and 3.4 percent per annum between 1999 and 2001,[33] financially Algeria had never been in such a good position.

With record oil revenues in 2003 and foreign reserves of more than $30 billion, President Bouteflika managed to tour the entire country just prior to the 2004 presidential election campaign and distribute, on average, the equivalent of $50–65 million to every *wilaya* he visited. It is widely believed that his ability to distribute so generously was in no small measure responsible for his overwhelming victory (Werenfels 2007: 139–40). As in the heady days of oil booms,

---

[31] Between 1985 and 1991, the price of oil fluctuated between $10 and $20 per barrel. After the 1991 spike, when the price increased briefly to $35, it again hovered between $10 and $23 through 1999.

[32] According to the EIA (2006), Algeria's foreign reserves at the end of 2005 were an impressive $56 billion (for a population of 31 million), having increased from $32 billion in 2003 and $43 billion in 2004. (They would reach more than $70 billion by spring 2007) Nonetheless, in 2002, the Algerian CNES reported that 13 million Algerians – more than 40 percent of the population – were living below the poverty threshold, on less than $1 per day.

[33] Most estimates suggest that to begin to address the acute unemployment situation in Algeria – in which 30–35 percent of the population remains unemployed, 60 percent of whom are young and unskilled – the economy would need to grow at roughly 7 percent per annum. For an analysis of macroeconomic conditions in Algeria since the mid-1980s and the relationship to politics, see Lowi (2007b).

burgeoning revenues contribute to the assiduous pursuit of regime goals. They also provide the means for purchasing loyalty and silencing opposition.

Algeria's hydrocarbon revenues are likely to remain high, given that there have been significant new oil and gas discoveries in recent years.[34] While analysts consider Algeria to be underexplored, there are plans for far more exploration drilling, largely by foreign companies. Indeed, Algeria, which in 2007 was ranked eighth among OPEC oil producers after Venezuela and Angola, and fourth among exporters of liquid natural gas after Qatar, Malaysia, and Indonesia, is bound to experience a sharp increase in hydrocarbon exports over the next few years.[35]

A budding relationship with the United States government has contributed to the regime's re-equilibration as well. For one, the United States is deeply implicated in the Algerian hydrocarbon industry. In fact, the largest foreign company engaged in hydrocarbon exploration and production in Algeria is the Houston-based Anadarko Petroleum Corporation. Involved in the Algerian oil industry since 1989, Anadarko is currently responsible for an output equivalent to more than one-quarter of total average annual hydrocarbon production in the country. Until recently, it had plans to extend its operations to include the exploitation of natural gas as well.[36] Another American firm, Halliburton, has recently signed an eight-year contract with the Algerian government for enhanced oil recovery (EIA 2006). Needless to say, American oil companies have an interest in protecting an ongoing partnership with the Algerian regime and hence an important stake in the stability of the country.

Beyond the oil and gas sector, the relationship with the United States has become far closer since 9/11. In an effort to position itself in the international "war on terror," the Algerian regime has insisted that it has tremendous experience fighting "Islamist terrorists" – not unlike those who targetted the World Trade Center and the Pentagon. The military has offered to share its expertise, at the same time as it has sought

---

[34] It was estimated in 2007 that Algeria contained 12.3 billion barrels of proven oil reserves, an increase of 1 billion in ten years. See BP: Statistical Review of World Energy 2008. See as well Chakib Khalil, "Energy Industry in MENA: An Algerian Perspective," conference entitled, *Middle East Energy 2008: Risk and Responsibility: The New Realities of Energy Supply*, Chatham House, London, UK, February 4–5, 2008.

[35] See www.bp.com and www.eia.doe.gov/emeu/cabs/algeria.html.

[36] Since 2007, Anadarko has been locked in a dispute with the Algerian government over a newly legislated tax on profits. See, in this regard, "Anadarko says talks to Algeria's Sonatrach on tax," May 5, 2007, www.reuters.com.

sophisticated equipment with which to wipe out its own insurgency once and for all.[37]

Indeed, a strategic alliance has developed between the two countries. Algeria works closely with the United States, in Algeria and neighboring states, on the United States Department of State-funded Trans-Sahara Counterterrorism Initiative (TSCTI). Launched in 2005, the TSCTI builds upon the successes and extends the mandate of the Pan Sahel Initiative (PSI) which began two years before "to prevent terrorists from setting up safe havens in Africa."[38] Through military and intelligence training provided by the United States, the aim is to foster regional cooperation and coordination in tracking the movement of "suspicious people and goods" across borders, and to enhance border capabilities and the sharing of information.[39]

Conclusion

The combination of factors described above – regime strategies to combat its opposition, plus international structural forces – allowed the Algerian regime to reassume the reins of power and assert its hegemony "after a crisis that had seriously threatened the continuity and stability of … the basic political mechanisms" (Linz and Stepan 1978b). The initial strategy of all-out repression was modified once the leadership recognized that resort to it, exclusive of other strategies, served only to undermine further its legitimacy and incite more defections to the opposition. From the middle of the 1990s, the regime employed a variety of distributive mechanisms and rhetorical devices to achieve its aims. Targetted violence was combined with manipulation of both the Algerian public and insurgents, as well as co-optation of (real and potential) forces of opposition.

Leadership strategies, of co-optation and manipulation especially, were decisive. The ability to rely on these strategies over the longer term was

---

[37] In October 2002, one year after 9/11, an international symposium on terrorism, entitled "Le Terrorisme: Le Précédent Algérien," was held in Algiers. Organized by the Algerian military and attended by high-ranking members of the intelligence communities of several Western countries, the aim of the meeting was to overturn the country's international isolation and assist the regime in positioning itself in the "war on terror." At the meeting, attended by this author, several Algerian "men in uniform" took the podium to outline the military's strategy vis-à-vis the insurgents, and make a plea to the international community, and especially the United States, for equipment such as infrared night lights.

[38] For further detail on the strategic alliance, see Lowi and Werenfels (unpublished ms).

[39] The PSI was lauded for its apprehension of Abderrazak al-Para, a key figure in the GSPC who was turned over to the Algerian government in 2004. Nonetheless, the PSI was replaced with the TSCTI that was to be much better funded; apparently it has an annual budget of $100 million. See www.globalsecurity.org/military.

facilitated by the financial support of European powers as of the mid-1990s. Then, at the end of the decade and into the new century, once the regime had brought the insurgency more or less to heel, international structural forces – among them, rising oil prices and the "war on terror" – appeared vigorously in its favor. They contributed to regime efforts to defeat its opponents and dominate the political landscape virtually uncontested.

Part III

Comparisons and conclusions

7 Variations on a theme: comparators in the Muslim world

With the story of Algeria as the backdrop, how can we account for the variation in stability in high-growth, development-oriented, oil-exporting countries in the aftermath of an economic shock? If we consider a sample of oil-exporting states that share certain commonalities with Algeria, how can we explain that in some, contentious politics provoked regime collapse, while in others it did not, and in still others, weakened states confronted for some time by determined challengers managed to re-stabilize?

Recall that Iran and Indonesia succumbed to regime breakdown and system change, in 1979 and 1998 respectively, although Indonesia had successfully weathered previous economic shocks. Saudi Arabia, in contrast, remained stable, despite a severe economic downturn in the late 1980s, and the regime has prevailed. Like Algeria, Iraq became acutely unstable after the 1986 shock, but the regime was able to re-equilibrate into the 1990s. What accounts for regime breakdown and change in Iran in 1979 and in Indonesia in 1998? Why was Saudi Arabia spared a similar outcome to Iran or Indonesia, and how has it managed to remain relatively stable? Why was Indonesia able to weather earlier shocks – in 1986, for example – but not later ones? Furthermore, why were Algeria and pre-Gulf War Iraq, despite suffering acute instability and regime crisis from the late 1980s, able to eventually step back from the brink and re-equilibrate?

I noted, in the first chapter, that there are two critical junctures in the trajectory of the oil-exporting LDC and for its political stability: the inception of oil-based development and the occurrence of an (exogenous) economic shock. The inception of oil-based development can be thought of as a foundational moment, precisely because it is at this time and with the availability of important rents that leaders make consequential decisions about the form, shape, and strength of institutions. What's more, the choices made set the country along a particular course.

As for the occurrence of an economic shock, it too is a critical juncture for the oil-exporting state. As a rentier state that interacts with society

147

largely through distribution, a precipitous change in its revenues impacts both its distributive capacities and the choices it makes, hence its relationship with society.[1] The decisions of leaders regarding the distribution of resources in the aftermath of an economic shock have, just as in the case of the inception of oil-based development, profound consequences for political institutions. They play a major role in establishing outcomes: political stability or instability. In short, those states that remain relatively stable in "bust" periods, or eventually manage to re-equilibrate after a period of instability, do so because of astute leadership choices regarding the reform or adaptation of political and socio-economic arrangements: choices that acknowledge social preferences and, by distributing resources in particular ways, neutralize domestic challengers.

In this chapter, I first compare the five cases in terms of the institutional origins of the state and the robustness of institutional foundations. I do so with two aims: first, to give a sense of the variation in context within which leaders act, and second, to show how contextual features may be manipulated to impact outcomes. Second, I consider the inception of oil-based development. I explore the decisions of leaders at this juncture regarding distributive arrangements and the incorporation of social cleavages. This discussion provides a tableau of the institutional development of the five states at a foundational moment.

Third, I turn my attention to economic shocks – both those with boom and with bust effects. I compare the decisions of leaders at this juncture: in principle, decisions are aimed at easing the effects of shocks on society and maintaining or restoring domestic peace. I conclude with a brief summary of the comparative evidence, highlighting the centrality of leadership choice in effecting outcomes. I leave to the last chapter a more developed exposition of the significance of the comparisons in terms of the capacities of states to remain stable in the face of economic shocks.

Institutional origins of the state

In all five cases, foreign intervention and/or the force of arms assisted regimes in assuming power. Coercion, but also distribution and manipulation, would contribute to their remaining in power. In four of the five cases, powerful nationalist movements took root, and the sentiments they expressed would figure prominently in the process of state formation.

---

[1] Moreover, thriving as it does on the distribution of favors, an authoritarian regime with patrimonial structures is especially challenged at moments of fiscal crisis, while it flourishes during boom periods (Médard 1982: 162–92).

In Algeria, a revolutionary nationalist movement fought and eventually routed the French colonial power that had occupied and ruled the country for 130 years.[2] Until the 1950s, the movement embraced a variety of political tendencies. Over time, however, the leadership of the movement became increasingly authoritarian and intolerant; by the mid-1950s, and despite reference to a National Liberation *Front* (FLN) – as if it were an umbrella organization, gathering up the multiplicity of nationalist voices – a militarized, minority tendency with praetorian inclinations pushed aside all other nationalist forces. At independence in 1962, it would seize power in a fratricidal struggle, and ruthlessly eliminate all other competing power centers. The political elite was fractured, and with the FLN a hollow shell, the only strong institution of the state was the military. The reliance on force, the denial of diversity, and the silencing of debate, that had characterized political life as of 1949, would persist.[3] And despite the populist rhetoric, the militarized regimes of independent Algeria would remain viscerally suspicious of the Algerian masses, in large measure because of the manner in which they had come to power and how deeply alienated they remained from those they governed.

In Iraq and Indonesia, as well, nationalist forces of a variety of political tendencies fought the colonial power – Britain and the Netherlands, respectively – and were eventually victorious.[4] In Iraq, as in Algeria, there had been a fairly rich political spectrum; it was composed of Kurdish nationalists, religious traditionalists, pan-Arab and Iraqi nationalists, Communists, among others. While the country became nominally independent in 1932, British intervention in Iraqi affairs persisted.[5] It would take a coup, orchestrated in 1958 by a clandestine officers' movement within the military, to overthrow the British-backed monarchy and install a military-dominated, republican government. However, rather than devolve power or create popular institutions of representation, the republican government, formed by the populist 'Abd al-Karim Qasim, maintained patrimonial networks, silenced the opposition, and tightened its control over society (Tripp 2007: 150–5).

---

[2] Note that although three of the five cases – Algeria, Indonesia, and Iraq – were *de jure* colonies, Algeria was the only settler colony. Europeans moved *en masse* to Algeria, as of the middle of the nineteenth century, to establish themselves and build a life there, not as European civil servants, but rather as residents of the colony.

[3] Above, chapter 3.

[4] On the Dutch in Indonesia, see Cribb (1999); on the Japanese occupation and resistance to it, see Anderson (1972).

[5] On state formation and the early years of state-building in Iraq, see Batatu 1978; Dodge 2003; Sluglett and Farouk-Sluglett 1987/2001; Tripp 2007.

In Indonesia, the nationalist leader, Sukarno, would be named president when the country gained its independence in 1949 and a constitutional democracy was established. For the sake of remaining all-inclusive and nurturing unity in this vast, multi-ethnic archipelago, the nationalist movement chose to remain vague about a political program. In fact, the "ideology" it propounded – *Pancasila* – espoused principles that were palatable to the broad spectrum of tendencies within Indonesian nationalism (Cribb 1999: 15–17).[6]

After overthrowing parliamentary democracy with the help of the military at the end of the 1950s – avowedly to resolve persistent social conflicts – Sukarno created a system of personalist authoritarian rule, which he called "Guided Democracy." Despite his efforts, he was unable to bring order to the country; he would be pushed out of office by his own military following a bloody, country-wide anti-communist witch-hunt. At the helm of the brutal pacification effort, General Suharto assumed power for himself (Crouch 1979: 573–4). As of 1966, he was in absolute command, and officers from every branch of the army could be found in all parts of government and the civil service.

Suharto purchased the loyalty of what had been a factionalized military with oil money and a host of political and economic favors. The military would remain rich, powerful, and devoted to Suharto. A bought-off military secured Suharto's tenure, while a ubiquitous repressive force, combined with creative ways to coopt key social forces, ensured the political quiescence of the population (Crouch 1979).[7] Suharto would construct a system, which he called the "New Order," founded on army-based authoritarian development. *Pancasila* and developmentalism (*pembangunan*), touted as unifying forces, were the only tolerated ideologies, while communism, Islamism, and ethno-nationalism were vigorously combated (Liddle 1999b: 39–52).

While force and coercion, but also co-optation and collaboration, were integral to state formation in Iran and Saudi Arabia as well, their experiences were quite distinct from the other three cases, and from each other. For one, neither had been a colony in the proper sense of the term, but in both, foreign involvement was considerable. Furthermore, in Saudi Arabia,

---

[6] *Pancasila* expresses five principles: belief in one god, unity of Indonesia, humanitarianism through justice and civility, democracy through deliberation, social justice for all.

[7] Suharto institutionalized the army's new role through *dwi fungsi*, the idea that the army enjoyed a dual function: to defend the state and its borders from foreign aggression, and to protect the country from domestic dangers of any kind. Indeed, threats from within were perceived to be at least as likely and severe as from without. Hence, traditional military responsibilities were combined with political ones for the sake of domestic security, broadly understood.

in contrast to the other cases, state formation had *not* been the result of an anti-colonialist, or even a nationalist, struggle.

Foreign powers had intervened in Persian affairs from the late nineteenth century, attracted primarily by the country's resource wealth and the possibility of managing it through concessions. Once oil was discovered in 1908, this tendency gained in importance.[8] Iranian nationalism, exemplified by the Constitutional Revolution of 1905/6, was a response to both the intervention of Britain and Russia in local affairs, and the perceived disloyalty – indeed, anti-nationalism – of Persian kings.[9] The demands that foreign domination and arbitrary rule be curtailed and property rights be established remained central to nationalist efforts (Abrahamian 1982: 50–80; Keddie 1999: 44–93). Nonetheless, both the first and second Pahlavi Shahs were placed on the throne by, or with the assistance of, foreign powers.

Relying upon the military, the bureaucracy, and court patronage, Reza Khan would establish an authoritarian state that he would oversee until his foreign benefactors removed him from power and replaced him with his son. Both he and Mohamad Reza consolidated power through programs of modernization and, with the assistance of generously funded, foreign-backed, military and security apparati, by leveling out the political landscape, silencing independent voices, and neutralizing forces of opposition (Keddie 2003: 87–91, 133–4).[10]

As for Saudi Arabia, Ottoman control did persist in some parts of the Arabian Peninsula into the twentieth century, but it was weak and uneven (Vassiliev 2000: 206–8, 235–40). Rather, the creation of the Saudi state in the second quarter of the twentieth century harks back to a powerful alliance that formed in the center of the peninsula – the Nejd – in the mid-eighteenth century between Mohamad ibn Sa'ud, a political figure and member of the Al Sa'ud clan, and Mohamad ibn 'Abd al-Wahhab, a religious reformer. The politico–religious alliance ensured that ibn 'Abd al-Wahhab would pay allegiance to, actively support, and promote the extension of the rule of ibn Sa'ud, as long as the latter continued to abide by, and impose in his political realm, the very particular interpretation of Islam propounded by ibn 'Abd al-Wahhab. Together, they would embark

---

[8] The British had been exploring for oil in Persia since 1901. While clear evidence of oil had been found in 1904, it was in May 1908 that it was officially struck by the British-owned Burmah Oil in Masjid-i-Suleiman (Yergin 1991: 142–7).

[9] The first mobilized expression of these twin sentiments was the tobacco protest of 1891–2. See Keddie (1966).

[10] Shah Reza Pahlavi did much to develop the country's infrastructure, educate the population, and promote industrialization. Nonetheless, his social reforms struck hard at the traditional fabric of society (Farmanfarmaian and Farmanfarmaian 1997: 113–20).

upon an expansionist enterprise of domination, indoctrination, and control, in which submission to the authority of the Al Sa'ud and the tenets of Wahhabi Islam was central. The price of resistance was conquest (Al-Rasheed 2002: 44–69; Vassiliev 2000: 73–111).[11]

In the first decades of the twentieth century, "Ibn Sa'ud" ('Abd al-Aziz ibn 'Abd al-Rahman Al Sa'ud), a direct descendant of Mohamad ibn Sa'ud, wrested control over the peninsula, then under prominent families of the Ottoman empire. He did so through coercion and conquest, but also via co-optation of key social forces, collaboration with prominent families and tribes, and religious indoctrination (Steinberg 2005: 20–2). Wahhabism was revived as the state religion and key organizing principle of the country. As in the past, a powerful alliance developed between Ibn Sa'ud and the religious authorities, trained in the Wahhabi tradition (Vassiliev 2000: 254–306). In 1926, a monarchy was established under Ibn Sa'ud, and in 1932 it was renamed the Kingdom of Saudi Arabia.

The convergence, in the creation of the state, of historic claims, conquest, and an alliance that cemented two key social forces and demanded submission, suggests fairly robust institutional foundations. Furthermore, as suggested above, Ibn Sa'ud, displaying considerable political acuity, was careful to incorporate into the state-building process, and thereby neutralize, not only both sedentary and tribal/nomadic elements but also former, or potential, rivals and alternate centers of power.[12] He did so through a variety of innovative and highly personalized means, including marriage, gift-giving, the disbursement of offices, and other forms of distribution of both material favors and political resources (Al-Rasheed 2002: 60–85; Salamé 1993: 582). Incorporation entailed distribution, and distribution implied co-optation.

When exploring the consolidation of state power, I note that in all five cases, the leadership enjoyed a fairly narrow social base. In Saudi Arabia, however, the problem of questionable legitimacy, and potentially weak

[11] The emirate (or princedom) survived until 1818, when it was crushed by Mohamad Ali of Egypt. There was a second Sa'udi-Wahhabi emirate from 1843–91, but it was brought down by forces of the Ottoman Empire in alliance with a rival regional power – the Rashidi emirate in Ha'il. Then, from 1902–21, the Al-Rashid and the Al Sa'ud competed for control of central Arabia, with the latter eventually holding sway. With the outbreak of World War I and the fall of the Ottoman Empire, a power struggle developed between the Hashemite family of the Hejaz and the Al Sa'ud of the Nejd, with the latter intent on expanding their control over the peninsula once again. With the help of the British, who had already betrayed the Hashemites in a duplicitous deal, the Al Sa'ud emerged victorious, while the Hashemites went into exile in Iraq, Syria, and Jordan (Fromkin 1989; Vassiliev 2000: 192–250, 260–4).

[12] Subduing tribes by putting an end to their land rights and raiding activities was essential for state-building insofar as undermining the tribal economy allowed for the settlement and co-optation of tribal leaders. (I am grateful to Steffen Hertog for this insight.)

institutions that derive therefrom, was mitigated by two key contextual features: first, the centrality of imposed "conversion" in state formation, and second, the "marriage," in conquest and control, to a very particular religio-political arrangement, between two prominent social forces. Moreover, while leadership in the five countries worked to counter its narrow social base by trying to nurture a compliant public, and did so largely through mechanisms of co-optation that combined distribution with repression, the Al Sa'uds, as we will see below, would prove exemplary in the elaboration and mobilization of these powerful survival strategies. Indeed, they lay at the very crux of the state-building enterprise.[13]

Inception of oil-based development

In Algeria and the four comparators, authoritarian regimes with patrimonial structures have endured from the inception of oil-based development in the 1950s or 1960s. With access to new and important sources of income from the sale of oil, regimes embarked upon massive, state-led development programs of growth and modernization. They adopted national industrialization programs of broad scope, and financed ambitious social and economic projects at the same time as they sustained fairly generous welfare systems. The investment foci varied from case to case: Algeria, with its *industries industrialisantes* concept of development, was engaged from the start in the promotion of very big, capital-intensive industries; Iran, as well, concentrated on heavy industry, but also on huge investments in military expansion (Amirahmadi 1995: 195; Amuzegar 1977). Iraq focused on infrastructural development and import substitution industrialization (Chaudhry 1999: 317–42; Farouk-Sluglett and Sluglett 1987/2001: 216–54). Indonesia proceeded more cautiously, pursuing a "balanced growth" policy of close attention to rural as well as urban development of the economy and administrative apparatus (Booth 1999; Campos and Root 1996: 64–7). Saudi Arabia, from its rudimentary beginnings, embarked on a broad-based program of bureaucratic and infrastructural development, as well as modernization in the economic, social, and military spheres (Chaudhry 1997: 65–100, 139–85).

Of the development programs pursued, Indonesia's was decidedly egalitarian – if not populist – in intent, and attentive to social preferences.

---

[13] The absence, in Saudi society, of a history of struggle to achieve collective goals contributes in some measure to regime stability. Successful collective action in the past, exemplified by an indigenous nationalist movement, poses a challenge to regimes insofar as the people can draw inspiration from a history of having mobilized against unjust authority and emerged victorious.

There appeared to be something for everybody in Suharto's program: it addressed the needs of the countryside and the cities, and aimed to achieve food security, administrative reach, as well as macroeconomic stabilization. The program was geared explicitly to promoting order and addressing the fundamental problems that had marred the tenure of Suharto's predecessor (Gelb *et al.* 1988: 203–4).[14] Order would be achieved by distributing oil revenues in such a way that all would benefit from growth and development, at the same time as the center gained a foothold in all regions. Retaining an extractive capacity of note, despite burgeoning oil revenues – unique among the five cases – assisted Suharto's regime in its efforts to gain access to information across the archipelago and build institutional capacity (Smith 2007: 129–32).[15] To be sure, pursuing his "balanced growth" agenda with the assistance of a very able team of economic advisors and achieving positive results were of enormous benefit to Suharto, earning for him what Liddle (1991) has so aptly termed "performance legitimacy." Besides, Suharto's rhetoric, that stressed development, stability, and equality, and insisted on their inter-relatedness, contributed to "inspiring" the public and "persuading" them of the beneficence of his program (Liddle 2007: 34).[16]

In contrast, in Algeria, Iran, and somewhat less so in Iraq, the rural sector was sorely neglected, yet reconfigured in such a way as to engender much hardship in both the short and long term. With the inception of oil-based development, Boumedienne, espousing the demands of social justice, and the Shah, cynically kowtowing to the suggestions of the United States' administration, adopted agrarian reform programs. In Algeria, rather than break up large landholdings and redistribute plots in an egalitarian fashion among the peasantry, the latter were denied legal ownership of land and forced onto cooperatives, while members of the wartime *Armée de la frontière* were awarded the most desirable plots.

---

[14] Suharto had understood that, for the sake of stability, the needs of the rural environment, where more than 80 percent of the Indonesian population lived in 1966, could not be ignored.

[15] Also distinct from most other oil-exporting LDCs, Indonesia's non-oil exports grew significantly in the 1970s' boom years. Following the advice of his technocrats, Suharto accepted that Indonesia devalue its currency so as to prevent exchange rate appreciation that, via the Dutch Disease, would discourage non-oil exports. The devaluations at the end of boom periods, in 1978 and 1983, boosted the non-oil tradable sectors. Manufactured exports, for example, increased by 260 percent after the first large devaluation (Gelb *et al.* 1988: 220–1).

[16] Samuels (2003: 8) notes that to build and maintain power, leaders "appeal to affect, by *inspiring* ... to material interests, by *buying* ... And, by *bullying*, they may appeal to fear." This is roughly equivalent to my manipulation, co-optation, repression. See, as well, McAdam *et al.* (2001).

In Iran, the White Revolution (1963) land reform undercut the power of the traditional landed elite which included the Shi'a clergy, favored the concentration of land in the hands of the big peasantry, and thoroughly bureaucratized the rural economy (Hooglund 1982; Katouzian 1978). The historic alliance between the landed upper class and the monarchy was dissolved, tensions hardened in the relations between the state and the clergy, and the state assumed a far more interventionist role in the rural economy than ever before. Concurrently, the monarchy experienced a profound narrowing of the social basis of its support (McLachlan 1977: 136–7; Parsa 2000: 34–5).[17]

In both Iran and Algeria, rural policy promoted the centralizing ambitions of the regime, at the same time as a new landless class of peasants was created. In the absence of incentives to produce and with living standards depressed, they had little choice but to migrate to the cities, swelling the ranks of the urban poor and intensifying pressures on urban resources. Social inequalities widened and social ills deepened. Migrants would form an important segment of the opposition in the late 1970s in Iran, and in the late 1980s and 1990s in Algeria (Keddie 2003: 228; Lowi 2005: 231–2).

Indeed, oil rents financed distribution, and distribution engaged both development and exclusion. Perhaps most clearly in Algeria and Iraq, institutional frameworks that consolidated politicized distributional arrangements were elaborated. In Algeria, massive redistribution, from independence through the early years of oil-based development, nourished the state's egalitarian discourse. Nonetheless, redistribution, beginning with the *biens vacants*, was carried out in a hierarchical fashion: "old guard" militants, their allies, and those closest to the regime enjoyed privileged access.

The promotion by the regime of arabo–islamism belied the inclusivist rhetoric through its marginalization of specific social categories: Berbers were formally excluded from the Algerian "nation," while religious traditionalists were coopted by the state, and arabophones, who in principle were favored over francophones, would find themselves marginalized in the labor market. Again, members of the pre-independence *Armée de la frontière* remained the most privileged category.

The system of redistribution reinforced clientelism, which itself bolstered the already strong collegial, kinship, and regional ties that carried over from the colonial period, while aggravating social conflicts. As they competed for, and at times were denied, access to resources,

---

[17] For a more positive appraisal of the land reform program and its outcomes, see Majd (1992).

key cleavage structures were weakly incorporated into the Algerian state. Those same social forces which had been denied inclusion in the post-1949 period remained on the margins at the inception of oil-based development. Nonetheless, Boumedienne, like Suharto until the 1990s, "appeal(ed) to affect by inspiring" (Samuels 2003: 8): there was a widely shared sentiment in Algeria that the leader had a social project and was genuinely committed to building what *he* referred to as the "new Algeria."

In Iraq, as well, exclusion, financed through oil-based development that had begun in the 1950s, became the preferred ordering principle of one narrowly based, military-backed ruling clique after another. Beginning with Prime Minister Nuri al-Sa'id, who dominated Iraqi politics from 1939–58, and mimicking a pattern introduced by the British mandate authority (1921–32), Iraqi leaders used oil revenues to cement alliances, coopt challengers, and destroy intransigent adversaries (Farouk-Sluglett and Sluglett 1987/2001: 21; Tripp 2007: 133–4, 206–7). Through selective distribution and repression, they would push aside movements that enjoyed popular support – notably, the Iraqi Communist Party and the *al-Da'wa* (Shi'a) movement[18] – and suppress Kurdish demands for autonomy. The aim was to increase the maneuverability of the regime and dominate politics uncontested.

The army, dominated by Sunni officers, was the centerpiece of the regime from 1958 onward, while under B'ath rule (1968–2003), the private sector enjoyed privileged access to the regime and was, with the military, the principal recipient of state largesse. Much effort was devoted to breaking the power of the traditional landed and commercial elite – the majority of whom were Shi'a – and gaining direct control over economic resources (Chaudhry 1999: 327).[19] Despite a generous distributive state welfare system, especially after the nationalization of the oil industry in 1972, ethnic, religious, and ideological communities remained poorly integrated.

In Iran and in Saudi Arabia, selective allocations signified the favoring of some over others, the consolidation of the regime's alliance with only certain sectors of society, the neglect of specific social categories, the fabrication of new elites. By the mid-1950s, Iran's complex political landscape was being systematically leveled out. Forces of opposition were silenced: rebellious regions with ethnic minorities (Arabs of Khuzistan, Kurds of Mahabad) and tribal formations (Qashqai and Bakhtiari of the southwest) had been

---

[18] See below, p. 159.
[19] On economic development programs from 1958, see Farouk-Sluglett and Sluglett (1987/2001: 216–54).

subdued, powerful liberal–nationalists (Musaddiq) had been removed, opposition movements with mobilizational capacity (Tudeh Party) had been outlawed, and even strong, independent-minded prime ministers, whether of the opposition (Musaddiq) or pro-Shah (General Zahedi), were ousted (Cottam 1964/79: 59–90).[20]

At the inception of oil-based development in the 1960s, the Shah pushed aside the traditional elite – bazaari merchants and the clergy – and excluded them from access to state resources. Moreover, he denied the clergy their traditional function as educators, service providers, and moral authorities, while bestowing favors on the modern middle classes in general and the private sector in particular (Farmanfarmaian and Farmanfarmaian 1997: 113–20). With burgeoning oil revenues as of the early 1970s, however, the increasingly interventionist state began to hamstring private sector activity as well, even though it would remain the principal recipient of state largesse.[21]

In Saudi Arabia, state revenues were, from the outset, the critical tool for cementing relationships of dependence on and acquiescence to the Al Sa'ud.[22] Far more so than in the other cases, an array of basic commodities and utilities has been subsidized for consumers, and enormously broad, cradle-to-grave social welfare programs – including pensions and social security benefits, public employment, free education and health care, and generous scholarships – have been available to Saudi nationals (Al-Rasheed 2002: 125–7; Chaudhry 1997: 147–55).[23]

Through the vast redistributive network, the Al Sa'ud have pursued several implicit goals: first, by consolidating the dependency of the subject population upon state largesse, they have silenced popular demands and purchased loyalty, or at least fairly broad compliance to their rule. Second, as some forms of distribution, such as social welfare programs, were available to all citizens, while others, such as contracts and gifts, were accessible only to some, distribution became the principal means for

---

[20] In the early 1960s, Ebtehaj, head of the Plan Organization, and Arsanjani, the popular Minister of Agriculture, would be forced to resign from their positions (Keddie 2003: 137–8, 152). On the Musaddiq era and the 1953 coup, see Gasiorowski and Byrne (2004).

[21] As the state reserved heavy industry for itself, there was not much of an industrial bourgeoisie to speak of in Iran. Rather, the bourgeoisie was mainly financial and mercantile. See Karshenas (1990: 99–105); Parsa (2000: 56–7).

[22] Until the discovery of oil in Al-Hasa (Al-Mintaqa al-Sharqiyya – the Eastern Province) in 1938 and its commercial exploitation as of 1946, revenues were drawn mainly from the pilgrimage and from zakat (alms), but also from foreign subsidies. By the mid-1940s, oil revenues, extracted from the major oil companies, had become the primary source of state revenues (Al-Rasheed 2002: 89; Vassiliev 2000: 401).

[23] However, Saudi Shi'a have been denied, for example, certain positions in government and in the oil industry. See below.

marking difference. Indeed, unequal access to oil wealth was glaring, and reflected the major sociological and regional cleavages in the country: urban Najdi businessmen and high-ranking civil servants were favored and received substantial material rewards, the 'ulama were courted and coddled, while the Shi'a minority faced sweeping discrimination in the economic, social, and cultural spheres (Chaudhry 1997: 156–61; Abir 1993: 82; Hertog 2005: 112–30). In fact, access to wealth was itself an important social cleavage, alongside region, tribe, dialect, and "confession"/sect.

In Algeria and the comparators, development was promoted as a good: as the means to bring growth and modernization, and end backwardness and dependence. In Saudi Arabia, the leadership favored growth for the sake of growth; there were no ideological or developmentalist underpinnings to its pursuits, other than a commitment to the free market. In Algeria, Indonesia, and to a lesser extent Iraq, where development did include an ideological component, it was championed more or less explicitly as a channel through which to bypass politics. Boumedienne's and Suharto's *modus operandi* suggested that, just like Nuri al-Sa'id, Iraq's Prime Minister during the monarchical period, they believed that the "hard choices" at the core of the modern state – representation, recognition of identities, inclusion, accountability – could be avoided altogether through massive economic development funded by oil money (Tripp 2007: 106). In their view, as long as populations enjoyed rising standards of living and improved quality of life, they would forgo making demands upon the state and insisting upon their primordial ties.

Suharto, in fact, transformed development (*pembangunan*) into state ideology to which the entire country had to adhere. Development ensured stability and represented the New Order's promise of a better life for all Indonesians (Liddle 1991). In Algeria, the population was itself engaged in the all-out development strategy through the severe austerity measures it was subjected to for the sake of maximizing investment. Development had become a way of not simply circumventing politics, but more pointedly, "engaging in politics by other means" (El-Kenz 1997: 332). The populist rhetoric adopted by the Algerian, Indonesian, and Iraqi regimes reinforced these efforts.

In all five countries and to varying degrees, institutional arrangements were put into place that did away with pluralism, while providing the illusion of popular incorporation. Only in Saudi Arabia was political participation of any sort illegal; political parties simply do not exist and government rallies do not take place. The lacuna of participation has been filled by a politics of massive redistribution accompanied, when necessary, by repression, and buttressed by religious discourse which itself represents an enforced discipline. Nonetheless, a perception that there exists the possibility of access to those in power has remained an important element of the system, as well as a source of legitimacy for the Al Sa'ud. It has provided the leadership with a means for both gauging social preferences and dispensing patronage.[24]

In Algeria and Iraq, political parties did exist at the inception of oil-based development, but in the case of Algeria, all but the former Communist Party, renamed the *Parti de l'avant garde socialiste* (PAGS), were mere phantom institutions. In Iraq, it was not until the mid- to late 1970s that the Communist Party and the *al-Da'wa* movement were either decimated or forced underground. And while the two Kurdish nationalist parties, the Kurdistan Democratic Party (KDP) and the Patriotic Union of Kurdistan (PUK), remained more or less active, they too had suffered persecution intermittently.[25]

In Indonesia, Suharto outlawed political activity of significance in all but the official sanctioned form. GOLKAR was the quintessential mobilizational government party, with considerable patronage-providing and information-gathering capacity (Smith 2007: 86–91); adherence to it, as to the FLN in Algeria and in later years the B'ath Party in Iraq, was the avenue to social promotion.[26] Even the Shah of Iran created two sham political parties, *Melli* and *Mardom*, to provide a veneer of incipient democracy in the form of multipartyism. He did so once he had eliminated all organized forces of opposition in the post-Musaddiq period, coinciding with the inception of oil-based development. Then in 1963, *Iran Novin* replaced *Melli* and became the Shah's personal mouthpiece, while *Mardom* functioned as the "official" opposition. In short, at the inception of oil-based development, leaders sought to weaken all channels of interest articulation, inhibit sub-national ties, and establish a mono-loyalty to the state, while offering the impression of popular engagement.

---

[24] I am grateful to an anonymous reader for this insight.

[25] On the Iraqi Communist Party, see Batatu (1978); on the *al-Da'wa* movement, see Batatu (1986); on the Kurdish nationalist movement, see McDowall (1996).

[26] Moreover, while GOLKAR brought people into politics whom Suharto wanted in and whose support he was anxious to have, it was also a vehicle for suppressing the mobilization of competing cleavage structures. Furthermore, while in the 1971 elections as many as nine parties, plus GOLKAR, were competing, Suharto in 1973 forced the nine to fuse into two, with one representing secular nationalism and the other, Islam. This was indeed a repressive move, but it allowed a measure of real contestation (I am grateful to Bill Liddle for sharing these insights with me).

    Interestingly, both the Algerian and Indonesian regimes allowed religious traditionalists some freedom of association and a restricted voice, especially in religious and educational matters, at the same time as they worked hard at coopting them or diluting their mobilizational capacities.

When faced with dissent, the Shah of Iran responded with force. In the years following the 1953 coup that ousted Musaddiq, members of the National Front and the Tudeh Party were subjected to severe repression. Indeed, among the principal activities of the newly created security apparatus, the SAVAK (National Organization of Information and Security), were the dismantling of both organizations and prevention of their revival (Abrahamian 1982: 324–5, 457; Smith 2007: 70–1, 99). Then, when the Muharram riots of 1963 quickly evolved into a popular protest movement, the Shah had his military fire on the crowds; hundreds, if not thousands, were killed (Zonis 1971: 63).[27] He also had Ayatollah Khomeini, assumed to be an instigator, arrested and sent into exile (Abrahamian 1982: 426). Repression prevailed. It brought social peace for some time, but the Shah remained alienated from a broad cross-section of the population. In the absence of institutional reach, he enjoyed no strong presence within society and little access to information about social preferences.

In contrast, the Saudi regime's response to the emergence of a "secular opposition" at the inception of oil-based development would become something of a trademark – a virtually institutionalized practice – for dealing with dissent.[28] First, King Faisal sought to win over those elements of society whom he feared would be attracted to secular ideologies; he did so via material hand-outs and incorporation into government services, as well as promises of political participation through a national *majlis al-shura* (consultative council) (Abir 1993: 60–3, 114–16). Second, he tried to eclipse the secularists and their appeal. He insisted upon both his own Islamic credentials and the compatibility of religiosity with modernization. In addition, he actively courted "Islamic fundamentalists" who were being persecuted elsewhere in the Muslim world (Al-Rasheed 2002: 123).[29] Third, he pursued the dissidents with a vengeance, subjecting them to severe punishment (Abir 1988: 96; Al-Rasheed 2002: 133). In sum, distribution – which was heedful of the interests of key cleavage

[27] Anti-Shah rebellions broke out in tribal areas, while in the major cities, those hardest hit by the structural changes wrought by the White Revolution – the lower and lower-middle classes – took to the streets. They were joined by nationalist students, consistently opposed to the Shah, as well as bazaari merchants and clerics, among whom a certain Ayatollah Ruhollah Khomeini. On the Muharram riots see, *inter alia*, Abrahamian (1982: 422–6).

[28] For a discussion of the various movements within the secular opposition and their platforms, see Salamé (1993: 596–8).

[29] For example, he offered sanctuary in the kingdom, as well as generous stipends, to members of the Egyptian Muslim Brotherhood. He began a practice, followed by his successors, of providing material support to *salafiyya* movements across the region. The decision to welcome and support them would come back to haunt the Al Sa'ud at the turn of the century when those very movements and their adherents would call for the overthrow of the monarchy.

structures – and manipulation combined with repression to silence "voice," purchase loyalty, and secure stability.

Economic shocks

With the 1973 oil boom, euphoria among policy-makers in some oil-exporting states led to over-ambitious development programs. Such was the case in Algeria and Iran, and, to a lesser extent, Indonesia. Tensions emerged in the policy communities in Algeria and Indonesia, as Boumedienne and Suharto were easily seduced by the more extravagant of their advisors into adopting highly capital-intensive, grandiose projects.

In Algeria, the policy community had already begun to unravel as Boumedienne favored the audacious Belaid Abdesselam, his Minister of Industry and Energy, over the more cautious Kamal Abdallah-Khodja, Secretary of State for the Plan.[30] By 1974, Boumedienne's project for the "new Algeria" seemed to be coming apart. The president himself was increasingly removed from his advisors and closest collaborators. SONATRACH, the state-owned oil company, was becoming an ever more autonomous institution. Corruption and nepotism were on the rise.

While there was, in Indonesia, a similar development in the policy community, with Suharto favoring B. J. Habibie over Widjojo Nitisastro, there were three significant differences. First, through the boom years, Indonesia retained a focus on both diversifying the economy into non-oil exports and attending to the rural sector (Campos and Root 1996: 65–7).[31] Indonesia attained self-sufficiency in rice production in the early 1980s, with positive effects on stability (Booth 1999: 114), while Algeria, Iran, and Iraq moved from self-sufficiency in food production to become net importers of food (Abrahamian 1982: 447; Tripp 2007: 198). Second, the Indonesian state maintained its extractive capacity well into the boom, despite burgeoning oil revenues; this provided it with revenues, but also undisturbed access to information about social preferences (Smith 2007: 135–6). Third, a financial crisis, caused by the extravagant practices of Pertamina, the state-owned oil company, rocked the Indonesian economy in the middle of the decade; it provided a timely lesson to the regime about the need for policy restraint and tempered ambitions even in boom times.[32]

---

[30] Above, chapter 4.

[31] In 1976, non-oil exports constituted no more than 3 percent of total exports in Iran and 9 percent in Algeria, but as much as 30 percent in Indonesia (Amuzegar 1999: 245–6).

[32] On the Pertamina crisis, see Bresnan (1993: 165–84); Winters (1996: 83–91). Until the mid-1970s, Pertamina was the most important source of Suharto's patronage funds. After

With rapidly increasing oil revenues, the Shah of Iran had become, like Saddam Hussein of Iraq, his very own policy community.[33] He ignored the opinions of his economic advisors and simply multiplied investment targets with no attention to the economy's "absorptive capacity." Plagued with huge distortions, the economy spun out of control (Amirahmadi 1995: 197–8). Furthermore, the newfound wealth fed the Shah's political ambitions. He disbanded the two existing parties that he himself had created, replacing them, in 1975, with the Rastakhiz party, his personal mouthpiece, to which membership for all Iranians was mandatory. The aim was "to transform the ... military dictatorship into a totalitarian-style one-party state" (Abrahamian 1982: 441).

It was through the party that the Shah, assisted by his feared security apparatus, the SAVAK, would infiltrate economic, social, and even cultural life.[34] Nonetheless, while it controlled all organizations, imposed new legislation and codes of behavior, extorted "taxes" from target groups, and even dictated artistic production, Rastakhiz would turn out to be entirely ineffectual in imposing the Shah's rule and bringing stability to the country.[35] Through it, the Shah could gain neither access to information about society, nor a presence within society. Rather, he simply created new enemies for his regime from within the population. This was, indeed, a weakly institutionalized state with, by the mid-1970s, little other than repressive capacity.

In response to the very high inflation, accompanied by recession, as of the middle of the decade, the Shah failed to find ways to mitigate the economic hardship faced by important segments of the population (Table 7.1). He instructed ministries to cut back on spending, placed new international contracts on hold, and borrowed from world money markets. At the same time, corruption was both widespread and mounting, and private Iranian investors were sending large sums

---

the crisis, that role devolved primarily to the business community and state agencies. For example, prominent cronies such as Bob Hasan, Liem Sioe Liong, and Suharto's children, who had become very rich through import and trading monopolies granted to them by Suharto, financed the latter's patronage activities and even bailed out the state at times of economic crisis (Liddle 1991: 418; Schwarz 1994: 53).

[33] Charles Tripp (2007: 209) writes that, "(I)n September 1977 Saddam Hussein took control of all aspects of Iraq's oil policy, giving him unquestioned access to the key resource of the Iraqi state. He determined levels of production and controlled the disbursement of oil revenues. Only Saddam Hussein knew the exact levels of income and expenditure and it was from this period that a fixed percentage of Iraq's oil revenues was systematically transferred to deposits abroad ... which was to serve his regime well in the coming decades."

[34] On the Shah's intervention in cultural life, see Baraheni (1977).

[35] Smith (2007: 142–3, 145–6) describes how the Rastakhiz Party functioned as a sort of tax collector: it organized groups of thugs to seize money from bazaaris.

Table 7.1 *Iran: economic indicators, 1975–9*

	1975	1976	1977	1978	1979
GDP (US$ billions)	49.5	64.4	75.9	74.8	87.4
% change in GDP	5.4	16.9	−1.1	−11.0	−7.9
GNI per capita (US$ billions)	2670	3200	3260	3010	2900
% change in GNI per capita	...	19.8	1.9	−7.7	−3.6

Source: World Bank: World Development Indicators

abroad (Abrahamian 1982: 437–8; Halliday 1978: 155; Katouzian 1998: 199–200).[36]

The Shah's principal effort, however, was to lash out at those social forces he detested and that posed, in his view, a challenge to his domination of the domestic political economy. Through his anti-profiteering campaign and new price controls, he targetted the bazaari merchants especially. He imposed debilitating regulations and harsh fines on their economic activities, and conducted massive arrests. In contrast, he would ignore the activities of the few big industrialists and large importers (Abrahamian 1982: 444–5; Parsa 2000: 206–8). In this way, the Shah tantalized and radicalized his opposition, rather than pacifying it. He managed, inadvertently, to push together disparate forces, many of which had given up hopes for reform – their initial demand – in favor of revolution.

In the five cases, the boom years of the 1970s, followed by the mild recession toward the end of the decade, provide rich comparative material for addressing the management of dissent. Indonesia was unique among the comparators to experience massive popular unrest at the height of the boom. When protestors took to the streets in 1974, denouncing the favoritism shown to the Sino–Indonesian business elite in economic affairs, the growing presence of foreigners in the economy, and the blatant corruption in the institutions of governance, Suharto responded quickly and on several fronts.[37]

Not unlike the Saudi regime when faced with dissent, the Indonesian regime became increasingly authoritarian and patrimonial, but as before, attentive to social preferences. On the one hand, Suharto, through his military, employed severe repression: broad arrests were

---

[36] According to Parsa (2000: 201), as much as $50 million were leaving Iran every day by the end of October 1978.

[37] On the Malari incident and its aftermath, see Bresnan (1993: 135–63); Robison (1986: 165–7); Winters (1996: 107–9).

carried out and 'outspoken' newspapers were summarily closed down. On the other hand, he conceded somewhat to protestors' demands by implementing sweeping measures to protect indigenous business, while still allowing the Sino–Indonesians creative ways to circumvent the new regulations and continue to prosper (Bresnan 1993: 233–4). He went even further by investing generously in local-level infrastructural and institutional development throughout the country (Liddle 1992: 449–50).

Boumedienne also handled dissent fairly effectively by investing in institutions in ways that altered distribution. Keenly aware that his development strategy was causing hardship for important segments of the population, he called for a national debate so that grievances could be aired – albeit under close surveillance.[38] He believed that an increase in political participation – no matter how slight or superficial – would reinvigorate support for the regime and ease domestic suffering. Indeed, the regime was overwhelmed by the scope and extent of popular discontent. In response, Boumedienne used gentle manipulation and the provision of political resources to appease the population: in 1977, as the economy was in a mild recession, he unveiled a new constitution that described rights and responsibilities, and reasserted the regime's commitment to social justice and the "new Algeria." Moreover, he implemented structural reforms within the bureaucracy to give the impression of real changes in governance. The results in terms of domestic peace were positive.

Saddam Hussein worked assiduously to rein in forces of opposition throughout the decade in ways that share similarities with both Suharto and the Al Sa'uds. He would begin with manipulation by offering to distribute political resources in novel ways. This he did with the Iraqi Communist Party when he tried to get them to adhere to the National Front government (Farouk-Sluglett and Sluglett 1987/2001: 182–7). He would then combine manipulation with co-optation, through the distribution of economic resources and a variety of personal and/or professional favors. This he did with the al-Da'wa movement in the late 1970s when he invested generously in religious institutions, distributed gifts of money in public in the Shi'a south, and demonstrated increasing deference to Islam in his public pronouncements (Tripp 2007: 208–9; Sluglett and Farouk-Sluglett 1992: 270–2). If that strategy failed, he would then repress ferociously. By the end of the decade, the communist opposition had been literally eliminated, while al-Da'wa was forced underground or into exile

---

[38] Above, chapter 4.

and its leadership was executed.[39] But the ultimate resource for addressing dissent was the one Saddam Hussein would use for the first time in 1980 – the initiation of war. It rallied the population behind the regime, unified the country in support of the war effort, directed attention away from domestic ills, and transformed open opposition to the state into an unmitigated act of treason.[40]

In comparison with Suharto, Boumedienne, and Saddam Hussein, the Shah's method of dealing with dissent was woefully inadequate. Rather than work systematically to coopt popular forces by extending political resources, the Shah had a tendency to first hesitate and then simply repress (Keddie 2003: 231–8).[41] After having pursued the bazaari merchants, he targetted the clergy and sought, through the Rastakhiz Party apparatus that had become an instrument of his despotism, to impinge upon their status in society (Abrahamian 1982: 443–5). In doing so, he not only trampled over the population's traditional attachments and destroyed whatever links remained between himself and society, but also antagonized further key forces that had resources and organizational capacity. Recall that the bazaari merchants and Shi'a clergy controlled and managed independent, and independently wealthy, networks, emanating from the bazaars and the mosques.[42] Moreover, when protestors took to the streets – whether clerical students in Qom in 1975, or the mass-based mobilizations across the country beginning in January 1978 – the Shah had his military fire on the crowds. Indeed, until almost the very end, he maintained the capacity and will to use force. When he finally accepted to negotiate in mid-November 1978, after almost one year of recurrent demonstrations, the Shah chose as his interlocutors the "marginalized moderates among the opposition," displaying, yet again, the extent of his alienation from social preferences (Smith 2007: 160).

Debilitated by illness and poor judgement, and faced with a broad-based movement that enjoyed mobilizational capacity and charismatic

[39] As for the Kurds, they had militated for decades either for self-government or for an array of political and cultural rights. Their tenacity, beginning in the 1970s, provoked a brutal campaign against them that took on genocidal proportions in the late 1980s. On the gassing of Halabja in 1988 and the al-Anfal campaigns see, among others, Hiltermann (2007).

[40] See, in this regard, Tilly (1985); Al-Khafaji (2000).

[41] Throughout 1978, the Shah vacillated between repression and conciliation. Some scholars – among them Mark Gasiorowski (personal communication: November 3, 2007) and Eva Bellin (personal communication: October 18, 2007) – suggest that had he been more ruthless during this period, he may have been able to prevent the revolution from spreading. In contrast, see Nikki Keddie (2003) and Benjamin Smith (2007).

[42] I am grateful to an anonymous reader for stressing the importance of this factor.

leadership, the Shah could not respond effectively to social demands.[43] He refused real political reform. Having thoroughly "mismanaged Iranian culture and nationalism" in addition to the domestic political economy,[44] and without anything to offer the people, he could do nothing to reverse the groundswell of opposition to his rule. No sooner had the military put down its arms in the face of the revolutionary upsurge than the Pahlavi monarchy crumbled.

Most adept at dealing with dissent in the 1970s were the Al Sa'uds. Their method refined what they had employed against the secular opposition in the 1960s, and reflected the "tried and true patrimonial strategy" (van de Walle 1994: 148) pursued by Suharto (and Saddam Hussein) as well. In response to the Shi'a opposition which had emerged in reaction to the economic, social, and cultural discrimination they were subjected to, the regime employed a two-pronged strategy.[45] First, it began to invest important sums in the economic and infrastructural development of the Eastern Province, where the Shi'a constituted at least 40 percent of the population. Second, it persecuted the Shi'a opposition and, especially since the Iranian Revolution, it has maintained vigilant security in the region (Abir 1993: 82–8, 112–13; Nehme 1995: 58–9). In these ways, it silenced overt dissent.[46]

As for the neo-*Ikhwan* movement of Juhayman al-Utaibi, the regime pursued the leadership and its followers with a vengeance, summarily executing those who survived the military re-occupation of the mosque.[47] It also sought to coopt the *salafists* in Saudi society. It did so in two ways: first, it strengthened the regime's alliance with the 'Ulama so as to consolidate, in the eyes of the Saudi public, the Al Sa'uds' Islamic credentials; second, via the intervention of the *mutawwa'a*, it intensified the surveillance of society, so as to insist upon the kinds of moral behavior that

---

[43] On Khomeini's "revolutionary" views, see Abrahamian (1993: 21–32).

[44] Mark Gasiorowski, personal communication March 11, 2007.

[45] On the Shi'a opposition, see Goldberg (1986).

[46] The monarchy has continued to invest in regional development ever since. Sager (2005: 242) notes that the principal Shi'a opposition organization disbanded in 1993, after having reached an understanding with the Al Sa'ud regarding the community's welfare.

[47] In the 1970s, an Islamist movement that had formed in Medina in the mid-1960s was gaining momentum. Known as al-*Jama'a al-Salafiyya al-Muhtasiba* (JSM – The Salafi Group that Commands Right and Forbids Wrongdoing), it was inspired in part by the arrival of foreign-born *salafis* into the country and had subsequently become prominent in Saudi religious universities. The movement was strongly critical of the "westernization" of Saudi Arabia, and the "moral corruption" of the Saudi ruling class and Saudi society. In 1979, Juhayman al-Utaibi, a *salafi* preacher and leader of a radicalized branch of the original JSM, laid siege to and occupied the Great Mosque of Mecca, along with a few hundred followers. The aim of the group was to name one of its adherents as the *mahdi* and demand the end of the Al Sa'ud monarchy. See Hegghammer and Lacroix (2007).

salafists themselves would advocate (Abu Dharr 1980; Hegghammer and Lacroix 2007; Okruhlik 1999: 299).[48] In these ways, the regime both responded indirectly to social preferences and at the same time enhanced its domination, infiltration, and monitoring of domestic society.

Even more challenging for the political stability of oil-exporting states was the exogenous shock of 1986 when the price of oil plummeted to $10 per barrel; apart from a brief spike in 1991, it would remain low until the end of the 1990s (Figure 7.1). Iraq, and Algeria especially, were highly destabilized. In the early 1990s, the Algerian regime appeared to be on the verge of breakdown. In contrast, Indonesia and Saudi Arabia seemed to weather the shock masterfully. However, by the time Indonesia was hit with the Asian financial crisis in 1997, the aging Suharto had lost the capacity and the will to respond effectively to social conflict. Like Iran twenty years earlier, Indonesia would undergo regime breakdown and change.[49] The Saudi regime, for its part, has faced repeated challenges, most notably from an Islamist opposition.[50] Nonetheless, it has fine-tuned its trademark strategy for neutralizing dissent, which combines distribution, co-optation, and repression. So far, the regime has withstood the offensive, remaining relatively stable.

Coupled with the debilitating effects of the oil price downturn, Iraq had been engaged in an eight-year war that ended in 1988, at the height of economic malaise and a stringent reform program.[51] For much of the decade, the coincidence of declining oil revenues and dwindling foreign reserves with escalating war costs, surging levels of imports of foodstuffs and military supplies, and an ongoing war with no clear victor had put Iraq in a very difficult position. By 1986, the state was bankrupt and heavily in debt, while society experienced crippling inflation and acute shortages

---

[48] *Mutawwa'a* are the "religious police," members of the so-called "Committees for Enjoining Good and Forbidding Evil" (*Hay'at al-'amr bi-l-ma'ruf wa-nahy 'an al-munkar*).

[49] It is interesting to note that both Suharto and the Shah were considerably depleted when acute social conflict took hold: Suharto was old and increasingly frail, and the Shah was sick with cancer. (I am grateful to William Liddle and Mark Gasiorowski for stressing the importance of this factor on decision-making and outcomes.)

[50] For a discussion of the emergence in the kingdom of two different types of Islamism, the reformist *Sahwa* (or "Islamic Awakening") tendency and the rejectionist "neo-*salafi*" tendency, and their impacts on later Islamist groups, especially the "jihadists" of the 1980s and beyond, see ICG (2004b). For more on the Islamist opposition in Saudi Arabia, see Dekmeijan (1994); Fandy (1999); Lacroix (2005: 35–56); Okruhlik (2002: 22–8).

[51] On the origins of the Iran–Iraq war see, among others, Ismael (1982); El-Azhary (1984). On its evolution and outcome, see Karsh (1987); Farouk-Sluglett and Sluglett (1989/ 2001: 257–74). On its economic costs to Iraq, see Tripp (2007: 226–7, 239); Kanovsky (1987: 234–5).

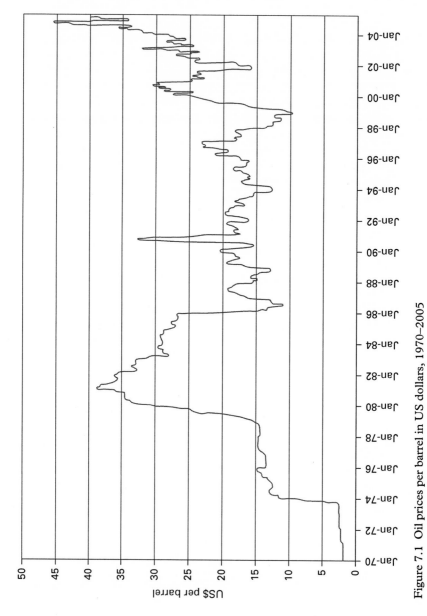

Figure 7.1 Oil prices per barrel in US dollars, 1970–2005

Source: Energy Information Administration

Table 7.2 *Socio-economic effects on Iraq of war with Iran, 1980–8*

Year	GDP (%Δ)	Inflation rate (%)
1980	−18.0	6.2
1981	−39.6	17.7
1982	−12.7	32.5
1983	41.7	100.0
1984	0.0	558.1
1985	−14.3	2627.5
1986	−19.3	2241.3
1987	−1.5	2759.0
1988	−10.0	3167.4

Source: Economist Intelligence Unit (EIU), Online Country Data

(Table 7.2). The reform strategy, that included privatization and price liberalization, combined with declining wages, hit consumers the hardest (Siemsen 1995/96: 36–7; Tripp 2007: 241–2).

With close to one-quarter of the labor force conscripted into the army, war termination represented a serious challenge. On the one hand, former conscripts found that their peace-time jobs had been filled by cheaper, imported labor. On the other hand, the military, that had benefitted from the statist policies of the earlier boom period and had remained the regime's most important base of support during the war years, found itself "unemployed" at the height of the fiscal crisis and the economic reform program (Chaudhry 1999: 334–5).

Via the omnipresent B'ath Party network, the regime was keenly aware of social preferences. In response to the staggering discontent which expressed itself largely through an upsurge in random urban violence and criminality, and to reassert his control over an increasingly insecure domestic political economy, Saddam Hussein stepped up repression against traditional forces of opposition.[52] In addition, he fell back on the strategy that had served him well ten years earlier: he remobilized his military, and this time invaded Kuwait (Al-Khafaji 2000; Tripp 1996: 21–38). War-making was a strategy not only for extracting resources, but also for addressing domestic discontent, and promoting social cohesion

---

[52] It was around this time that he launched, for example, the genocidal al-Anfal campaigns against the Kurdish population (Human Rights Watch 1995).

and support for the regime. For Saddam Hussein, it was a preferred response to shocks and social conflicts.

In the 1990s, the combination of distribution and repression would help Saddam Hussein consolidate his power once again, and this, despite seven years of United Nations-imposed sanctions – a quintessential exogenous shock. Through the "shadow economy" that had been created to circumvent the embargo, Saddam managed to generously line the pockets of his supporters, and coopt potential opponents with funds most cleverly diverted from the notorious "oil for food" program (Tripp 2007: 263–4). Moreover, as his power base became increasingly narrow, confined to the most tightly knit elements of his inner circle of family and closest associates, surveillance and repression became far more pervasive. When, with the encouragement of the United States' government and other Western powers, the Shi'a in the south and the Kurds in the north rose up in an effort to bring down the regime, Saddam's elite Republican Guard crushed the uprisings ferociously as the foreign powers looked on (Tripp 2007: 244–9).[53]

While the Algerian regime also resorted to co-optation and repression to reassert its control, it would take it longer and along a far more checkered path than the B'athists in Iraq. President Benjedid's first response to the post-1986 domestic dissent was to open up the political system to multipartyism. However, in comparison to Boumedienne before him, Benjedid was a weak and easily manipulated leader. Under his leadership, the regime had lost, by 1986 and the oil price downturn, the institutional resilience it had enjoyed in 1977/8 in the face of acute social conflict. Once it became clear, in 1991, that the FLN was going to lose power and to an Islamist party, the military, the strongest institution in the country, put a stop to the electoral process and the democratic transition, and deposed the president. Following that, it pursued the Islamist opposition with utmost brutality for several years, with the result that the insurgency grew tremendously, factionalized, and radicalized.[54]

On its own, repression, as was seen in the case of Iran, is an ineffective – indeed, counter-productive – strategy. When combined with co-optation, however, targetted repression can produce positive results for incumbents. In a variety of ways, the Algerian leadership successfully appropriated and defused the political agendas of both the Islamist and Berberist oppositions such that by the end of the 1990s, it had reasserted control over the domestic political economy. Nurturing an

---

[53] It was via a combination of generous salaries, professional perks, and institutional coherence that the Republican Guard remained fiercely loyal to Saddam Hussein.
[54] Above, chapters 5 and 6.

Table 7.3 *Indonesia: economic data, 1985/6 and 1995/6*

	1985/6	1995/6
Non-oil exports as % of total exports	25	80
Manufacturing as % of GDP	12	24
Share (%) of gov't revenues from oil	>70	<25
Incidence of poverty (% of pop.)	60 (early 1980s)	15.1 (1990)

Sources: Booth 1999: 112; Hill 2000: 118; World Bank 1996: 1

"official" Islamist opposition and incorporating it into electoral politics, extending amnesty to insurgents, transforming the Kabyle protest movement into an "ethnic" phenomenon and preventing it from spreading beyond the region of Kabylia proved to be powerful means for recuperating dissenting forces.[55]

At the same time, the leadership, through clever manipulation of the Algerian public, the international community, and conjunctural forces, delegitimized the insurgents and reclaimed its hegemony. No doubt, surging oil revenues as of 1999 allowed the regime to consolidate its gains and fatten its political ambitions. Hence, through a combination of targetted violence, co-optation, and manipulation of key forces, and facilitated eventually by a set of enabling features of the international conjuncture, both the Algerian and the Iraqi regimes were able to re-equilibrate after periods of tremendous upheaval.

Quite rare among oil-exporting LDCs, Suharto's technocrats ensured Indonesia's macro-economic stability despite the 1986 price shock. They did so through a variety of measures including devaluation, deregulation, stepped-up taxation, and foreign borrowing. Unlike most other oil exporters, the country experienced positive GDP growth through the mid-1990s (Booth 1999: 109–35; Soesatro 1989: 860–9). But unlike Algeria and the other comparators, Indonesia was no longer an oil-dependent economy; by then it had diversified successfully into competitive manufacturing (Gelb *et al.* 1988: 220–1) (Table 7.3).

Nonetheless, economic liberalization and privatization, combined with declining government revenues, had loosened central control over the economy and the regions (Liddle 1992: 452). Reinforced by the technocrats' inability to target patronage and clientelism in the highest

---

[55] While the Shi'a uprising in Saudi Arabia could be easily quarantined in the Eastern Province and enjoyed little sympathy from the broader Saudi public, the Algerian regime had to work hard to quarantine the Kabyle uprising of 2001 and delegitimize a movement that was quickly gaining national support.

echelons of the state, the reforms also enhanced the wealth of a tiny but powerful elite, which included the Suharto family and its close associates, and a complicit private sector.[56]

In response to growing dissent in the early 1990s, Suharto initially did what Chadli Benjedid had done: he made space for free but controlled expression, only to backpedal, in 1993, when social forces began to mobilize. Suharto reasserted control, with repression; press freedoms were curtailed and opponents of the regime were meted out harsh punishments (Aspinall 1999: 133–5). He proved inflexible in the face of mounting popular demands, thereby (re-)igniting social conflicts of various sorts. Violent (ethnic) conflicts and regional rebellions – in Aceh, Irian Jaya, Kalimantan, and East Timor, to name a few – contributed to the political turbulence of the mid-1990s.[57] Many of them had their origins in earlier periods, were responses to government policies, and faced severe repression. Once the Asian financial crisis hit the country in 1997, Suharto's regime was already seriously weakened.

Excessive short-term private debt, plus growing pressure on the rupiah sparked very high inflation and the loss of investor confidence. Domestic private capital, that had been favored by the reforms of the 1980s, fled the country. There was a snowballing effect: defaults on private foreign debts combined with the plummetting value of the rupiah, frequent bank failures, and the regime's cancellation of billions of dollars worth of investment projects – all with severe distributional consequences. Unemployment soared, and the incidence of poverty rose to an alarming 40 percent from 11.3 percent before the crisis (Hill 2000: 124–5; Pincus and Ramli 1998: 723, 725–8). At the same time, massive forest fires engulfing much of Sumatra and Kalimantan wiped out human habitat as well as hundreds of miles of valuable timber, another major export item; environmental catastrophe exacerbated the distributional crisis (Emmerson 1999: 317–19). By the end of January 1998, the economy had collapsed.

As his and his cronies' fortunes grew from the mid-1980s, Suharto identified his own interests increasingly with those of his kin (in business)

---

[56] Some analysts suggest that aspects of the reforms – for example, the dominant role given to the private sector, the preservation of the Suharto family's monopolies – plus Suharto's subsequent abandoning of the technocrats during the early 1990s' boom, laid the groundwork for the breakdown at the end of the decade (Hill 2000: 128, 131; Pincus and Ramli 1998: 729–33).

[57] On the conflict between the Dayaks and Madurese in West Kalimantan, see Peluso and Harwell (2001: 83–116). On the Acehnese struggle, see ICG (2003a); Malley (1999: 93–5); Ross (2005). On the resistance to Indonesian rule on Irian Jaya, see ICG (2001b); Malley (1999: 96–7); Ross (2005). For the anti-colonial struggle in East Timor, see Malley (1999: 97–101); Taylor (1991).

and close Sino–Indonesian business associates.[58] Thus, when offered an IMF bailout in the face of the country's staggering economic predicament, Suharto would not accept the conditions imposed on him; they would have undone the material benefits he and his entourage had been enjoying (Liddle 2007).[59] And while he hoarded material resources in this period of severe economic constraint, he refused to distribute political resources that could have appeased social forces. Suharto was no longer committed to investing in institutions that fostered redistribution and the fabrication of a broad base of support for the state. He had lost touch with social preferences, yet he feared the consequences of the crisis to the structure of power. Old, tired, and captive of the increasingly narrow and brittle institutional foundations of his rule, the leader lost his former resilience in the face of mounting domestic unrest.

The Al Sa'ud are alone among the five cases to have remained more or less consistently stable throughout "bust" periods and without resorting to massive violence. Indeed, they have perfected strategies that served them well at the inception of statehood. Although government revenues in 1986 ($24 million) had plummetted by 99.97 percent from their 1980 level ($106 billion), while per capita income fell 85.7 percent (from $28,000 to $4,000), the regime maintained, and in some cases enhanced, key distributive arrangements. With the help of deficit financing, it managed to keep in place most subsidies and welfare services (Krimly 1999). In this way, the regime remained attentive to social preferences. Moreover, by cushioning the population from the full effects of the price shock, it could keep them in tow.

In the aftermath of the first Gulf War, the Al Sa'ud leadership responded to the rising tide of dissent in the kingdom by again extending distribution through institutional development.[60] It allowed for a degree of political space by tolerating the petitions of the 1990s, presented by

---

[58] For a rich and colorful discussion of the privileged business community and its links to Suharto, see Schwarz (1994: 99–155).

[59] In fact, Suharto behaved indecisively in response to the IMF bailout package in October 1997 and then again in January 1998. He first accepted to implement the reforms – even those impinging upon his family's and cronies' interests – and shortly thereafter either circumvented or rescinded many of them (MacIntyre 1999: 156–8). It was only later in the spring that he accepted, for example, the IMF demand that he lift fuel subsidies.

[60] The uneasy calm of the 1980s, when regional affairs – primarily, the emergence of the Islamic Republic of Iran and the eight-year Iran–Iraq war – combined with the crippling decline in oil revenues, dominated domestic concerns, incubated brewing dissent. Saudi society became increasingly polarized as the regime strengthened both its repressive apparatus and its ties with Western powers (Niblock 2006: 80–7). On the one hand, the middle class and technocratic elites despaired of being granted decision-making powers, while they and the university-educated junior 'ulama remained critical of royal policies, privileges, and excesses. On the other hand, there was generalized disdain for the laxity of

different social forces.[61] In response, King Fahd would reassert the Al Sa'uds' monopoly of power, and bring further into the fold those individuals or groups whom he deemed potentially threatening. Along with that, he approved of some regional decision-making power related to social and economic welfare so as to appease the "liberal" petitioners. In addition, he enhanced the visibility and prerogatives of the *'ulama* and the *mutawwa'a* in order to appease "Islamist" petitioners (Al-Rasheed 2002: 168–75; Rouleau 2002).

When petitioning persisted into the new century, the regime, mindful of the challenges it faced from both the radical *jihadi* front and the (domestic effects of the) United States' intervention in Iraq, sponsored a National Dialogue in 2003–4. It included not only "centrists" but popular *salafi* preachers, Shi'a, Sufis, and women as well (ICG 2004b: 16–18; Glosemeyer 2005: 228–30; Sager 2005: 254–5).[62] One year later, the regime, facing growing unrest – related, in large measure, to the ongoing war in Iraq and the utilization of bases inside Saudi Arabia by the US military – held municipal elections for the first time in nearly half a century. Investing in institutions by extending (however slight) political resources provided a hint of political incorporation and participation that could pacify the disgruntled, but relatively moderate social forces. However, the more radical *jihadi* opposition, and any force engaged in overtly hostile behavior, has been subjected to severe repression.[63]

Considered to be a major threat to the Al Sa'ud leadership, *jihadis* strike at the very core of the Saudi state, founded as it was on the basis of its politico–religious legitimacy. Not only do they challenge the Al Sa'ud on their own turf, but they also reject the regime's close alliance with the United States – which, paradoxically, was considered, until recently, a key

---

the wealthy, heavily armed, and profoundly compromised regime in the face of the Palestine imbroglio, the rising power of Imam Khomeini, and Saddam Hussein's seemingly effortless invasion of Kuwait next door. Domestic turmoil intensified with the Gulf War of 1991 (Abir 1993: 116–19; Nehme 1995; Al-Rasheed 2005: 190).

[61] For the texts of the so-called secular petition and religious petition, published in December 1990 and February 1991 respectively, see Middle East Watch (1992: 59–62). There was a second "religious petition" in 1992, and several more petitions between 1998 and 2003. See Okruhlik (1999: 306); Sager (2005: 246–8, 268–70); Niblock (2006: 92–6).

[62] On the National Reform Document, see Al-Rasheed (2005: 187). It was submitted to the Crown Prince in January 2003, signed by 103 intellectuals, liberals, and moderate Islamists, and demanded a constitutional monarchy in Saudi Arabia.

[63] For a thoughtful discussion of King Abdullah's two-track strategy – "the quiet transformation of Saudi institutions" and direct assaults on radical *jihadis* – see "Winds of Change in Saudi Arabia," *Jane's Islamic Affairs Analyst* (Jane's Information Group), December 1, 2007.

ingredient of the monarchy's security and durability.[64] Furthermore, *jihadis'* activities suggest that they are not cowed by the regime's capacity to employ repression. Typically, as noted above, investing in institutions through a clever politics of distribution and social control, combined with repression, had allowed the Al Sa'ud leadership to effectively rein in its opponents and ensure stability – much as had been the case with the Suharto regime through the mid-1980s. However, this new and somewhat elusive force may not submit to the regime's traditional strategies as readily as others have.[65] To be sure, the regime may be facing a more serious threat, at the beginning of the twenty-first century, than ever before: one that could rattle its erstwhile well-honed stability.

In response, the Al Sa'ud have elaborated a clever politics of manipulation via dissuasion. On the one hand, they have initiated a mediatic and discursive onslaught meant to sway the Saudi public away from the *jihadi* message and "towards a kinder, gentler Islam" (Sager 2005: 257). On the other hand, they have sought to integrate captured *jihadis* into government-sponsored and government-run voluntary programs of "rehabilitation." However, non-compliant *jihadis* and those "with blood on their hands" continue to face severe repression (Boucek 2007: 1–4). As in the past, discipline and punishment go hand in hand with distribution in the Al Sa'ud's skillful management of dissent.

Conclusion

Of the five cases, Saudi Arabia has been alone in maintaining stability. While consequential challenges to the regime have appeared at times over the past four decades, they were dealt with swiftly and unequivocally, such that opposition movements could neither mobilize the population nor enhance their own appeal. Through various institutional mechanisms, the Al Sa'ud have kept abreast of social preferences; and they have responded through institutional mechanisms – with paternalism, religious

---

[64] Tim Niblock (2006: 172–6) underscores three central problems faced by the regime – among them, that reliance on the United States, deemed to be essential for its security, is also a source of insecurity. The other two are the non-competitiveness of Saudi labor internationally and its dependence on migrants, and the non-incorporation of certain groups into the system.

[65] It is the case that *Sahwa* oppositionists were successfully coopted in the 1990s (Al-Rasheed 2007: 81–96). Apparently, several of them have received real-estate handouts in exchange for abandoning their struggle (I am grateful to Steffen Hertog for sharing this information). As for the more radical Islamists, many of whom eventually opted for exile whence they hoped to foment resistance to the regime, see Fandy 1999. On the globalist *jihadi* tendency, see Al-Rasheed (2007: 106–33); ICG (2004b); Hegghammer (2006, 2009).

discourse, and tried and true co-optation strategies – in ways that have neutralized real or potential opponents, and kept the peace.

In contrast, Iran in 1978/9 and Indonesia in 1998 succumbed to instability; both experienced regime – indeed, system – change. When faced with severe challenges to their power and privileges, both the ailing Shah and the aging Suharto were all but immobilized. Appearing tired, confused, and indecisive, they refused to extend political resources to appease social forces, even though Suharto had proved capable of doing so in the past. The Shah lost, over time, whatever linkages to society he had once enjoyed. Suharto, in turn, insulated himself increasingly in the final years of his rule as his troubles – and avarice – grew and he faced mounting opposition. Not only did the Shah lack the resources for managing dissent effectively, but whether he relied on conciliation or repression, his actions seemed to expand the forces of opposition, and invigorate the revolutionary rhetoric and mobilizational capacities of Ayatollah Khomeini and his followers.

As for Algeria and Iraq, the leadership was eventually able to regain its hold on power and re-stabilize, but only after the systematic co-optation and manipulation of competing social cleavages, accompanied by the threat of, or resort to, violence. Opponents, or potential opponents, of the regime were brought in line via access to political and/or economic resources, often through their integration into patronage and client networks. At times, in the case of Iraq, they were eliminated outright. In both cases, the leadership benefitted from the weak organizational capacities of the opposition. Indeed, government strategies were aimed at fracturing and fragmenting the opposition, precisely to prevent their consolidation and mobilization.

In both Algeria and Iraq, re-stabilization took time and was accompanied by tremendous violence. It was facilitated, as well, by developments in the international environment which incumbents could successfully exploit to shore up their "staying power." To be sure, the outcome of challenges to political stability hinges squarely upon the decisions of leaders, and their ability to mold and manipulate, to their advantage, structural features of the context they find themselves in.

8   Conclusions: oil wealth and the poverty of politics

Some final thoughts on Algeria

Having come full circle, how does the analytical framework employed in this book help make sense of Algeria's auspicious beginnings, acute social conflicts in the 1980s, a bloody and interminable civil war, and the fairly spectacular resurgence of the state in the late 1990s? Why did the domestic political economy unravel, and how did the regime manage to retain power and neutralize its opposition more or less successfully? And what does the Algerian experience teach us about the durability of patrimonial systems, the contingency of oil, as well as the integrated roles of structures and actor choice in political outcomes in oil-exporting states? What mechanisms have allowed the institutional arrangements that emerged out of the critical junctures in Algeria to sustain themselves over time such that the system reproduces itself and persists, rather than succumbs to hostile social forces?

In pondering the Algerian experience, one could argue that a profound contradiction lies at the heart of the country's political development. The leadership, in its efforts at fashioning a nation and as part of the post-independence developmentalist agenda, espoused an ideology and rhetoric of popular incorporation, and implemented policies – such as heavy industrialization, arabization, and the distribution of abandoned colonial property – that it insisted were inclusive in nature. However, not only did those policies fail to achieve their stated goals, but they were, in practice, highly exclusionary.

This contradiction, between the ideology and rhetoric of the political elite (and the expectations they gave rise to) on the one hand, and the reality of policies and practice on the other, first emerged within the nationalist movement in the late 1940s in response to intra-elite conflict. It remained integral to the political substructure and the social project of the tiny ruling elite during the war of liberation and the first twenty-five years of independence. Just as the war had appeared as a broad-based institution, encompassing almost all Algerians, while that same war was endlessly productive of personal and factional divisions and exclusions, so the leadership of independent Algeria has consistently insisted upon its commitment to popular incorporation, while reality has revealed systematic efforts to restrict the circle of power and define access to resources exclusively in terms of proximity to power. Since independence, rents have been manipulated to prop up the mythology of the state and "lubricate" its social project. Rents have financed the inclusion of some and exclusion of others, and the bolstering of those in power.

Because the revenue base of the oil-exporting state is hostage to fluctuations in the international market, and since distribution remains the source of regime legitimacy, this same contradiction, between the rhetoric of the leadership and the reality of its decisions, came to the fore in the face of the 1986 price shock which provoked a state fiscal crisis. In the new environment of relative scarcity and rising frustrations, social forces that heretofore had been marginalized (re-)aligned in an effort to capture the reins of power and (re-)define the nation. "Who are we, and what do we want to achieve together?" – the question that had appeared for the first time within the nationalist movement in the late 1940s, and since then had been either hijacked or deferred – re-emerged and occupied the limelight. The state weakened, the "nation" and its meaning would be fought over once again (McDougall 2006: 143).

Thus, the seeds of the instability that gripped Algeria in the late 1980s and evolved into civil war are not to be found in the oil endowment. Rather, they can be found in the particularities of state-building and of leadership choices – hence, the combination of structure and agency – that preceded the inception of oil-based development, in fact, but were invigorated by it. Furthermore, incorporated in those particularities was a persistent contradiction, eventually fueled by external rents, between inclusivist rhetoric and exclusivist practice. To be sure, in their efforts to remain in power, ruling elites, lacking popular legitimacy, chose to obscure the deep divisions in society. When oil rents were available, they would be distributed in ways to subdue divisions, fragment social formations, and defeat alternative threats to the ruling elite's hegemony. Clientelist practices of co-optation and manipulation have figured prominently in regime strategies.

In effect, what was fashioned in Algeria over time, and what became apparent with the end of state capitalism and then the market reforms of the 1980s and 1990s, was a patrimonial system of clan politics, elaborated by a military–bureaucratic oligarchy that, along with its clients, have been the principal beneficiaries. This is, as Werenfels (2007) illustrates, a vertically fashioned system, composed of intricate and overlapping networks of interests, and engaging military officers, government personnel, and business elites, and eventually *hittistes*, *trabendistes*, and insurgents as well. In this environment, some of the most lucrative economic trans-actions take place in the shadows, while the principal objective of all players is to increase their access to the rent and to power.

Since the 1960s, the backbone of state power in Algeria has been the hydrocarbon sector, while control over the rent and its distribution has been its principal instrument. SONATRACH, because of its critical economic and rent-channeling roles, has remained above supervision, regulation, and accountability; it successfully escaped the restructuring measures of the 1980s and 1990s. Perhaps more than any other state institution, SONATRACH is deeply enmeshed in a web of political, economic, and administrative relationships, while being systematically exploited by different government circles for special interests. This being the case, SONATRACH remains the locus of some of the most virulent political struggles, at the same time as it resists reform.

It is through the selective distribution of rent and other material favors that loyalties are bought, alliances are cemented, and networks are greased. Similarly, the withholding of material favors is itself a powerful means for destroying alliances and networks. The saga of the al-Khalifa financial and industrial empire, emblematic of the opaque interlacing of private interests with state power, is a case in point (Aubenas 2003). Apparently, the Khalifa Bank was used for money laundering and provid-ing credit to people close to the regime; it also was the repository for pension funds of several public institutions, including the labor union (UGTA). Although it enjoyed credits from public Algerian banks, it escaped Central Bank supervision because it was connected to President Bouteflika and his closest associates. When the bank developed an unfore-seen liquidity problem, it collapsed, virtually overnight, and with it the rest of the Khalifa business empire. It was rumored that Bouteflika failed to protect Rafiq Khalifa at this juncture because he had refused to openly support the president as he campaigned before the 2004 elections. The empire, that included both a bank and an airline, dissolved in a breath-taking fashion. This is a leadership that has not only deep pockets, but also entrenched concerns for its political survival and, it would appear, a remarkable capacity for revenge.

To be sure, substantial hydrocarbon rents in the hands of the regime have facilitated the consolidation over time of a vast, informal, clientelist organization that operates under the cover of official institutions. Indeed, market reform has done little to restructure power and access to resources in a salutary fashion. Rather, it has simply blurred further the already highly porous boundaries between the public and the private, the formal and the informal, the economic, the political, and the military (ICG

2001b; Werenfels 2007: 49–50).[1] By nurturing highly profitable patron–client networks, economic liberalization has strengthened predatory structures that remain at the core of the domestic political economy, and enhanced the power of the generals (Murphy 2001: 25–6). No doubt, vested interests in the status quo are both diverse and robust. This is a system that relies on clientelism – which is, by definition, exclusionary – and resists reform.

For roughly ten years as of 1992, Algeria was in the grip of civil war. The proximate cause for the outbreak of violence was the military's annulment of the results of the December 1991 legislative elections and its cancellation of the constitutionally decreed transition to a multiparty system. The military staged a coup d'état and declared a state of emergency. The FIS was outlawed and its leadership imprisoned. Thousands of real and suspected members and supporters of the FIS were rounded up and detained, and many were tortured. Outraged at the impunity with which the military had hijacked the transition and the ferocious repression it was meting out to its challengers, new militants were radicalized overnight. Algeria exploded.

The violence emerged as an expression of political contestation within the context of an obdurate political system and a brutal socio-economic crisis. For decades, political freedoms had been absent, but the population had been appeased and remained relatively comfortable through redistribution. However, with the fall in oil prices after 1982, the combination of a sharp decline in living standards, rising inequalities in a context of severe institutional rigidities, growing unemployment, and the end to redistribution brought acute social conflicts to the fore.

The insurgency took on a religious guise because Islam provided a persuasive critique of Algerian politics and society, and offered a more compelling formula for a better life than secular politicians had been able to. Furthermore, in Algeria as in other Muslim societies with authoritarian systems, shorn of politics, Islam has been one of few tolerated forms of (political) expression. Its messages resonate strongly with its adherents. Moreover, before it was outlawed, the FIS had become the

---

[1] Werenfels (2007: 49) describes the Algerian leaders' implementation of "market reforms" as "merely the conversion of public monopolies to private oligopolies, creating a situation of oligopoly and Mafia-like structures, with 'godfathers' found in or close to the military–bureaucratic apparatus and, particularly, among former army officers."

Note that while active or retired members of the military had been involved in private-sector activities from the 1960s, their implication in both the private and the informal sectors increased from the Chadli years, encouraged by both government legislation and the peculiar ways in which economic liberalization has been carried out. See Dillman (2000: 134).

most effective and best organized political party in the country, and the only one with broad appeal and mobilizational capacity. It came to represent a real threat to the hegemony of the military–bureaucratic oligarchy.

The discourse of contestation expounded from the pulpits attracted to its ranks not simply those who viewed an Islamic alternative as the preferred one; the insurgency became a magnet for those who felt excluded and viewed the *maquis* (armed resistance) as the antidote to their exclusion. As for incumbents, they fought to preserve their hold on power by all means. They eventually received external support from parties coveting the country's oil wealth and wary of "Islamic radicalism."

For the durability of the Algerian regime and reproduction of the system, reliance on what had become virtually institutionalized practice appears to have been critical.[2] To be sure, the past offers enormous capital. For example, the resort to force – the ultimate resource employed by leaders to achieve their goals – was built into not only the determination of *algériennité* (what it means to be Algerian), but also the formation of the Algerian (nation-)state. Indeed, coercion, combined with co-optation and manipulation, have been central to the practice of politics.[3] As such, these strategies are consistently being refined and reinvigorated by those in power.

During the civil war years, the violence itself became a source of political capital for the regime, with which to manipulate both Algerian society and the international community. For example, to vindicate itself for its resistance to the implementation of real reforms, the leadership drew attention to the unending insecurity in the country. It insisted that it would be an act of gross irresponsibility to accept significant changes to the distribution of power and resources as long as the insurgency persisted. Thus, the context of violence and insecurity was exploited so as to leave the impression that the military-backed government was indispensable. Since 1998, ongoing low-intensity conflict has allowed the leadership to hunker down, consolidate its power and access to resources, protect its right to decide how the oil rent is spent, and escape from even a minimum of regulation and accountability.

---

[2] The same is true in Saudi Arabia; and there, too, the past offers enormous capital. What is particular to Saudi Arabia, however, is that religious discourse in the kingdom is pervasive, persistent, and manipulative. In conjunction with classic means of co-optation, it neutralizes dissent by delegitimizing it outright.

[3] But as James McDougall (2006: 238) so poignantly points out: "(I)f it is true that the tradition of the dead generations has seemed to weigh nightmarish on Algeria, speaking to new generations in authoritarian, demagogic and utopian tones instead of enabling the creative, and inescapably complex, transformation of its future, Algerians are not thereby condemned forever grotesquely to repeat the tragedies of their forebears."

Furthermore, the recurrent regime practice of "recycling the dinosaurs" of the wartime FLN and integrating them systematically into the highest echelons of the state, as in the choice of Abdelaziz Bouteflika as president of Algeria in 1999, exemplifies the military-backed regime's dogged insistence on historic capital. It is, indeed, another form of coercion, but also manipulation, of the population and of the past. Moreover, encouraging and reinforcing the interlacing of interests between the public and the private, the formal and the informal, the economic, the political, and the military through coercion, co-optation, and manipulation have sponsored the reproduction of the system. The interlocking connections and mutual dependence of those invested in the system are thereby extended and intensified. Besides, because they are exclusionary in essence, co-optation and manipulation promote the fragmentation – hence neutralization – of (potential) forces of dissent. Fragmentation contributes to regime stability insofar as it inhibits mass mobilization and most forms of collective action.

It is via reliance on these strategies, and buttressed of late by favorable international structural forces, that the regime, the guardian of the status quo, persists – it is bolstered, in fact – and the system reproduces itself. To be sure, high and rising oil prices since the beginning of the new millennium, combined with the post 9/11 "war on terror," have played directly into the hands of the Algerian leadership. Important and ever-growing financial resources provide the regime with the wherewithal to invest and distribute generously, and in ways that further its objectives and its security. At the same time, the United States-sponsored "war on terror" and the Algerian regime's signing on to that effort by virtue of its avowed victim status lend credence to the strategies it has employed to advance its objectives and retain power.

The variation in outcomes and the capacities of states

How can we account for the variation in stability in high-growth, development-oriented, oil-exporting countries in the aftermath of an economic shock? The brief foray into comparative analysis enriches the argument advanced for Algeria about the relative impact of structure, context, and leadership choice on political (in)stability. It suggests that what matters most for (the variation in) outcomes is how leaders manage shocks and their impact: how they act in response to challenges to institutional arrangements and their distributive implications.

The Al Sa'ud monarchy has remained relatively stable precisely because it has consistently and selectively extended the distribution of (however meager) political and/or economic resources, and in that way invested in institutional development. Related to that, clientelism and the systematic reinforcement of societal dependence upon the state have been long-lasting regime strategies: indeed, the dominant mode of politics in the kingdom. Maintaining subsidies at a time of economic crisis fostered domestic peace, while accepting limited expression of domestic discontent in the early 1990s when the Gulf War was under way and foreign troops were based on Saudi soil, mollified dissent. Conceding to some degree of political participation in the form of municipal elections in the new millennium had salutary effects as well. Keenly aware of social preferences, which it gains access to through extensive institutional reach, the regime has been prepared to give a little politically, in order to stem the rising tide of grievances, without giving up very much. Nonetheless, while the regime has invested in institutional development, it has done so in conjunction with the administration of repression and other forms of social control – most notable among them the imposition of the uniforming doctrine of Wahhabism. This combination of strategies has resulted in (relative) political stability and regime continuity.

In contrast, both the Shah of Iran and Indonesia's President Suharto failed to distribute political resources in the late 1970s and the late 1990s respectively, when they were faced with domestic unrest. Disconnected from social forces, they retreated further into their shells, rebuffing real reform, determined to protect their power and privileges at all costs. To the end, the Shah enjoyed no institutional reach, and chose repression as his preferred strategy for countering popular unrest, while Suharto, by that time and largely because of policies and practices he had initiated in the 1980s, lost the institutional reach he had once enjoyed. Moreover, given the extent of corruption and his implication in it, Suharto no longer had the will to compromise on his policies or invest in institutions in ways that would alter distributive arrangements, even if that meant appeasing social forces. Besides, both leaders were physically depleted by illness or age. Their diminished state may well have affected their mental acuity, as well as their ability to appreciate the changing context, hence their decision-making. Both the Shah and Suharto succumbed to regime breakdown and change.

In Algeria and Iraq, it was the combination of targetted violence with the co-optation and manipulation of key forces in the domestic arena, as well as some manipulation in the international arena, that allowed the regimes to re-equilibrate after periods of tremendous upheaval. Both regimes engaged in selective distribution of political and economic resources, despite the environment of relative scarcity. In that way, they managed to recuperate (real or potential) forces of opposition and appropriate them for their own networks of support. They were also able to manipulate their populations by, among other things, vilifying the enemy within – that is, the Islamist insurgents in the case of Algeria – or the enemy without – the sanctions-imposing United Nations in the case of Iraq. Indeed, Saddam Hussein most cleverly manipulated the sanctions regime and the related "oil-for-food" program to his advantage. For its part, the Algerian regime was successful at manipulating the international community and international structural forces to its advantage. It did so by signing onto the "war on terror," and drawing parallels between its own domestic experience with "Islamist terror" and the global challenge.

To wit, severe repression, on its own, is an ineffective – in fact, a counter-productive – strategy, as we have seen in the Shah's Iran. However, when selectively meted out and joined to targeted co-optation and clever manipulation, as mastered by the Saudi monarchy and practiced by the Algerian and Iraqi regimes, it can produce positive results for those in power.

In short, neither structures nor the institutions or resources they encompass are sufficient for determining outcomes. Rather, political outcomes are shaped by leadership decisions in the face of shocks. Decisions are shaped in part by the structural features of the context leaders find themselves in, but also by the degree to which leaders can envisage institutional change – that is, changes to the distribution of power and resources.

Among the five cases I explore, there have been variations over time within a single case, such that the same leader (Suharto) responded at one juncture in a salutary fashion for domestic peace, but in a destructive manner at another. Variation has much to do with context – that may include, for example, a new distribution of power and resources within the state, derivative of a changed environment and/or policy agenda, or new international structural forces. But variation has to do with context *combined* with both the leader's perception of the resources available to him at that particular juncture and his capacity to respond effectively. It is for this reason that an economic shock can provoke either the weakening of a regime or its consolidation (Englebert and Ron 2004). Economic crisis does not determine outcomes.[4]

As the experience of Algeria in the 1990s demonstrates, at issue is precisely whether leaders have the will and the capacity to seize the opportunities presented by (new) structural forces and work them to their advantage. Insofar as regime stability is concerned, effective leadership decisions are those that transform the constraints presented by the

---

[4] The seven years of economic sanctions that Iraq was subjected to in the 1990s actually strengthened the regime of Saddam Hussein in some ways, and perhaps domestic support for it as well; they did not incite the regime's demise.

context leaders find themselves in into possibilities for promoting their own incumbency and diminishing support for alternative centers of power. To be sure, the ongoing violence in Algeria was, in principle, a constraint. However, it was effectively transformed into an opportunity by the leadership, for the purpose of consolidating its power and obstructing (real and potential) challengers.

No doubt, the availability of rents can enhance the efficacy of leadership strategies. It provides additional resources with which to carry out the tasks of nation-building and institutional development. However, oil, in and of itself, is nothing but a *machine à sous* ("cash cow"). It is what leaders do with it – the decisions they make – that count.

Alternate explanations

There are, indeed, other possible explanations for the variation in (in)stability of oil-exporting states in the aftermath of an economic shock. Among them, I have identified five hypotheses that turn on the following factors: (1) the ratio of oil revenues to population size; (2) regime type; (3) the role of the international community; (4) the prevailing distribution of power between the regime and the opposition; (5) the degree of repression by the state. I suggest, however, that while these factors may shape the context, they matter only insofar as they resonate and reinforce leadership choice. On their own, they can provide, at best, only partial explanations for the divergent outcomes. I address each alternate explanation in turn.

First, the higher the ratio of oil revenues to population size, the better equipped the state may be for managing crises of distribution. Hence, the persistence of stability derives, in this view, from a powerful "cushion effect" in the form of sufficient funds with which to buy time. I suggest, however, that the "cushion effect" promotes stability and offsets the harmful consequences of either weak institutional foundations or poorly incorporated social forces, only if the leadership responds to shocks and distributes economic and/or political resources effectively. Indeed, how oil revenues are distributed, as well as whether citizens have other opportunities for earning income besides oil, would be key intervening variables between this ratio and political stability. The mere availability of funds matters less for outcomes than what regimes choose ultimately to do with them.[5]

---

[5] Recall that President Ahijo (1960–82) of Cameroon kept the state's oil revenues in his own personal accounts outside the country. Above, chapter 1, fn. 25. The case of oil in Equatorial Guinea, and the choice of that country's leadership, is also quite remarkable. See McSherry (2006).

Per capita revenues in Saudi Arabia were $4,000 in 1986, having fallen from $28,600 in 1981 – a drop of more than 85 percent in five years. In Iraq, per capita revenues in 1980 were $2,000, having dropped from $4,200 one year before. By 1988, however, the per capita figure had plummeted to $611 – a fall of roughly 85 percent in nine years (Tripp 2007: 235; al-Khafaji 2003: 93). In Algeria, per capita income was only $500 in 1988, having dropped almost 80 percent from its 1980 figure of $2,268. While per capita revenues in the three countries declined in similar fashion, Saudi Arabia remained stable, and Algeria, for one, faced an acute political crisis that persisted for several years. Nonetheless, the Saudi regime drew down its reserves at this time and borrowed from the domestic banking system as well;[6] it used those funds to maintain subsidies in place. Algeria and Iraq either chose not to do the same or they did not have the capacity to do so. As for Indonesia, the least oil-dependent of the five countries, it was the only one in which per capita income continued to grow during this period.[7] Like Saudi Arabia, it remained stable in the years immediately following the 1986 price shock. Hence, there appears to be no direct causal link between per capita oil revenues and regime stability in the absence of leadership decision. All regimes and all societies have had to confront relative scarcity.

Second, the greater the degree of power sharing and internal dispute resolution, the greater the degree of regime stability. To be sure, sharing power and resolving disputes internally would contribute to the stability of any regime – monarchical or not, dynastic or not. However, the focus on regime type as the explanatory variable for outcomes following economic shocks conceals what are shared, key features of governance in the contemporary Muslim world.

It is, indeed, modern authoritarianism that characterizes political systems in the Middle East and North Africa (Hammoudi 2008). Government comprises a large bureaucracy, linked to a small and narrow group – often from a single ethnic, tribal/kin, "cultural," confessional, or regional community. And government enjoys remarkable forms of monopoly power and control of resources, which include new and sophisticated means for exercising coercion – but also, mobilization and intimidation – and limiting distribution.[8]

---

[6] Indeed, Saudi debt exceeded 100 percent of GDP as late as 2000. (I am grateful to an anonymous reader for this information.)

[7] In fact, growth continued through 1996 before plummetting in 1997/8.

[8] No doubt, there are attributes to these political systems that reflect patrimonial structures of old, as described by Max Weber and reinterpreted by some to explain contemporary politics in the region. However, by projecting the past into the present and insisting upon

Algeria and the four comparators share the same basic characteristics of modern authoritarianism, admittedly with some regionally specific features. In each country, however, there exists a very particular formula at the core of the governing structure. (In Algeria, for example, a military-dominated, single-party state with a populist ideology was in control for much of its history as an independent state.) The formula adopted, in each case, derives from a distinctive appreciation of how best to manage resources and conflicts over access to resources. In the case of Saudi Arabia, the pact between the Al Sa'ud and the (Wahhabi) 'Ulama is a function of leadership decisions, within a particular context, about how best to ensure the monarchy's survival.[9] It is, I would argue, the formula at the core of the governing structure, and not regime type *per se*, that is noteworthy when accounting for outcomes.

Third, the greater and more sustained the interest of the international community in a particular oil-exporting state, the more likely it is to intervene in ways that shore up the regime and avert civil violence. A foreign power may choose to abandon a beleaguered regime in a crisis, or it may decide, rather, to reinvigorate it through different means of support. The trajectories of Algeria, Indonesia, Iran, Iraq, and Saudi Arabia suggest that the role of external actors has effects far too varied to make overarching claims.[10] In Algeria and the four comparators, the presence of the international community has been noteworthy, but in no case, except for the United States' intervention in Iraq in 2003, has it been decisive for outcomes – political stability and regime durability.

For one, the strong alliance between the Al Sa'ud monarchy and the United States' government bolsters the confidence with which the former implements policies. However, United States' backing has not been put to the test in the face of acute domestic unrest. Besides, it is unclear how close cooperation between the monarchy and the United States helps foster domestic peace; it may well be a potential source of instability, as the growth of an Islamist opposition in Saudi Arabia in the post-Gulf War environment suggests (Gresh 2002: 207; Niblock 2006: 172–6).

Although the United States' government continued to support the Shah of Iran until just days before his downfall, it could neither keep him in

---

patrimonialism, traditionalism, tribalism, and even dynasticism, the similarities between authoritarianism in the Middle East and North Africa and in other parts of the world in the twentieth and twenty-first centuries are obscured.

[9] Recall Peter Sluglett's suggestion (2002: 152) that the Saudi monarchy reinvented itself so as to conform to the exigencies of the modern state. Above, chapter 1, fn. 12.

[10] This view contrasts with Brownlee (2002b).

power nor dampen the revolutionary upsurge. Besides, there is no indi-cation whatsoever that the withdrawal of American support for the Shah in his final days was crucial for the success of the revolution. Most likely, the revolution would have succeeded without the last-minute exit of the Shah's "foreign patron."

As for Indonesia, the IMF refused to bail out the Suharto regime because Suharto had rejected the conditions imposed by the IMF.[11] Hence, while the absence of financial resources certainly did contribute to destabilizing the regime, it was leadership choice – not to cave in to international actors and not to cede economic fiefdoms – rather than the role played by international actors that sealed the regime's fate.

The case of Algeria is slightly more complex. International financial institutions in the mid-1990s were indeed crucial for bailing out the Algerian regime from the depths of a several years-long fiscal crisis. The intervention provided the beleaguered regime with the wherewithal to both administer repression and engage in co-optation: strategies that would eventually help neutralize insurgents. However, the international community did not play a role in the success of the extensive strategies of manipulation, except inadvertently: part of the regime's tactics was to manipulate new, international structural forces, such as the "war on terror."

For Iraq, as well, international structural forces – among them, the imposition of sanctions against the country – inadvertently contributed to the regime's ability to re-establish its hold on power.[12] In short, external actors may facilitate particular outcomes, but overall their role in the persistence or collapse of domestic political arrangements is indetermi-nate. Besides, they are themselves responsive to the decisions of leaders. Moreover, how leaders respond to the possibility of using the interna-tional community to promote their own interests matters as well.[13]

Fourth, the stronger the regime, in terms of its capacity to achieve its goals, relative to forces of opposition, the greater the likelihood that it will remain stable. Regimes that enjoy broad-based legitimacy and/or possess

---

[11] Besides, business opportunities for foreign investors were stifled in the 1990s through the cronyism and greed of Suharto and his entourage.

[12] It is interesting to note in this regard that while the United States actively supported Saddam Hussein for much of the war with Iran, that support was not sufficient to ensure Iraq's success; the war ended with a stalemate. Some analysts have argued that that outcome may have been the United States' government's preference.

[13] With changes to the international environment since 9/11, a new pattern has been emerging: Western powers are interested in supporting and stabilizing regimes that cooperate in the "war on terror" and comply on the issue of nuclear proliferation. Whether or not they have the capacity to stabilize regimes is, indeed, open to question, as the case of Pakistan under Pervez Musharraf, for example, demonstrated.

effective means for extending their domination and control are best equipped for neutralizing an opposition and promoting stability. Indeed, this hypothesis is tautological. In the countries I have studied, legitimacy was purchased largely through distribution, and it was accompanied by repression.

Through the 1970s and 1980s, Suharto of Indonesia enjoyed what William Liddle (1991) has referred to as "performance legitimacy." He did so by investing heavily in economic and social development, and improving the standard of living and life chances of a broad cross-section of the Indonesian people. That, combined with a powerful repressive apparatus, quelled domestic dissent, forcing underground or into exile whatever existed of meaningful opposition.

All the regimes I have studied have been more or less repressive; all have mobilized vast resources to silence dissent. Some regimes, however, were unable to achieve their goals relative to forces of opposition, and incapable of neutralizing challengers. The Shah of Iran was forced out of office and out of the country on the heels of revolutionary mobilization that drew inspiration from the charismatic leadership of Ayatollah Khomeini. The Algerian regime seemed to have been tottering on the edge of breakdown for several years in the early 1990s, even though for decades it insisted upon its "revolutionary legitimacy." There is no doubt that of the five cases, the Saudi monarchy – that harps upon its "historic legitimacy" – has been most effective at achieving its goals and ensuring domestic stability. However, the explanation for outcomes is more complex than a simple matrix comparing the relative strengths and weaknesses of the state and forces of opposition. Besides, in all cases, regimes have worked assiduously to affirm, if not shore up, their own legitimacy, and to weaken real and potential forces of opposition.[14]

Fifth, the more severe the constraints on collective action, the more stable the regime and the system remain. This hypothesis suggests that when state repression deters most forms of popular mobilization, the state thereby preserves itself, averts domestic opposition, and maintains

---

[14] While Kurzman (2004) is correct when he says that there was a viable alternative to the Shah in the person of Khomeini, and that contributed enormously to the success of the revolution, it is important to note that the recognition of a viable alternative emerged only late in the day: during the initial months of political upheaval, the Iranian masses were demanding reforms and *not* the end of the Pahlavi monarchy. It was, in large measure, the way in which the Shah responded to popular demands that caused social preferences to shift radically. In other words, the Shah was the source of his own undoing. Besides, the availability of a viable alternative is itself a clear indication of the failure of leadership choice.

stability. I insist, however, that repression can deter explicit opposition to the state, but it cannot preclude it altogether.

Of the five cases in this book, the political system in Saddam Hussein's Iraq was the most blatantly repressive. In Saudi Arabia, the political system is profoundly repressive at its core, even though the regime's resort to overt violence is uncommon. While both the Iraqi and the Saudi regimes managed (have managed) to deter explicit opposition to the state, neither was (has been) able to prevent it altogether. Besides, the Saudi state has remained relatively stable, while Iraq, despite severe repression, underwent an acute crisis. It eventually managed to re-stabilize, albeit not via the resort to repressive tactics alone. Furthermore, the Saudi regime has tended to prefer coopting its opposition, rather than repressing it outright (Hertog 2007).

In sum, constraints on collective action may be one of several "facilitators" for regime stability, but they do not explain it. As the last years and final months of the Shah's leadership illustrate in no uncertain terms, repression alone is not sufficient for fostering stability or even re-equilibrating a system in crisis.[15] Moreover, the curious suggestion that the Shah's regime collapsed because it was not repressive enough overlooks, if nothing else, the systematic brutalization of, among others, members and sympathizers of the Tudeh Party from the mid-1950s and the relentless persecution of the religious establishment from the mid-1960s.

Conclusions

The in-depth study of Algeria's political trajectory, punctuated by a focus on critical junctures and buttressed by a brief excursion into comparative analysis, has highlighted the significance of both context and leadership choice in outcomes. It has demonstrated that oil, oil rents, and oil-based development – and, of course, economic shocks – do pose challenges to the domestic political economy. Nonetheless, those same challenges can either be mitigated or exacerbated by the decisions of leaders against the backdrop of the institutional arrangements that leaders construct and rely upon.

It is precisely through a historical narrative that traces the interaction between structure and agency that we can link challenges and constraints, and responses to them, to future outcomes. As with the analysis of Algeria's trajectory, the foray into comparativism has corroborated that

---

[15] As Smith (2006: 66) points out, the Shah's regime used repression until the very end and had the support of the United States until the very end; it collapsed nonetheless.

the genesis of particular structures derives, in large measure, from choice and contingency. In other words, macro- and domestic-structural variables interact in ways that strain regimes, while actors, through the choices they make, either bring strains to crisis point or keep them in check. As noted by Rotberg (2004: 25), "institutional fragilities and structural flaws contribute to failure ... but those deficiencies usually hark back to decisions or actions by men." Choice interacts with structure; it is the interaction between them that decides the effect.

Although rentier states, and especially oil-exporting LDCs, are often treated as exceptional, their experiences shed light on the study of post-colonial states and the challenges they face more generally. Indeed, when exploring the trajectories of Algeria and the four comparators from the inception of oil-based development through economic shocks, the first two explanatory variables, a weakly institutionalized state and weakly incorporated societal cleavages – common features of post-colonial states – recede in importance if independent of and disassociated from the third variable.

The study of Algeria, complemented by within-case and cross-case comparisons with Indonesia, Iran, Iraq, and Saudi Arabia, elucidates the centrality in outcomes of the decisions of leaders. Stability was maintained when leaders, at critical junctures and in the absence of economic resources, extended political resources via the creation of, however meager, crude, or illusory, participatory political structures. Invariably, co-optation, manipulation, and (some degree of) bounded repression went hand in hand with the process. Hence, "investing" in the development of (political) institutions, through what are essentially redistributive measures, may be a useful strategy for leaders to adopt when faced with domestic challenges on the heels of economic shocks.

Bibliography

Aarts, Paul and Nonneman, Gerd (eds.) 2005. *Saudi Arabia in the Balance*. New York: New York University Press

Abdi, Nourredine 2001. "Origine et Fondement de la Subordination du Politique au Militaire en Algérie," *AWAL* 24: 3–19

Abdoun, Rabah 1990. "Algeria: the Problem of Nation-Building," in Azzam, Mahjoub (ed.), pp. 14–48

Abir, Mordechai 1988. *Saudi Arabia in the Oil Era: Regime and Elite, Conflict and Collaboration*. Boulder, CO: Westview Press

1993. *Saudi Arabia: Government, Society and the Gulf Crisis*. London: Routledge

Aboud, Hichem 2002. *La Mafia des Généraux*. France: JC Lattès

Abrahamian, Ervand 1982. *Iran Between Two Revolutions*. Princeton, NJ: Princeton University Press

1993. *Khomeinism: Essays on the Islamic Republic*. Berkeley, CA: University of California Press

Acemoglu, Daron, Johnson, Simon, and Robinson, James A. 2003. "An African Success Story: Botswana," in Rodrik, Dani (ed.), pp. 80–119

Addi, Lahouari 1990. *Impasse du populisme: l'Algérie: Collectivité et état en construction*. Algiers: ENAL

1992. "Algérie: Le Dérapage," *Le Monde Diplomatique*, February

2004. "Réformes Economiques et Obstacles Politiques," *Le Quotidien d'Oran*, June 24

Aden, Jean Bush 1988. "Oil and Politics in Indonesia, 1945–1980," PhD Dissertation, Cornell University

Ageron, Charles-Robert 1964. *Histoire de l'Algérie Contemporaine: de l'insurrection de 1871 au déclenchement de la guerre de libération (1954)*. Paris: Presses Universitaires de France

Al-Ahnaf, Mustafa, Botiveau, Bernard, and Frégosi, Franck 1991. *L'Algérie par ses Islamistes*. Paris: Karthala

Aissaoui, Ali 2001. *Algeria: The Political Economy of Oil and Gas*. Oxford, UK: Oxford University Press

Ait-Ahmed, Hocine 1983. *Mémoires d'un combattant: L'Esprit d'indépendance 1942–1952*. Paris: Sylvie Messinger

1964. *La Guerre et l'Après-Guerre*. Paris: Editions de Minuit

Ait-Larbi, M., Ait-Belkacem, M. S., Belaid, M., Nait-Redjam, M. A., and Soltani, Y. 1999. "An Anatomy of the Massacres," in Bedjaoui, Youcef *et al.* (eds.), pp. 13–195

Akre, Philip J. 1992. "Algeria and the Politics of Energy-Based Industrialization," in Entelis, John P. and Naylor, Philip C. (eds.), pp. 73–96

Algeria, Democratic and Popular Republic of: Ministère de la Planification et de l'Aménagement du Territoire 1966/7, 1976, 1980–1, 1985/6, 1994–2001. *Annuaire Statistique de l'Algérie.* Algiers: Direction des Statistiques et de la Comptabilité Nationale

1987. *Algérie: Le Deuxième Plan Quinquénnal, 1985–1989.* Algiers: Ministère de la Planification et de l'Aménagement du Territoire

1970. "Aspects of the Algerian Oil Policy," Algiers: Ministry of Industry and Power

Algeria Watch: www.algeria-watch.org

Algerian Oil Policy 1965–1972. *President Houari Boumedienne's Speeches*

Aminzade, Ronald R., Goldstone, Jack A., McAdam, Doug, Perry, Elizabeth J., Sewell Jr, William H., Tarrow, Sidney, and Tilly, Charles 2001. *Silence and Voice in the Study of Contentious Politics.* New York: Cambridge University Press

Amirahmadi, Hooshang 1995. "The Political Economy of Iran's Oil Policy," in Gillespie, Kate and Henry, Clement Moore (eds.), pp. 185–227

Amirsadeghi, Hossein (ed.) 1977. *Twentieth Century Iran.* New York: Holmes and Meier Publishers

Amnesty International 1997. "Algeria: Civilian Population Caught in a Spiral of Violence," MDE 28/23/97

2000. "Algeria: Truth and Justice Obscured by the Shadow of Impunity." MDE 28/011/2000

Amuzegar, Janhangir 1977. *Iran: an Economic Profile.* Washington, DC: the Middle East Institute

1982. "Oil Wealth: A Very Mixed Blessing," *Foreign Affairs* **60**: 814–35

1999. *Managing the Oil Wealth: OPEC's Windfalls and Pitfalls.* London: IB Tauris

Anderson, Benedict 1972. *Java in a Time of Revolution: Occupation and Resistance, 1944–46.* Ithaca, NY: Cornell University Press

1990. *Language and Power: Exploring Political Cultures in Indonesia.* Ithaca, NY: Cornell University Press

Anderson, Lisa 1987. "The State in the Middle East and North Africa," *Comparative Politics* **20**: 1–18

Anderson, Perry 1974. *Lineages of the Absolutist State.* London: Verso

Angoustures, Aline and Pascal, Valérie 1996. "Diasporas et Financement des Conflits," in Jean, François and Rufin, Jean-Christophe (eds.), pp. 494–542

Aouli, Smaïl and Redjala, Ramdane 1995. "La Kaybylie face à la dérive intégriste," *Les Temps Modernes* **50**: 197–208

Arab Communication Consult (ACC), "Algeria Investment Report, 2002," www.arabcomconsult.com/algeria2002

Asad, Talal and Owen, Roger (eds.) 1983. *The Middle East: the Sociology of 'Developing Societies'.* New York: Monthly Review Press

Aspinall, Ed 1999. "Opposition and Elite Conflict in the Fall of Soeharto," in Forrester, Geoff and May, Ronald James (eds.), pp. 130–53

Aubenas, Florence 2003. "Khalifa, un empire en désintégration," *Libération* March 20

Aussaresses, Paul 2001. *Services Spéciaux: Algérie, 1955–1957*. Paris: Perrin

Auty, Richard 1993. *Sustaining Development in Mineral Economies: The Resource Curse Thesis*. London: Routledge

1997. "Natural Resources, the State, and Development Strategy," *Journal of International Development* **9**: 651–63

1998. *Resource Abundance and Economic Development: Improving the Performance of Resource-rich Countries*. Helsinki: UNU World Institute for Development Economics Research

2002a. "Integrating Industrialising Oil-Exporting Countries into the Global Economy: Egypt and Algeria." Working Paper 0102, prepared for MNSIF, World Bank, May 13

2002b. "Reforming Acutely Distorted Industrialising Economies: Egypt and Algeria," paper prepared for IESG Meeting, University of Birmingham, April 11–12

nd. "How Natural Resources Can Generate Civil Strife," Working Paper, Lancaster University

Auty, Richard and Gelb, Alan 2000. *The Political Economy of Resource Abundant States*. Helsinki: World Institute for Development Economics Research

Auty, Richard and Mikesell, Raymond 1998. *Sustainable Development in Mineral Economies*. Oxford, UK: Clarendon Press

Avin, Rose-Marie 1986. "Money Windfalls and Oil-Exporting Developing Countries: A Comparative Study of Algeria, Ecuador, Trinidad and Tobago, and Indonesia," Ph.D. dissertation, University of Maryland

El-Azhary, M. S. (ed.) 1984. *The Iran–Iraq War*. London: Croom Helm

Azzam, Mahjoub (ed.) 1990. *Adjustment or Delinking?: the African Experience*. Tokyo: United Nations University Press

Baer, Robert 2003. "The Fall of the House of Saud," *Atlantic Monthly* **291**: 55–65

Balta, Paul and Rulleau, Claudine 1981. *L'Algérie des Algériens, vingt ans après*. Paris: Les éditions ouvrières

Baraheni, Reza 1977. *The Crowned Cannibals: Writings on Repression in Iran*. New York: Vintage Books

Barakat, Halim (ed.) 1985. *Contemporary North Africa: Issues of Development and Integration*. Georgetown, DC: Center for Contemporary Arab Studies

Batatu, Hana 1978. *The Old Social Classes and the Revolutionary Movements of Iraq*. Princeton, NJ: Princeton University Press

1986. "Shi'i Organizations in Iraq: al-Da'wah al-Islamiyah and al-Mujahidin," in Cole, Juan and Keddie, Nikki (eds.), pp. 179–200

Bates, Robert H. 1989. *Beyond the Miracle of the Market: the Political Economy of Agrarian Development in Kenya*. New York: Cambridge University Press

2001. *Prosperity and Violence: The Political Economy of Development*. New York: W.W. Norton & Co.

Bates, Robert H. and Krueger, Anne O. (eds.) 1993. *Political and Economic Interactions in Economic Policy Reform*. Cambridge, UK: Blackwell Publishers

Bauchard, Denis, Hammoudi, Abdellah and Leveau, Rémy (eds.) 2007. *La démocratie est-elle soluble dans l'islam?* France: Centre National de la Recherche Scientifique

Beaugé, Florence 2002. "Antar Zouabri, chef du GIA algérien, a été tué par les forces de sécurité, vendredi, à Boufarik," *Le Monde* p. 5, February 2

Beblawi, Hazem 1987. "The Rentier State in Arab States," in Beblawi, Hazem and Luciani, Giacomo (eds.), pp. 49–62

Beblawi, Hazem and Luciani, Giacomo (eds.) 1987. *Nation, State, and Integration in the Arab World, Vol 2: The Rentier State.* London: Croom Helm

Bedjaoui, Youcef 1999. "On the Politics of the Massacres," in Bedjaoui *et al.* (eds.), pp. 305–72

Bedjaoui, Youcef, Aroua, Abbas and Ait-Larbi, Meziane (eds.) 1999. *An Inquiry into the Algerian Massacres.* Geneva: Hoggar Books

Behdad, Sohrab 1996. "The Post-Revolutionary Economic Crisis," in Rahnema, Saeed and Behdad, Sohrab (eds.), pp. 97–128

Belhoucine, Mabrouk 1987. "L'Algérie Libre Vivra," *Sou'al* 6: 130–41

Bellin, Eva 2004. "The Robustness of Authoritarianism in the Middle East: Exceptionalism in Comparative Perspective," *Comparative Politics* 36: 139–57

2005. "The Political–Economic Conundrum: The Affinity of Economic and Political Reform in the Middle East and North Africa," in Carothers, Thomas and Ottaway, Marina (eds.), *Uncharted Journey: Promoting Democracy in the Middle East.* Washington, DC: Carnegie Endowment for International Peace

Ben, Djamel 1998. "Mitidja: La Contre-Attaque des 'Patriotes'," *Le Nouvel Observateur* pp. 33–4, April 15

Benachenou, Abdellatif 1987. "L'Evolution de la Doctrine Economique de l'Etat Algérien," in *Aspects du Changement Socio-culturel en Algérie*, conference papers, Paris: Centre Culturel Algérien

Benderra, Omar 2002. "Economie Algérienne 1986–1998: Les réseaux aux commandes de l'Etat," www.algeria-watch.de/farticle/analyse/benderra_2002. htm

2003. "Les Réseaux au Pouvoir: Effondrement de l'état de prédation," *Confluences Méditerranée* 45: 81–94

Benheddi, Zemri 1992. "Algérie: Origines et Aspects Géopolitiques de la Crise Actuelle," *Hérodote* 65: 50–62

Bennett, Andrew and Elman, Colin 2006. "Complex Causal Relations and Case Study Methods: The Example of Path Dependence," *Political Analysis* 14: 250–67

Bennoune, Mahfoud 1985. "The Industrialization of Algeria: an Overview," in Barakat, Halim (ed.), pp. 178–213

1988. *The Making of Contemporary Algeria, 1830–1987.* New York: Cambridge University Press

Bennoune, Mahfoud and El-Kenz, Ali 1990. *Le hasard et l'histoire: entretiens avec Belaid Abdesselam.* Algiers: ENAG

Berger, Anne-Emmanuelle (ed.) 2002. *Algeria in Others' Languages.* Ithaca, NY: Cornell University Press

Berman, Bruce 1998. "Ethnicity, Patronage, and the African State: The Politics of Uncivil Nationalism," *African Affairs* 97: 305–41

Bhattacharya, Amar and Pangestu, Mari 1993. *Indonesia: Development Transformation and Public Policy* (series entitled: *The Lessons of East Asia*). Washington, DC: World Bank

Binder, Leonard (ed.) 2007. *Rebuilding Devastated Economies in the Middle East.* New York: Palgrave/Macmillan

Boix, Carles 2003. *Democracy and Redistribution.* Cambridge, UK and New York: Cambridge University Press

Boone, Catharine 1990. "The Making of a Rentier Class: Wealth Accumulation and Political Control in Senegal," *Journal of Development Studies* 26: 425–49

Booth, Anne 1998. *The Indonesian Economy in the Nineteenth and Twentieth Centuries: A History of Missed Opportunities.* New York: St. Martin's Press
     1999. "Development: Achievement and Weakness" in Emmerson, Donald K. (ed.), pp. 109–35

Boucek, Christopher 2007. "Extremist Reeducation and Rehabilitation in Saudi Arabia," *Terrorism Monitor* 5: 1–4

Boudiaf, Mohamed 1964. *Où va l'Algérie?* Paris: Librairie de l'Etoile

Boukhobza, M'hammed 1991. *Octobre 88: Evolution ou Rupture?* Algiers: Editions Bouchène

Bourdieu, Pierre 1961. *The Algerians.* Boston, MA: Beacon Press

Bouzghaia, Djamel E. (Colonel) 2002. "Le Terrorisme Islamiste: une Menace Transnationale," paper prepared for the International Symposium on Terrorism, Algiers, October 26–8

Bozarslan, Hamit 2001. "Le Phénomène Milicien: Une Composante de la Violence Politique en Turquie des Années 70," *Turcica* 31: 185–244
     2003. "Pouvoir et Violence dans l'Irak de Saddam Hussein" in Dawod, Hosham and Bozarslan, Hamit (eds.), pp. 31–46

BP: Statistical Review of World Energy. www.bp.com

Brahimi, Abdelhamid 2000. *Aux Origines de la Tragédie Algérienne (1958–2000): Témoignage sur 'hizb França'.* Switzerland: Hoggar

Brahimi, Mohamad 1990. "Les Evenements d'Octobre 1988: La Manifestation Violente de la Crise d'une Idéologie en Cessation de Paiement," *Revue algérienne des sciences juridiques, économiques, et politiques* 28: 681–703

Bratton, Michael and van de Walle, Nicolas 1997. *Democratic Experiments in Africa.* Cambridge, UK and New York: Cambridge University Press

Bresnan, John 1993. *Managing Indonesia: The Modern Political Economy.* New York: Columbia University Press

Brownlee, Jason 2002a. "Low Tide after the Third Wave: Exploring Politics under Authoritarianism," *Comparative Politics* 34: 477–98
     2002b. "… And Yet They Persist: Explaining Survival and Transition in Neopatrimonial Regimes," *Studies in Comparative International Development* 37: 35–63

Brynen, Rex, Korany, Bahgat and Noble, Paul (eds.) 1995. *Political Liberalization and Democratization in the Arab World.* Boulder, CO: Lynne Rienner

Burgat, François 1996. "Islamists in Algeria: Armed Resistance, Terrorism and Politics," *MSANEWS* May 31

Burgat, François and Dowell, William 1993. *The Islamic Movement in North Africa.* Austin, TX: University of Texas

Byman, Daniel L. and Pollack, Kenneth M. 2001. "Let Us Now Praise Great Men: Bringing the Statesman Back In," *International Security* **25**: 107–46

Byrd, William 2003. "Algérie: Contre-Performances Economiques et Fragilité Institutionnelle," *Confluences Méditerranée* **45**: 59–79

Campos, Edgardo and Root, Hilton L. 1996. *The Key to the East Asian Miracle: Making Shared Growth Credible.* Washington, DC: The Brookings Institution

Carlier, Omar 1995. *Entre Nation et Jihad: Histoire sociale des radicalismes algériens.* Paris: Presses de la Fondation Nationale des Sciences Politiques

1998. "D'une guerre à l'autre, le redéploiement de la violence entre soi," *Confluences Méditerranée* **25**: 135–50

2002. "Civil War, Private Violence, and Cultural Socialization: Political Violence in Algeria (1954–1988)," in Berger, Anne-Emmanuelle (ed.), pp. 81–106

Capoccia, Giovanni and Kelemen, R. Daniel 2005. "The Study of Critical Junctures: Theory, Narrative, and Counterfactuals in Institutional Theory," paper presented at the annual meeting of the American Political Science Association, Washington, DC, September 1–4

Cashin, Paul and McDermott, C. John 2002. "Terms of Trade Shocks and the Current Account: Evidence from Five Industrial Countries," *Open Economics Review* **13**: 219–35

Centre des Hautes Etudes de l'Armement (CHEAr) 1992–7. "Reflections on the Crisis in Algeria," *Laboratoire Minos no. 16*, Paris

Chaker, Salem 1987. "L'Affirmation identitaire berbère à partir de 1900: Constantes et mutations (Kabylie)," *Revue de l'Occident musulman et de la Méditerranée* **44**: 14–33

Chaliand, C. and Minces, J. 1972. *Algérie Indépendante.* Paris: Maspero

Charef, Abed 1994. *Algérie: Le Grand Dérapage.* Paris: Editions de l'Aube

1998. *Algérie: autopsie d'un massacre.* Algiers: Editions de l'Aube

Chatterjee, Pratap 1993. "The World Bank Under Fire," *World Press Review* **40**: 38

Chaudhry, Kiren Aziz 1994. "Economic Liberalization and the Lineages of the Rentier State," *Comparative Politics* **27**: 1–25

1997. *The Price of Wealth: Economies and Institutions in the Middle East.* Ithaca, NY: Cornell University Press

1999. "Prices, Politics, Institutions: Oil Exporters in the International Economy," *Business and Politics* **1**: 317–42

Cheema, G. Shabbir and Rondinelli, Dennis A. (eds.) 1983. *Decentralization and Development.* Beverly Hills, CA: Sage Publications, Inc.

Chehabi, Houchang E. and Linz, Juan (eds.) 1998. *Sultanistic Regimes.* Baltimore, MD: Johns Hopkins University Press

Chérif, Hachemi 1998. "La Lumière et les Ténèbres," *Confluences Méditerranée* **25**: 83–92

Chikhi, Said 1991. "Désindustrialisation et Crise de Société en Algérie," *Africa Development* **16**(2): 57–71

Chouet, Alain 1994. "L'Islam Confisqué: Stratégies dynamiques pour un ordre statique," in Bocco, Ricardo and Djalili, Mohammed Reza (eds.), *Moyen Orient: Migrations, Démocratisation, Médiations.* Paris: Presses Universitaires de France

Clapham, Christopher (ed.) 1982. *Private Patronage and Public Powers*. London: Pinter

1985. *Third World Politics: An Introduction*. Madison, WI: University of Wisconsin Press

2004. "The Global–Local Politics of State Decay," in Rotberg, Robert (ed.), pp. 77–93

Clark, John 1997. "Petro-Politics in Congo," *Journal of Democracy* **8**(3)

Clegg, Ian 1972. *Workers' Self-Management in Algeria*. London: Allen Lane

Cole, Juan and Keddie, Nikki (eds.) 1986. *Shi'ism and Social Protest*. New Haven, CT: Yale University Press

Collier, David and Norden, Deborah L. 1992. "Strategic Choice Models of Political Change in Latin America," *Comparative Politics* **24**: 229–43

Collier, Paul and Hoeffler, Anke 2001. "Greed and Grievance in Civil War," World Bank/DECRG, October 21

2004. "Greed and Grievance in Civil War," *Oxford Economic Papers* **56**: 563–95

Collier, Paul and Sambanis, Nicholas (eds.) 2005. *Understanding Civil War: Cases and Analyses*. Vols. 1 and 2. Washington, DC: World Bank

Collier, Ruth B. and Collier, David 1991. *Shaping the Political Arena*. Princeton, NY: Princeton University Press

Conway, Patrick and Gelb, Alan 1988. "Oil Windfalls in a Controlled Economy: A 'Fix-price' Equilibrium Analysis of Algeria," *Journal of Development Economics* **28**: 63–81

Cook, Michael A. (ed.) 1970. *Studies in the Economic History of the Middle East*. Oxford, UK: Oxford University Press

Corden, W. Max and Neary, J. Peter 1982. "Booming Sector and De-Industrialisation in a Small Open Economy," *Economic Journal* **92**: 825–48

Corm, Georges 1993. "La Réforme Economique Algérienne: une Réforme Mal Aimée?" *Maghreb-Machrek* **139**: 9–27

Cottam, Richard W. 1964. *Nationalism in Iran*. Pittsburgh, PA: University of Pittsburgh Press [updated version 1979]

Cribb, Robert 1999. "Nation: Making Indonesia," in Emmerson, Donald K. (ed.), pp. 3–38

Crone, Donald K. 1988. "State, Social Elites, and Government Capacity in Southeast Asia," *World Politics* **40**: 252–67

Crouch, Harold 1979. "Patrimonialism and Military Rule in Indonesia," *World Politics* **31**: 571–87

Crystal, Jill 1990. *Oil and Politics in the Gulf: Rulers and Merchants in Kuwait and Qatar*. Cambridge, UK and New York: Cambridge University Press

Danspeckgruber, Wolfgang and Tripp, Charles (eds.) 1996. *The Iraqi Aggression against Kuwait*. Boulder, CO: Harper-Collins

Daoud, Zakya 1992. "Algérie: Le Dérapage – Dans l'étau de la Dépendance Financière," *Le Monde Diplomatique*, Paris February 22

David, Paul 1985. "Clio and the Economics of Qwerty," *American Economic Review* **75**: 332–7

Davies, Victor A. B. and Fofana, Abie 2002. "Diamonds, Crime, and Civil War in Sierra Leone," paper prepared for the World Bank and Yale University case study project *The Political Economy of Civil Wars*

Davis, Graham A. 1995. "Learning to Love the Dutch Disease: Evidence from the Mineral Economies," *World Development* 23(10): 1765–79

Davis, Jeffrey, Ossowski, Rolando, Daniel, James and Barnett, Steven 2001. "Stabilization and Savings Funds for Nonrenewable Resources: Experience and Fiscal Policy Implications," *International Monetary Fund: Occasional Papers* 205

Dawod, Hosham 2003. "Société et Pouvoirs en Irak: Une Approche Anthropologique" in Dawod, Hosham and Bozarslan, Hamit (eds.), pp. 9–30

Dawod, Hosham and Bozarslan, Hamit (eds.) 2003. *La Société Irakienne: Communautés, pouvoirs et violences*. Paris: Editions Karthala

Dazi-Héni, Fatiha 2002. "Bahrain et Koweit: La Modernisation des Dynasties Al Khalifa et Al Sabah," in Leveau, Rémy and Hammoudi, Abdellah (eds.), pp. 215–38

Dekmeijan, Richard 1994. "The Rise of Political Islamism in Saudi Arabia," *Middle East Journal* 48: 627–43

Delacroix, Jacques 1980. "The Distributive State in the World System," *Studies in Comparative International Development* 15: 3–21

de Soysa, Indra 2000. "The Resource Curse: Are Civil Wars Driven by Rapacity or Paucity?" in Berdal, Mats and Malone, David (eds.) *Greed & Grievance: Economic Agendas in Civil Wars*. Boulder, CO: Lynne Rienner

   2002. "Paradise Is a Bazaar? Greed, Creed, and Governance in Civil War, 1989–99," *Journal of Peace Research* 39: 395–416

Dessler, David 1989. "What's at Stake in the Agent–Structure Debate?" *International Organization* 43: 441–73

Dharr, Abu 1980. *Thawra fi Rihab Makka*. Kuwait: Dar Sawt al-Tali'a

Diamond, Larry 2002. "Thinking about Hybrid Regimes," *Journal of Democracy* 13: 21–35

Dillman, Bradford L. 2000. *State and Private Sector in Algeria: the Politics of Rent-Seeking and Failed Development*. Boulder, CO: Westview Press

Djerbal, Daho 1991. "Le Discours Identitaire de l'Intégrisme Culturel à l'Intégrisme Religieux," *Mediterranean Congress of Historical Ethnology*, Lisbon, Portugal November 4–8

Dodge, Toby 2003. *Inventing Iraq: The Failure of Nation-Building and a History Denied*. New York: Columbia University Press

Doner, Richard 1992. "Limits of State Strength: Toward an Institutionalist View of Economic Development," *World Politics* 44: 398–431

Dridi, Daikha 2001. "Algérie: La Fin des Mensonges?" *Courrier International* 539: 34–9

Dunning, Thad 2005. "Resource Dependence, Economic Performance, and Political Stability," *Journal of Conflict Resolution* 49: 451–82

   2008. *Crude Democracy: Natural Resource Wealth and Political Regimes*. Cambridge, UK and New York: Cambridge University Press

Economist Intelligence Unit (EIU), *Algeria Country Profile* (1989–90), www.eiu.com

Ehteshami, Anoushiravan and Murphy, Emma 1996. "Transformation of the Corporatist State in the Middle East," *Third World Quarterly* 17: 753–72

Eifert, Benn, Gelb, Alan and Tallroth, Nils Borje 2003. "Managing Oil Wealth: The political economy of oil-exporting countries – why some of them have done so poorly," *Finance and Development*. www.worldbank.org/fandd

Eisenstadt, Shmuel N. 1978. *Revolution and Transformation of Societies: A Comparative Study of Civilizations*. New York: Free Press

Elbadawi, Ibrahim and Sambanis, Nicholas 2002. "How Much War Will We See? Explaining the Prevalence of Civil War," *Journal of Conflict Resolution* 46(3): 307–334.

Elkins, Caroline and Perdersen, Susan (eds.) 2005. *Settler Colonialism in the Twentieth Century: Projects, Practices, Legacies*. New York: Routledge

Emmerson, Donald K. (ed.) 1999. *Indonesia Beyond Suharto: Polity, Economy, Society, Transition*. Armonk, NY: M. E. Sharpe

Energy Information Administration (EIA), *Algeria: Country Analysis Briefs*, February 2006, Department of Energy, United States Government, www.eia.doe.gov

Englebert, Pierre 2000. "Pre-Colonial Institutions, Post-Colonial States, and Economic Development in Tropical Africa," *Political Research Quarterly* 53: 7–36

Englebert, Pierre and Ron, James 2004. "Primary Commodities and War: Congo-Brazzaville's Ambivalent Resource Curse," *Comparative Politics* 37: 61–81

Entelis, John 1983. "Algeria: Technocratic Rule, Military Power," in Zartman, William (ed.), pp. 92–143
    1986. *Algeria: the Revolution Institutionalized*. Boulder, CO: Westview Press
    1988. "Algeria under Chadli: Liberalization without Democratization," *Middle East Insight* 6: 47–64
    1994. "Islam, Democracy, and the State: the Reemergence of Authoritarian Politics in Algeria," in Ruedy, John (ed.), pp. 219–54
    1999a. "SONATRACH: The Political Economy of an Algerian State Institution," *Middle East Journal* 53: 9–27
    1999b. "Bouteflika's Algeria: Prospects for a Democratic Peace," *Middle East Insight* 14: 7–10

Entelis, John P. and Arone, Lisa J. 1992. "Algeria in Turmoil: Islam, Democracy and the State," *Middle East Policy* 1: 23–35

Entelis, John P. and Naylor, Philip C. 1992. *State and Society in Algeria*. San Francisco, CA: Westview Press

Ertman, Thomas 1997. *Birth of the Leviathan: Building States and Regimes in Medieval and Early Modern Europe*. Cambridge, UK: Cambridge University Press

Esty, Daniel C., Goldstone, Jack A., Gurr, Ted Robert, Harff, Barbara, Levy, Marc, Dabelko, Geoffrey D., Surko, Pamela T., and Unger, Alan N. 1998. *State Failure Task Force Report: Phase II findings*. McLean, VA: Science Applications International Corporation, July 31

Etienne, Bruno 1996. "L'Algérie Entre Violence et Fondamentalisme," *Revue des Deux Mondes* 47–56

Evans, Peter 1995. *Embedded Autonomy: States and Industrial Transformation*. Princeton, NJ: Princeton University Press

Evans, Peter B., Rueschemeyer, Dietrich, and Skocpol, Theda (eds.) 1985. *Bringing the State Back In*. Cambridge, UK and New York: Cambridge University Press

Al-Fahad, Abdulaziz H. 2004. "The *'Imama* vs. the *'Iqal*: *Hadari*–Bedouin Conflict and the Formation of the Saudi State," in Al-Rasheed, Madawi and Vitalis, Robert (eds.), pp. 35–76

Fakhri, Nahid 2002. "L'Echec de la Concorde Civile: le retour de la Violence?" *Les Notes de l'IFRI* [Institut Français des Relations Internationales], special issue. *L'Algérie: une Improbable Sortie de la Crise?*, 37: 19–30

Fandy, Mamoun 1999. *Saudi Arabia and the Politics of Dissent*. New York: St. Martin's Press

Fanon, Franz 1963. *The Wretched of the Earth*. New York: Grove Press
   1965. *A Dying Colonialism*. New York: Grove Press

Fardmanesh, Mohsen 1991. "Dutch Disease Economics and the Oil Syndrome: An Empirical Study," *World Development* 19: 711–17

Fargues, Philippe 1994. "Demographic Explosion or Social Upheaval?" in Salamé, Ghassan (ed.), pp. 155–81

Farmanfarmaian, Manucher and Farmanfarmaian, Roxane 1997. *Blood and Oil: Inside the Shah's Iran*. New York: The Modern Library

Farouk-Sluglett, Marion and Sluglett, Peter 1987/2001. *Iraq since 1958: From Revolution to Dictatorship*. London: I.B. Tauris

Farouk, M., Ait-Larbi, M., Hocine, M., Lalioui, M. S., Waliken, R. and Salem-Badis, L. 1999. "Voices of the Voiceless," in Bedjaoui *et al.* (eds.), pp. 196–265

Farsoun, Karen 1975. "State Capitalism in Algeria," *MERIP Reports* 35: 3–30 February

Fearon, James 2004. "Why Do Some Civil Wars Last So Much Longer Than Others?" *Journal of Peace Research* 41(3): 275–301
   2005. "Primary Commodity Exports and Civil War," *Journal of Conflict Resolution* 49: 483–507

Fearon, James D. and Laitin, David D. 2003. "Ethnicity, Insurgency, and Civil War," *The American Political Science Review* 97: 75–90

Foran, John (ed.) 1997. *Theorizing Revolutions*. New York: Routledge

Forrester, Geoff and May, R. J. (eds.) 1999. *The Fall of Soeharto*. Bathurst, AU: Crawford House Publishing

Francos, Ania and Séréni, Jean-Pierre 1972. *Un Algérien nommé Boumedienne*. Paris: Stock

Frieden, Jeff 1981. "Third World Indebted Industrialization: International Finance and State Capitalism in Mexico, Brazil, Algeria, and South Korea," *International Organization* 35: 407–31

Fromkin, David 1989. *A Peace to End All Peace: Creating the Modern Middle East, 1914–1922*. New York: Henry Holt & Co.

Galtung, Johan 1964. "A Structural Theory of Aggression," *Journal of Peace Research* 1: 95–119

Gandolfi, Paola (ed.) 2008. *Le Maroc Contemporain*. Venice: Université Frascati

Garçon, José 1997. "Quatre Questions sur la Tragédie," *Libération* August 30
   1998. "La Dérive Sanglante des Milices en Algérie," *Libération* April 15

Garçon, José and Affuzi, Pierre 1998. "L'Armée Algérienne: Le Pouvoir de l'Ombre," *Pouvoirs* **86**: 45–56

Garon, Lise 1994. "Crise économique et consensus en Etat rentier: le cas de l'Algérie socialiste," *Revue Etudes Internationales* **25**: 25–45

Gasiorowski, Mark 1995. "Economic Crises and Political Regime Change: An Event History Analysis," *American Political Science Review* **89**: 882–97

Gasiorowski, Mark and Byrne, Malcolm 2004. *Mohammad Mosaddeq and the 1953 Coup in Iran*. Syracuse, NY: Syracuse University Press

Geddes, Barbara 1999. "What Do We Know About Democratization After Twenty Years?" *Annual Review of Political Science* **2**: 115–45

Geertz, Clifford 1971. *Islam Observed: Religious Development in Morocco and Indonesia*. Chicago, IL: University of Chicago Press
  1973. *The Interpretation of Cultures*. New York: Basic Books

Geertz, Clifford 1973. "After the Revolution: the Fate of Nationalism in the New States" in Geertz, Clifford, pp. 234–54

Gelb, Alan H. 1986. "Adjustment to Windfall Gains: A comparative analysis of oil-exporting countries," in Neary, J. Peter and Van Wijnbergen, Sweder (eds.), pp. 54–93

Gelb, Alan. *et al.* 1988. *Oil Windfalls: Blessing or Curse?* New York: Oxford University Press

Gellner, Ernest 1974. "The Unknown Apollo of Biskra: The Social Base of Algerian Puritanism," *Government and Opposition* **9**: 277–310

Gerschenkron, Alexander 1962. *Economic Backwardness in Historical Perspective*. Boston, MA: Belknap

Ghilès, Francis 1998. "L'Armée a-t-elle un Politique Economique? Chronique de Douze Années de Compromis Incertains," *Pouvoirs* **86**: 85–106

Gillespie, Kate and Henry, Clement Moore (eds.) 1995. *Oil in the New World Order*. Gainesville, FL: University Press of Florida

Giugni, Marco, McAdam, Doug and Tilly, Charles (eds.) 1998. *From Contention to Democracy*. Larham, MD: Rowman and Littlefield Publishers

Glosemeyer, Iris 2005. "Checks, Balances and Transformation in the Saudi Political System," in Aarts, Paul and Nonneman, Gerd (eds.), pp. 214–233

Goldberg, Ellis, Wibbels, Erik and Mvukiyehe, Eric 2008. "Lessons from Strange Cases: Democracy, Development and the Resource Curse in the U.S. States: 1929–2002," *Comparative Political Studies* **41**: 4–5 (April–May): 477–527

Goldberg, Jacob 1986. "The Shi'i Minority in Saudi Arabia," in Cole, Juan and Keddie, Nikki (eds.), pp. 230–46

Goldstone, Jack 1991. *Revolution and Rebellion in the Early Modern World*. Berkeley, CA: University of California Press
  (ed.) 1994. *Revolutions: Theoretical, Comparative, and Historical Studies*, 2nd edition. New York: Harcourt Brace
  1998. "Social Movements or Revolutions? On the Evolution and Outcomes of Collective Action," in Giugni, Marco, McAdam, Doug, and Tilly, Charles (eds.), pp. 125–45
  1999. "Demography, Domestic Conflict, and the International Order," in Paul, T. V. and Hall, John (eds.), pp. 352–72

2001. "Toward a Fourth Generation of Revolutionary Theory," *Annual Review of Political Science* 4: 1–71

2003. "Comparative Historical Analysis and Knowledge Accumulation in the Study of Revolutions," in Mahoney, James and Rueschemeyer, Dietrich (eds.), pp. 41–90

Goldstone, Jack, Gurr, Ted Robert and Moshiri, Farrokh (eds.) 1991. *Revolutions of the Late Twentieth Century.* Boulder, CO: Westview Press

Goodwin, Jeff 1997. "State-Centered Approaches to Social Revolutions: Strengths and Limitations of a Theoretical Tradition," in Foran, John (ed.), pp. 11–37

2001. *No Other Way Out: States and Revolutionary Movements, 1945–1991.* Cambridge, UK: Cambridge University Press

Goodwin, Jeff and Skocpol, Theda 1989. "Explaining Revolutions in the Contemporary Third World," *Politics and Society* 17: 489–509

Goumeziane, Smaïl 1994. *Le Mal Algérien: Economie politique d'une transition inachevée, 1962–1994.* Paris: Fayard

Graham, Robert 1978. *Iran: The Illusion of Power.* London: Croom Helm

Grandguillaume, Gilbert 1979. "Langue, Identité, et Culture Nationale au Maghreb," *Peuples Méditerranéens* 9: 3–28

1995. "Comment a-t-on pu en arriver là?" *Esprit* 208: 12–34

Gresh, Alain 2002. "Arabie Saoudite: Les Défis de la Succession," in Leveau, Rémy and Hammoudi, Abdellah (eds.), pp. 205–14

Greif, Avner, Bates, Robert and Singh, Smita 2002. "Organizing Violence," *The Journal of Conflict Resolution* 46(5): 599–628

Gurr, Ted Robert 1970. *Why Men Rebel.* Princeton, NJ: Princeton University Press

Haber, Stephen and Menaldo, Victor 2007. "Do Natural Resources Fuel Authoritarianism?" unpublished paper, August 11

Hadj Nacer, Abderrahmane (ed.) 1989. *Les Cahiers de la Réforme.* Algiers: En A.P.

Hadjadj, Djillali 1999. *Corruption et Démocratie en Algérie.* Paris: La Dispute/Snédit

Hadjeres, Sadek 1984. *Culture, independance, et revolution en Algerie.* Paris: Temps Actuels

1998. "La Crise du PPA de 1949 et l'Actualité Algérienne: Part II – De Crise en Crise, les interactions perverses," *El Watan* August 29

Haggard, Stephan and Kaufman, Robert R. 1995. *The Political Economy of Democratic Transitions.* Princeton, NJ: Princeton University Press

Hainsworth, Geoffrey B. 1987. "Indonesia's Economic Downswing and Political Reform," *Current History* 86: 172–83

Halliday, Fred 1978. *Iran: Dictatorship and Development.* New York: Harmondsworth

Hammoudi, Abdellah 2001. *Maîtres et disciples: genèse et fondements des pouvoirs autoritaires dans les sociétés arabes: essai d'anthropologie politique.* Chicago, IL: University of Chicago Press

2008. "Sortie d'Autoritarisme? Le Maroc à la recherche d'une voie," in Gandolfi, Paola (ed.)

Hammoudi, Abdellah and Schaar, Stuart 1995. *Algeria's Impasse*. Princeton, NJ: Center of International Studies

Hamon, Hervé and Rotman, Patrick 1979. *Les Porteurs de Valise: La résistance française à la guerre d'Algérie*. Paris: Albin Michel

Harbi, Mohamad 1975. *Aux Origines du FLN: Le populisme révolutionnaire en Algérie*. Paris: Bourgeois

1980. *Le FLN Mirage et réalité: des origines à la prise du pouvoir (1945–1962)*. Paris: Editions Jeune Afrique

1981. *Les archives de la Révolution algérienne*. Paris: Editions Jeune Afrique

1984. *La Guerre Commence en Algérie: 1954*. Paris: Editions Complexe

2001. *Une Vie Debout: Mémoires Politiques, 1945–1962*. Paris: Arcantère

Hargrove, Erwin C. 2004. "History, Political Science, and the Study of Leadership," *Polity* 36: 579–93

Harik, Iliya and Sullivan, Denis J. (eds.) 1992. *Privatization and Liberalization in the Middle East*. Bloomington, IN: Indiana University Press

Haroun, Ali 2000. *L'Eté de la Discorde: Algérie 1962*. Algiers: Casbah éditions

Hashim, Ahmed 1992. "Iraq, the Pariah State," *Current History* 91: 11–16

Hassan 1996. *Algérie, Histoire d'un Naufrage*. Paris: Le Seuil

Hassner, Pierre 1997. *Violence and Peace: From the Atomic Bomb to Ethnic Cleansing*. Budapest and New York: Central European University Press

Haughton, Jonathan 1998. "The Reconstruction of War-Torn Economies," *Consulting Assistance on Economic Reform II*, Discussion Paper no. 23

Hays, Sharon 1994. "Structure and Agency and the Sticky Problem of Culture," *Sociological Theory* 12(1): 57–72

Hefner, Robert 2000. *Civil Islam*. Princeton, NJ: Princeton University Press

Hegghammer, Thomas 2006. "Global Jihadism After the Iraq War," *Middle East Journal* 60(1): 11–32

2009. "The Origins of Global Jihad: Explaining the Arab Mobilization to 1980s Afghanistan," Policy Memo, International Security Program, Belfer Center for Science and International Affairs, Kennedy School of Government, Harvard University, January 22

Hegghammer, Thomas and Lacroix, Stephane 2007. "Rejectionist Islamism in Saudi Arabia: the Story of Juhayman al-'Utaybi Revisited," *International Journal of Middle East Studies* 39: 103–21

Hegre, Havard 2003. "Disentangling Democracy and Development as Determinants of Armed Conflict," paper presented at the Annual Meeting of the International Studies Association, Portland, OR, February 27

Henni, Ahmed 1991. *Essai sur l'Economie Parallèle*. Algiers: ENAG

1992. *Le Cheikh et le Patron*. Algiers: OPU

1995. "Le Capitalisme de Rente: Nouvelles Richesses Immatérielles et Dévalorisation du Travail Productif," *Les Temps Modernes* 50: 98–131

1998. "La Production des Elites Economiques en Algérie: Elites Gestionnaires et Elites Missionnaires," in Kilani, Mondher (ed.), pp. 261–77

n.d. *Algérie: Violences, Pétrole et Société*. Unpublished manuscript

Henry, Clement M. and Springborg, Robert 2001. *Globalization and the Politics of Development in the Middle East*. Cambridge, UK: Cambridge University Press

Herb, Michael 1999. *All in the Family: Absolutism, Revolution, and Democracy in the Middle Eastern Monarchies*. Albany, NY: State University of New York Press
  2005. "No Representation without Taxation? Rents, Development, and Democracy," *Comparative Politics* **37**: 297–316
Hertog, Steffen 2005. "Segmented Clientelism: the Political Economy of Saudi Economic Reform Efforts" in Aarts, Paul and Nonneman, Gerd (eds.), pp. 11–43
  2006. "Segmented Clientelism: the Politics of Economic Reform in Saudi Arabia," unpublished dissertation, Department of Politics and International Relations, Oxford University
  2007. "Shaping the Saudi State: Human Agency's Shifting Role in Rentier State Formation," *International Journal of Middle East Studies* **39**: 539–63
Heydemann, Steve (ed.) 2000. *War, Institutions, and Social Change in the Middle East*. Berkeley, CA: University of California Press
Hidouci, Ghazi 1995. *Algérie: La Libération Inachevée*. Paris: Editions La Découverte
Hill, Hal 1990. "Indonesia's Industrial Transformation Part I," *Bulletin of Indonesian Economic Studies* **26**: 79–105
  1992. "Regional Development in a Boom and Bust Petroleum Economy," *Economic Development and Cultural Change* **40**: 351–80
  (ed.) 1994. *Indonesia's New Order: The Dynamics of Socio-economic Transformation*. Honolulu, HI: University of Hawaii Press
  2000. "Indonesia: The Strange and Sudden Death of a Tiger Economy," *Oxford Development Studies* **28**: 117–39
Hiltermann, Joost 2007. *A Poisonous Affair: America, Iraq, and the Gassing of Halabja*. Cambridge, UK: Cambridge University Press
Hirschman, Albert 1958. *The Strategy of Economic Development*. New Haven, CT: Yale University Press
  1977. "A Generalized Linkage Approach to Development, with Special Reference to Staples," *Economic Development and Cultural Change* **25**: 67–98
Hooglund, Eric 1982. *Land and Revolution in Iran, 1960–1980*. Austin, TX: University of Texas Press
Horne, Alistair 1977. *A Savage War of Peace: Algeria, 1954–62*. London: Macmillan
Human Rights Watch 1995. *Iraq's Crime of Genocide: the Anfal Campaign Against the Kurds*. New Haven, CT: Yale University Press
Humphreys, Macartan 2002. "Economics and Violent Conflict," working paper, Harvard University
  2005. "Natural Resources, Conflict and Conflict Resolution: Uncovering the Mechanisms," *Journal of Conflict Resolution* **49**: 508–37
Humphreys, Macartan, Sachs, Jeffrey D. and Stiglitz, Joseph E. (eds.) 2007. *Escaping the Resource Curse*. New York: Columbia University Press
Humphreys, Macartan and Sandbu, Martin E. 2007. "The Political Economy of Natural Resource Funds," in Humphreys, Macartan, Sachs, Jeffrey D., and Stiglitz, Joseph E. (eds.), pp. 194–233

Huntington, Samuel P. 1968. *Political Order in Changing Societies.* New Haven, CT: Yale University Press

Ibrahimi, Ahmed Taleb 1973. *De la décolonisation à la révolution culturelle.* Algiers: S.N.E.D.

Ilchman, Warren F. and Uphoff, Norman T. 1969. *The Political Economy of Change.* Berkeley, CA: University of California Press

International Crisis Group 2000. "The Algerian Crisis: Not over Yet," *Africa Report 24,* www.crisisgroup.org, 20 October

2001a. "The Civil Concord: A Peace Initiative Wasted," *Middle East and North Africa Report 31,* www.crisisgroup.org, 9 July

2001b. "Indonesia: Ending Repression in Irian Jaya," *Asia Report 23,* www.crisisweb.org, 20 September

2001c. "Algeria's Economy: the Vicious Circle of Oil and Violence," *Middle East and North Africa Report 36,* www.crisisgroup.org, 26 October

2003a. "Aceh: A Fragile Peace," *Asia Report 47,* www.crisisweb.org, 27 February

2003b. "Algeria: Unrest and Impasse in Kabylia," *Middle East and North Africa Report 15,* www.crisisgroup.org, 10 June

2004a. "Islamism, Violence, and Reform in Algeria: Turning the Page," *Middle East and North Africa Report 29,* www.crisisgroup.org, 30 July

2004b. "Saudi Arabia Backgrounder: Who Are the Islamists?" *Middle East and North Africa Report 31,* www.crisisgroup.org, 21 September

International Monetary Fund 1994. "Algeria: Recent Economic Developments," SM/94/124 23 May

1995. "Algeria: Background Paper," SM/95/108. 17 May

1998. "Algeria: Selected Issues and Statistical Appendix," *IMF Staff Country Report 98/87,* September

2000. "Algeria: Recent Economic Developments," *IMF Staff Country Report 00/105,* August

Ismael, Tareq 1982. *Iraq and Iran: Roots of Conflict.* Syracuse, NY: Syracuse University Press

Izel, B., Wafa, J. S. and Isaac, W. 1999. "What is the GIA?" in Bedjaoui *et al.* (ed.), pp. 373–457

Jabar, Faleh A. 2002. "Sheikhs and Ideologues: Deconstruction and Reconstruction of Tribes under Patrimonial Totalitarianism in Iraq, 1968–1998," in Jabar, Faleh A. and Dawod, Hosham (eds.), pp. 69–109

Jabar, Faleh A. and Dawod, Hosham (eds.) 2002. *Tribes and Power: Nationalism and Ethnicity in the Middle East.* London: Saqi Books

Jacquemot, Pierre and Raffinot, Marc 1977. *Le Capitalisme d'Etat Algérien.* Paris: Maspéro

Jean, François and Rufin, Jean-Christophe (eds.) 1996. *Economie des Guerres Civiles.* Paris: Hachette

Joffé, George 2002. "The Role of Violence within the Algerian Economy," *Journal of North African Studies* 7: 1–20

Jones, Toby "The Iraq Effect in Saudi Arabia," *Middle East Report Online,* www.merip.org/mer/mer237/jones.html

Julien, Charles-André 1964. *Historie de l'Algérie Contemporaine: La Conquête et les Débuts de la Colonisation (1827–1871)*. Paris: Presses Universitaires de France

el Kadi, Ihsane 1998. "L'Administration, Eternel Butin de Guerre," *Pouvoirs* **86**: 57–66

Kail, Michel 1995. "Indépendance et Dépendance," *Les Temps Modernes* **50**: 269–85

Kaldor, Mary, Karl, Terry Lynn and Said, Yahia (eds.) 2007. *Oil Wars*. London: Pluto Press

Kalyvas, Stathis N. 1999. "Wanton and Senseless? The Logic of Massacres in Algeria," *Rationality and Society* **11**: 243–85

Kanovsky, E. 1987. "Economic Implications for the Region and the World Market," in Karsh, Efraim (ed.), pp. 231–52

Karl, Terry Lynn 1997. *The Paradox of Plenty: Oil Booms and Petro-States*. Berkeley, CA: University of California Press

2007. "Ensuring Fairness: The Case of a Transparent Fiscal Social Contract," in Humphreys, Macartan, Sachs, Jeffrey D., and Stiglitz, Joseph E. (eds.), pp. 256–85

Karsh, Efraim (ed.) 1987. *The Iran–Iraq War: Impact and Implications*. London: Macmillan

Karshenas, Massoud 1990. *Oil, State and Industrialization in Iran*. Cambridge, UK: Cambridge University Press

1994. "Environment, Technology and Employment: Towards a New Definition of Sustainable Development," *Development and Change* **25**: 723–56

Katouzian, Homa 1978. "Oil versus Agriculture: A Case of Dual Resource Depletion in Iran," *The Journal of Peasant Studies* **5**: 347–69

1981. *The Political Economy of Modern Iran: Despotism and Pseudo-Modernism, 1926–79*. New York: New York University Press

1990. *Mussadiq and the Struggle for Power in Iran*. London: I.B. Tauris

1998. "The Pahlavi Regime in Iran," in Chehabi, Houchang E. and Linz, Juan (eds.), pp. 182–205

Keddie, Nikki 1966. *Religion and Rebellion in Iran: the Tobacco Protest of 1891–1892*. London: Cass

1980. "Oil, Economic Policy and Social Change in Iran," *Race and Class* **21**: 13–29

1999. *Qajar Iran and the Rise of Reza Khan 1796–1925*. Costa Mesa, CA: Mazda Publishers

2003. *Modern Iran: Roots and Results of Revolution*. New Haven, CT: Yale University Press [updated version 2006]

El-Kenz, Ali (ed.) 1989a. *L'Algérie et la Modernité*. Dakar, Senegal: Codersia

1989b. "La Société Algérienne Aujourd'hui: Esquisse d'une Phénoménologie de la Conscience Nationale" in El-Kenz, Ali (ed.), pp. 1–31

1997. "Prometheus and Hermes," in Shinn, Terry, Spaapen, Jack B., and Krishna, Venni (eds.), *Science and Technology in a Developing World*. Dordrecht and Boston, MA: Kluwer Academic, pp. 323–48

Kepel, Gilles 2002. *Jihad: the Trail of Political Islam*. Cambridge, MA: Harvard University Press

al-Khafaji, Issam 2000. "War as a Vehicle for the Rise and Demise of a State-Controlled Society: the Case of Ba'thist Iraq," in Heydemann, Steve (ed.), pp. 258–91

al-Khafaji, Isam 2003. "A mi-Chemin de la Démocratie: Les Options de Transition de l'Iraq," in Dawod, Hosham and Bozarslan, Hamit (eds.), pp. 85–101

Khelladi, Aissa 1995. "Les Islamistes Algériens à l'Assaut du Pouvoir," *Les Temps Modernes* 50: 137–53

Khelladi, Aissa and Virolle, Marie 1995. "Les Démocrates Algériens ou l'Indispensable Clarification," *Les Temps Modernes* 50: 177–95

Kilani, Mondher (ed.) 1998. *Islam et Changement Social*. Lausanne: Editions Payot

Knauss, Peter R. 1980. "Algeria under Boumedienne: The Mythical Revolution, 1965–1978," in Mowoe, Isaac James (ed.), *The Performance of Soldiers as Governors: African Politics and the African Military*. Washington, DC: University Press of America, pp. 27–100

Krasner, Stephen 1984. "Approaches to the State: Alternative conceptions and Historical Dynamics," *Comparative Politics* 16: 223–46

Krimly, Rayed 1999. "The Political Economy of Adjusted Priorities: Declining Oil Revenues and Saudi Fiscal Policies," *Middle East Journal* 53: 254–67

Krueger, Anne O. 1974. "The Political Economy of the Rent-Seeking Society," *The American Economic Review* 64: 291–303

Kurth, James R. 1979. "The Political Consequences of the Product Cycle: Industrial History and Political Outcomes," *International Organization* 33: 1–34

Kurzman, Charles 2004. *The Unthinkable Revolution in Iran*. Cambridge, MA: Harvard University Press

Labat, Séverine 1994. "Islamism and Islamists: The Emergence of New Types of Politico–Religious Militants," in Ruedy, John (ed.), pp. 103–21
    1995. "Le FIS à l'épreuve de la lutte armée," in Leveau, Rémy (ed.), pp. 87–110

Lacoste, Yves, Nouschi, André and Prenant, André 1960. *L'Algérie: Passé et Présent*. Paris: Éditions Sociales

Lacoste-Dujardin, Camille 1992. "Démocratie Kabyles: Les Kabyles: Une Chance pour la Démocratie Algérienne," *Hérodote* 65: 63–74

Lacroix, Stephane 2005. "Islamo–Liberal Politics in Saudi Arabia," in Aarts, Paul and Nonneman, Gerd (eds.), pp. 35–56

Lahouari, Addi 1995. "Violence et Système Politique en Algérie," *Les Temps Modernes* 580: 46–70

Laitin, David D. 1992. *Language Repertoires and State Construction in Africa*. New York: Cambridge University Press

Lal, Deepak 1998. *Unintended Consequences: The Impact of Factor Endowments, Culture, and Politics on Long-Run Economic Performance*. Cambridge, MA: The MIT Press

Lawless, Richard 1984. "The Contradictions of Rapid Industrialism," in Lawless, Richard and Findlay, Allen (eds.), pp. 153–90

Lawless, Richard and Findlay, Allen (eds.) 1984. *North Africa: Contemporary Politics and Economic Development*. New York: St. Martin's Press

Lebjaoui, Mohamed 1970. *Vérités sur la Révolution algérienne*. Paris: Gallimard

Le Billon, Philippe 2001. "The Political Ecology of War: Natural Resources and
    Armed Conflicts," *Political Geography* **20**: 561–84
    2005. "Corruption, Reconstruction and Oil Governance in Iraq," *Third World
    Quarterly* **26**: 685–703
Leca, Jean 1975. "Algerian Socialism: Nationalism, Industrialization and State-
    Building," in Desfosses, Helen and Lévesque, Jacques (eds.), *Socialism in the
    Third World*. New York: Praeger Publishers, pp. 121–60
    1998. "Paradoxes de la Démocratisation: L'Algérie au Chevet de la Science
    Politique," *Pouvoirs* **86**: 7–28
Leca, Jean and Leveau, Rémy 1993. "L'Algérie: Démocratie, Politiques
    Economiques et Demandes Sociales," *Maghreb Machrek* **139**: 3–52
Leveau, Rémy 1993. *Le Sabre et le Turban: l'Avenir du Maghreb*. Paris: Editions
    François Bourin
    (ed.) 1995. *L'Algérie dans la Guerre*. France: Editions complexe
    1998. "Acteurs et Champs de Force," *Pouvoirs* **86**: 29–43
Leveau, Rémy and Hammoudi, Abdellah (eds.) 2002. *Monarchies Arabes:
    Transitions et Dérives Dynastiques*. Paris: La Documentation Française
Levine, Daniel 1973. *Conflict and Political Change in Venezuela*. Princeton, NJ:
    Princeton University Press
    1978. "Venezuela since 1958: The Consolidation of Democratic Politics," in
    Linz, Juan and Stepan, Alfred (eds.), pp. 82–109
Lewis, Peter 1994. "Economic Statism, Private Capital, and the Dilemmas of
    Accumulation in Nigeria," *World Development* **22**: 437–51
    2007. *Growing Apart: Oil, Politics, and Economic Change in Indonesia and Nigeria*.
    Ann Arbor, MI: University of Michigan Press
Lewis, W. Arthur 1977. *The Evolution of the International Economic Order*.
    Princeton, NJ: Princeton University Press
Liabès, Djilali 1989. "L'Entreprise entre économie politique et société," in
    el-Kenz, Ali (ed.), *L'Algérie et la Modernité*. Dakar, Senegal: Conseil pour
    le développement de la recherche économique et sociale en Afrique,
    pp. 213–39
Liddle, William R. 1985. "Soeharto's Indonesia: Personal Rule and Political
    Institutions," *Pacific Affairs* **58**: 68–90
    1991. "The Relative Autonomy of the Third World Politician: Soeharto and
    Indonesian Economic Development in Comparative Perspective,"
    International Studies Quarterly **35**: 403–27
    1992. "Indonesia's Democratic Past and Future," *Comparative Politics* **24**(4):
    443–62, July
    1999a. "Indonesia's Unexpected Failure of Leadership," in Schwarz, Adam and
    Paris, Jonathan (eds.), pp. 16–39
    1999b. "Regime: the New Order," in Emmerson, Donald K. (ed.), pp. 39–70
    2007. "Indonesia: A Muslim-Majority Democracy," in Shively, W. Phillips
    (ed.), 60 printed pages
Linz, Juan 2000. *Totalitarian and Authoritarian Regimes*. Boulder, CO: Lynne
    Rienner
Linz, Juan and Stepan, Alfred (eds.) 1978a. *The Breakdown of Democratic Regimes:
    Latin America*. Baltimore, MD: Johns Hopkins University Press

1978b. *The Breakdown of Democratic Regimes: Crisis, Breakdown, and Reequilibration.* Baltimore, MD: Johns Hopkins University Press

Listhaug, Ola. 2005. "Oil Wealth Dissatisfaction and Political Trust in Norway: A Resource Curse?" *West European Politics* 28: 834–51

Looney, Robert E. 1982. *Economic Origins of Iranian Revolution.* New York: Pergamon Press

Lorcin, Patricia M. E. 1999. *Imperial Identities: Stereotyping, Prejudice and Race in Colonial Algeria.* London: I.B. Tauris

Lowi, Miriam R. 1993/95. *Water and Power: The Politics of a Scarce Resource in the Jordan River Basin.* Cambridge, UK: Cambridge University Press

1997. "The Politics of Development in Oil-Exporting LDCs: Algeria, Indonesia, and Iran Compared," annual meeting of the American Political Science Association, Washington, DC, August 28–31

2000. "Oil, Institutions, and Political Breakdown: the Case of Algeria", panel entitled "The 'Resource Curse' in Developing States"; annual meeting of the American Political Science Association, Washington, DC, August 31– September 1

2003. "Algérie 1992–2002: une nouvelle économie politique de la violence," *Maghreb-Machrek* 175: 53–72

2004. "Oil Rents and Political Breakdown in Patrimonial States: Algeria in Comparative Perspective," *Journal of North African Studies* 9: 83–102

2005. "Algeria, 1992–2002: Anatomy of a Civil War," in Collier, Paul and Sambanis, Nicholas (eds.), 1: 221–47

2007a. "Algeria and the Resource Curse," in Olander, Lydia, Weinthal, Erika, and Binder, Gordon (eds.), *For Security's Sake: Can the United States help petroleum rich nations avoid the resource curse?* Durham, NC: Duke University: Nicholas Institute for Environmental Policy Solutions, pp. 12–14

2007b. "War-torn or Systemically Distorted? Rebuilding the Algerian Economy," in Binder, Leonard (ed.), pp. 127–51

Lowi, Miriam R. and Werenfels, Isabelle unpublished ms. "Demystifying Civil–military Dynamics in Algeria"

Lucas, Russell E. 2004. "Monarchical Authoritarianism: Survival and Political Liberalization in a Middle Eastern Regime Type," *International Journal of Middle Eastern Studies* 36: 103–19

Luciani, Giacomo 1987. "Allocation Versus Production States: A Theoretical Framework," in Beblawi, Hazem and Luciani, Giacomo (eds), pp. 63–82

1995. "Resources, Revenues, and Authoritarianism in the Arab World: Beyond the Rentier State?" in Brynen, Rex, Korany, Bahgat, and Noble, Paul (eds.), pp. 211–27

Luong, Pauline Jones 2003. "The Middle Easternization of Central Asia," *Current History* 102: 333–40

Luong, Pauline Jones and Weinthal, Erika 2001. "Prelude to the Resource Curse: Explaining Energy Development Strategies in the Soviet Successor States and Beyond," *Comparative Political Studies* 34: 367–99

2004. "Contra Coercion: Russian Tax Reform, Exogenous Shocks, and Negotiated Institutional Change," *American Political Science Review* 98: 139–52

Macintyre, Andrew 1990. *Business and Politics in Indonesia*. Australia: Allen & Unwin
  1999. "Political Institutions and the Economic Crisis in Thailand and Indonesia," in Pempel, T. J. (ed.), pp. 143–62
Mahdavy, Hossein 1970. "Patterns and Problems of Economic Development in Rentier States: The Case of Iran," in Cook, M. A. (ed.), pp. 37–61
Mahoney, James and Snyder, Richard 1999. "Rethinking Agency and Structure in the Study of Regime Change," *Studies in Comparative International Development* 34: 3–32
Mahoney, James and Rueschemeyer, Dietrich (eds.) 2003. *Comparative Historical Analysis in the Social Sciences*. Cambridge, UK: Cambridge University Press
Maiza, A. (General) 2002. "L'Engagement de l'Armée Nationale Populaire Face au Terrorisme," paper presented at the International Symposium on Terrorism, Algiers, October 26–8
Majd, Mohammad Gholi 1992. "On the Relationship Between Land Reform and Rural–Urban Migration in Iran, 1966–1976," *Middle East Journal* 46: 440–56
Malley, Michael 1999. "Regions: Centralization and Resistance," in Emmerson, Donald K. (ed.), pp. 71–105
Malley, Robert 1996. *The Call from Algeria: Third Worldism, Revolution, and the Turn of Islam*. Berkeley, CA: University of California Press
Mameri, Khalfa 1988. *Abane Ramdane, héros de la guerre d'Algérie*. Paris: L'Harmattan
Martinez, Luis 1998. *La Guerre Civile en Algérie*. Paris: Karthala
Marzahn, Michelle 1994. "Killing the Singer," *Al Jadid: A Review and Record of Arab Culture and Arts* 4: 3
Mazouni, M. 1993. "Rôle de l'Industrie Pétrolière dans le Développement de l'Algérie," *Revue Française de l'Energie* 25
McAdam, Doug, McCarthy, John D. and Zald, Mayer N. (eds.) 1996. *Comparative Perspectives on Social Movements: Political Opportunities, Mobilizing Structures, and Cultural Framings*. Cambridge University Press
McAdam, Doug, Tarrow, Sidney, and Tilly, Charles 2001. *Dynamics of Contention*. Cambridge, UK: Cambridge University Press
McDougall, James 2006. *History and the Culture of Nationalism in Algeria*. Cambridge University Press
McDowall, David 1996. *Modern History of the Kurds*. London: I.B. Tauris
McLachlan, Keith 1977. "The Iranian Economy, 1960–1976" in Amirsadeghi, Hossein (ed.), pp. 129–69
McSherry, Brendan 2006. "The Political Economy of Oil in Equatorial Guinea," *African Studies Quarterly* 8: 23–45
Médard, Jean-François 1982. "The Underdeveloped State in Tropical Africa: Political Clientelism or Neo-patrimonialism?" in Clapham, Christopher (ed.), pp. 162–92
Merad, Ali 1967. *Le Réformisme Musulman en Algérie de 1925 à 1940*. Paris: Mouton & Co.
Merah, Ahmed 1998. *L'Affaire Bouyali*. Algiers: Editions Merah

Meynier, Gilbert 1981. *L'Algérie Révélée*. Geneva: Librairie Droz
Middle East Watch 1992. *Empty Reforms: Saudi Arabia's New Basic Laws*. New York: Human Rights Watch
Migdal, Joel 1988. *Strong Societies and Weak States: State–Society Relations and State Capabilities in the Third World*. Princeton, NJ: Princeton University Press
Mokeddem, Mohamed 2002. *Les Afghans Algériens: de la Djemaa à la Qa'ida*. Algiers: Editions ANEP
Moore, Barrington 1966. *Social Origins of Dictatorship and Democracy*. Boston, MA: Beacon Press
Moore, Mick 2004. "Revenues, State Formation, and the Quality of Governance in Developing Countries," *International Political Science Review* 25: 297–319
Mortimer, Robert A. 1977. "Algeria and the Politics of International Economic Reform," *Orbis* 21: 671–700
    1990. "Algeria after the Explosion," *Current History* 89: 161–4
    2006. "Africa in International Politics: External Involvement on the Continent," *African Studies Review* 49: 145–6
Moussaoui, Abderrahmane 1994. "De la Violence au Djihad," *Annales HSS* 6: 1315–33
    2006. *De la Violence en Algérie: Les Lois du Chaos*. Arles, Fr.: Actes Sud
Mowoe, Isaac James (ed.) 1980. *The Performance of Soldiers as Governors: African Politics and the African Military*. Washington, DC: University Press of America
Munson, Henry 1988. *Islam and Revolution in the Middle East*. New Haven, CT: Yale University Press
Murphy, Emma C. 1996. "The Initiation of Economic Liberalization in Algeria, 1979–1989," in Nonneman, Gerd (ed.), pp. 181–97
    2001. "The State and the Private Sector in North Africa: Seeking Specificity," *Mediterranean Politics* 6: 1–28
Murray, Roger and Wengraf, Tom 1963. "The Algerian Revolution – Part 1," *New Left Review* I, 22: 14–41
Nashashibi, K. et al. 1994. "*Algeria – Recent Economic Developments*," Document of International Monetary Fund, May 19
Nashashibi, Karim, Alonso-Gamo, Patricia, Bazzoni, Stefania, Feler, Alain Laframboise, Nicole and Horvitz, Sebastian Paris 1998. "Algeria: Stabilization and Transition to the Market," IMF Occasional Paper 165, Washington, DC: International Monetary Fund
Ndikumana, Léonce and Emizet, Kisangani F. 2005. "The Economics of Civil War: the Case of the Democratic Republic of Congo," in Collier, Paul and Sambanis, Nicholas (eds.), pp. 63–87
Neary, J. Peter and van Wijnbergen, Sweder (eds.) 1986. *Natural Resources and the Macroeconomy*. Oxford, UK: Basil Blackwell
Nehme, Michel 1995. "The Shifting Sands of Political Participation in Saudi Arabia," *Orient* 36: 45–60
Nellis, John R. 1983. "Decentralization in North Africa: Problems of Policy Implementation," in Cheema, G. Shabbir and Rondinelli, Dennis A. (eds.), pp. 127–82

Niblock, Tim (ed.) 1982. *Iraq: The Contemporary State.* New York: St. Martin's Press
  2006. *Saudi Arabia: Power, Legitimacy, and Survival.* New York: Routledge
Nonneman, Gerd (ed.) 1996. *Political and Economic Liberalization: Dynamics and Linkages in Comparative Perspective.* Boulder, CO: Lynne Rienner Publishers
  2001. "Rentiers and Autocrats, Monarchs and Democrats, State and Society: The Middle East between Globalization, Human 'Agency', and Europe," *International Affairs* 77: 141–62
North, Douglass 1981. *Structure and Change in Economic History.* New York: W.W. Norton & Company
  1990. *Institutions, Institutional Change and Economic Performance.* Cambridge University Press
Nouschi, A. 1962. *La naissance du nationalisme algérien.* Paris: Editions de Minuit
O'Donnell, Guillermo A. 1973. *Modernization and Bureaucratic-Authoritarianism: Studies in South American Politics.* Berkeley, CA: Institute of International Studies
OPEC 1984. "Algeria: SONATRACH," *OPEC Bulletin* 15: 23–33
  1990. "Oil: Algeria's Engine of Development," *OPEC Bulletin* vol: 27–35
Okruhlik, Gwenn 1999. "Rentier Wealth, Unruly Law, and the Rise of Opposition: the Political Economy of Oil States," *Comparative Politics* 31: 295–315
  2002. "Networks of Dissent: Islamism and Reform in Saudi Arabia," *Current History* 101: 22–8
  2005. "The Irony of *Islah* (Reform)," *The Washington Quarterly* 28: 153–70
Paige, Jeffery M. 1975. *Agrarian Revolution: Social Movements and Export Agriculture in the Underdeveloped World.* New York: Free Press.
Parasiliti, Andrew 2003. "The Causes and Timing of Iraq's Wars: A Power Cycle Assessment," *International Political Science Review* 24: 151–65
Parsa, Misagh 2000. *States, Ideologies, and Social Revolutions: A Comparative Analysis of Iran, Nicaragua, and the Philippines.* Cambridge University Press
Paul, T. V. and Hall, John (eds.) 1999. *International Order and the Future of World Politics.* Cambridge University Press
Peluso, Nancy Lee and Harwell, Emily 2001. "Territory, Custom, and the Cultural Politics of Ethnic War in West Kalimantan, Indonesia," in Peluso, Nancy Lee and Watts, Michael (eds.), pp. 83–116
Peluso, Nancy Lee and Watts, Michael (eds.) 2001. *Violent Environments.* Ithaca, NY: Cornell University Press
Pempel, T. J. (ed.) 1999. *The Politics of the Asian Economic Crisis.* Ithaca, NY: Cornell University Press
Perlmutter, Amos 1969. "The Praetorian State and the Praetorian Army: Toward a Taxonomy of Civil–Military Relations in Developing Polities," *Comparative Politics* 1: 382–404
Perroux, François 1955. "Note sur la notion de 'pôle de croissance,'" *Economie appliquée* 8: 307–20

Pfeifer, Karen 1992. "Economic Liberalization in the 1980s: Algeria in Comparative Perspective," in Entelis, John P. and Naylor, Phillip C. (eds.), pp. 97–116

Philip, George 1982. *Oil and Politics in Latin America: Nationalist Movements and State Companies*. Cambridge, UK: Cambridge University Press
    1994. *The Political Economy of International Oil*. Oxford, UK: Oxford University Press

Pierson, Paul 2003. "Big, Slow-Moving, and ... Invisible: Macrosocial Processes in the Study of Comparative Politics," in Mahoney, James and Rueschemeyer, Dietrich (eds.), pp. 177–207

Pincus, Jonathan and Ramli, Rizal 1998. "Indonesia: From Showcase to Basket Case," *Cambridge Journal of Economics* 22: 723–34

Pinto, Brian 1987. "Nigeria During and After the Oil Boom: A Policy Comparison with Indonesia," *The World Bank Economic Review* 1: 419–45

Polanyi, Karl 1944. *The Great Transformation*. New York: Farrar and Rinehart

Quandt, William B. 1969. *Revolution and Political Leadership: Algeria, 1954–1968*. Cambridge, MA: The MIT Press
    1998. *Between Ballots and Bullets: Algeria's Transition from Authoritarianism*. Washington, DC: Brookings Institution

Radelet, Steven and Sachs, Jeffrey D. 1998. "The East Asian Financial Crisis: Diagnosis, Remedies, Prospects," Brookings Papers on Economic Activity

Rahnema, Saeed and Behdad, Sohrab (eds.) 1996. *Iran after the Revolution: Crisis of an Islamic State*. New York: I.B. Tauris

Ramli, Rizal 1992. *Preventing the Dutch Disease: the Case of Indonesia*. Ph.D. dissertation in Economics, Boston University

Al-Rasheed, Madawi 2002. *A History of Saudi Arabia*. Cambridge, UK: Cambridge University Press
    2005. "Circles of Power: Royals and Society in Saudi Arabia," in Aarts, Paul and Nonneman, Gerd (eds.), pp. 185–213
    2007. "Interdire le Politique: Le Discours Religieux Wahhabite en Arabie Saoudite," in Bauchard, Denis, Hammoudi, Abdellah, and Leveau, Rémy (eds.), pp. 147–65

Al-Rasheed, Madawi and Vitalis, Robert (eds.) 2004. *Counter-Narratives: History, Contemporary Society, and Politics in Saudi Arabia and Yemen*. New York: Palgrave/Macmillan

Razavi, Hossein and Vakil, Firouz 1984. *The Political Environment of Economic Planning in Iran, 1971–1983*. Boulder, CO: Westview Press

Remaoun, Hassan 1995. "Ecole, Histoire et Enjeux Institutionnels dans l'Algérie Indépendante," *Les Temps Modernes* 50: 71–93

Roberts, Hugh 1982. "The Unforeseen Development of the Kabyle Question in Contemporary Algeria," *Government and Opposition* 17: 312–34
    1983. "The Algerian Bureaucracy," in Asad, Talal and Owen, Roger (eds.), pp. 95–114
    1984. "The Politics of Algerian Socialism," in Lawless, Richard and Findlay, Allen (eds.), pp. 5–11
    1988. "The Embattled Arians of Algiers: Radical Islamism and the Dilemma of Algerian Nationalism," reprinted in Roberts, Hugh (ed.) 2003a, pp. 3–33

1991. "Algerian Islamism and the Gulf Crisis," reprinted in Roberts, Hugh (ed.) 2003a, pp. 63–81

1993. "Historical and Unhistorical Approaches to the Problem of Identity in Algeria," reprinted in Roberts 2003, pp. 138–50

1995. "Algeria's Ruinous Impasse and the Honourable Way Out," *International Affairs* **71**: 247–67, reprinted in Roberts, Hugh (ed.) 2003a, pp. 160–82

1998. "Algeria's Contested Elections," reprinted in Roberts 2003, pp. 191–9

2000. "The Labours of Bouteflika," reprinted in Roberts, Hugh (ed.) 2003a, pp. 271–86

2003a. *The Battlefield, Algeria 1988–2002: Studies in a Broken Polity.* London: Verso

2003b. "The Armed Rebellion and the Continuation of Politics," in Roberts, Hugh (ed.), pp. 127–37

2003c. "Problems of the Polity," in Roberts, Hugh (ed.), pp. 263–70

2003d. "The FLN: French Conceptions, Algerian Realities," in Roberts, Hugh (ed.), pp. 34–62

2007. "Demilitarizing Algeria," *Carnegie Papers: Middle East Program* no. 86, Washington, DC: Carnegie Endowment for International Peace

Robison, Richard 1986. *Indonesia: the Rise of Capital.* Sydney, AU: Allen & Unwin

1988. "Authoritarian States, Capital-Owning Classes, and the Politics of Newly Industrialising Countries: the Case of Indonesia," *World Politics* **41**: 52–74

1999. "Why Indonesia is Unraveling in the Wake of the Asian Crisis," Comparative Politics Seminar, Dept. of Politics/Woodrow Wilson School, Princeton University, February 25

Rodrik, Dani 1999a. "Where Did All the Growth Go? External Shocks, Social Conflict, and Growth Collapses," *Journal of Economic Growth* **4**: 385–412

1999b. *"The New Global Economy and Developing Countries: Making Openness Work,"* policy essay no. 24, Washington, DC: Overseas Development Council

(ed.) 2003. *In Search of Prosperity: Analytic Narratives on Economic Growth.* Princeton, NJ: Princeton University Press

Rogowski, Ronald 1989. *Commerce and Coalitions.* Princeton, NJ: Princeton University Press

Ross, Michael 1999. "The Political Economy of the Resource Curse," *World Politics* **51**: 297–322

2001. "Does Oil Hinder Democracy?" *World Politics* **53**: 325–61

2003. "Oil, Drugs, and Diamonds: The Varying Role of Natural Resources in Civil War" in Ballentine, Karen and Sherman, Jake (eds.) *Beyond Greed and Grievance: The Political Economy of Armed Conflict.* Boulder, CO: Lynne Rienner

2004. "How Does Natural Resource Wealth Influence Civil War? Evidence from Thirteen Cases," *International Organization* **58**: 35–67

2005. "Resources and Rebellion in Aceh, Indonesia," in Collier, Paul and Sambanis, Nicholas (eds.), 2: 35–58

2006. "Is Democracy Good for the Poor?" *American Journal of Political Science* **50**: 860–74

Rotberg, Robert 2003. "Failed States, Collapsed States, Weak States: Causes and Indicators," in Rotberg, Robert (ed.), pp. 1–25

(ed.) 2003. *State Failure and State Weakness in a Time of Terror*. Washington, DC: World Peace Foundation

(ed.) 2004. *When States Fail: Causes and Consequences*. Princeton, NJ: Princeton University Press

Rothchild, Donald and Chazan, Naomi (eds.) 1988. *The Precarious Balance: State and Society in Africa*. Boulder, CO: Westview Press

Rouleau, Eric 2002. "Trouble in the Kingdom," *Foreign Affairs* **81**: 4 (July–August)

Ruedy, John 1992. *Modern Algeria: The Origins and Development of a Nation*. Bloomington, IN: Indiana University Press

(ed.) 1994. *Islamism and Secularism in North Africa*. New York: St. Martin's Press

Sachs, Jeffrey D. 2007. "How to Handle the Macroeconomics of Oil Wealth" in Humphreys, Macartan, Sachs, Jeffrey D., and Stiglitz, Joseph E. (eds.), *Escaping the Resource Curse*. New York: Columbia University Press [see p.431, line 9]

Sachs, Jeffrey D. and Warner, Andrew M. 1995. "Natural Resource Abundance and Economic Growth," National Bureau of Economic Research (NBER) working paper 5398, Cambridge, MA.

Sager, Abdulaziz 2005. "Political Opposition in Saudi Arabia," in Aarts, Paul and Nonneman, Gerd (eds.), pp. 234–70

Saikal, Amin 1980. *The Rise and Fall of the Shah*. Princeton, NJ: Princeton University Press

Salamé, Ghassan 1993. "Islam and the West," *Foreign Policy* **90**: 22–38

(ed.) 1994. *Democracy Without Democrats? The Renewal of Politics in the Muslim World*. London: I.B. Tauris

1994. "Small is Pluralistic: Democracy as an Instrument of Civil Peace," in Salamé, Ghassan (ed.), pp. 84–111

Salgon, Jean-Michel 2001. "Le Groupe salafite pour la prédication et le combat (GSPC)," *Les Cahiers de l'Orient* **62**: 53–74.

Sambanis, Nicolas 2004. "What is a Civil War? Conceptual and Empirical Complexities of an Operational Definition," *Journal of Conflict Resolution* **48**: 814–58

Samuels, Richard J. 2003. *Machiavelli's Children: Leaders and their Legacies in Italy and Japan*. Ithaca, NY: Cornell University Press

Schwarz, Adam 1994. *A Nation in Waiting: Indonesia in the 1990s*. Boulder, CO: Westview Press

Schwarz, Adam and Paris, Jonathan (eds.) 1999. *The Politics of Post-Suharto Indonesia*. New York: Council on Foreign Relations

Schedler, Andreas (ed.) 2006. *Electoral Authoritarianism: the Dynamics of Unfree Competition*. Boulder, CO: Lynne Rienner Publishers

Scott, Catherine V. 1992. "International Capital and the Oil-Producing States in Africa: An Analysis of Angola, Nigeria, and Algeria," *Journal of Developing Societies* **3**: 179–93

Seers, Dudley 1967. "The Meaning of Development," *International Development Review* **19**: 2–7

Seton-Watson, Hugh 1977. *Nations and States: An Enquiry into the Origins of Nations and the Politics of Nationalism*. Boulder, CO: Westview Press

Sewell, William 1992. "A Theory of Structure: Duality, Agency, and Transformation," *The American Journal of Sociology* 98: 1–29

Shafer, D. Michael 1994. *Winners and Losers: How Sectors Shape the Developmental Prospects of States*. Ithaca, NY: Cornell University Press

Shambayati, Hootan 1994. "The Rentier State, Interest Groups, and the Paradox of Autonomy: State and Business in Turkey and Iran," *Comparative Politics* 26: 307–31

Sharabi, Hisham 1988. *Neopatriarchy: A Theory of Distorted Change in Arab Society*. New York: Oxford University Press

Shatz, Adam, 2003. "Algeria's Ashes," *The New York Times Book Review*. July 18

Shively, W. Phillips (ed.) 2007. *Comparative Governance*. New York: McGraw-Hill Primis online

Siemsen, Cynthia 1995. "Oil, War, and Semiperipheral Mobility: the Case of Iraq," *Studies in Comparative International Development* 30: 24–45

Skocpol, Theda 1979. *States and Social Revolutions: A Comparative Analysis of France, Russia, and China*. Cambridge University Press
   1982. "Rentier State and Shi'a Islam in the Iranian Revolution," *Theory and Society* 11: 265–83

Slackman, Michael 2005. "Top Algerians Prefer Amnesia to Accountability on War," *New York Times* 26 September p. A3

Sluglett, Peter 2002. "La Monarchie dans le Monde Arabe: Mythes et Réalités," in Leveau, Rémy and Hammoudi, Abdellah (eds.), pp. 143–58
   and Farouk-Sluglett, Marion 1992. "Sunnis and Shi'is Revisited: Sectarianism and Ethnicity in Authoritarian Iraq," in Spagnolo, John (ed.), pp. 259–73

Slyomovics, Susan 1995. "'Hassiba Ben Bouali, If You Could See Our Algeria': Women and Public Space in Algeria," *Middle East Report* 192: 8–13

Smith, Adam 1776. *The Wealth of Nations*. (multiple re-issues), Bantam Classics, 2003

Smith, Benjamin 2003. "'If I Do These Things, They Will Throw Me Out': Economic Reform and the Collapse of Indonesia's New Order," *Journal of International Affairs* 57: 113–28
   2004. "Oil Wealth and Regime Survival in the Developing World," *American Journal of Political Science* 48: 232–46
   2006. "The Wrong Kind of Crisis: Why Oil Booms and Busts Rarely Lead to Authoritarian Breakdown," *Studies in Comparative International Development* 40: 55–76
   2007. *Hard Times in the Lands of Plenty: Oil Politics in Iran and Indonesia*. Ithaca, NY: Cornell University Press

Snyder, Richard 1992. "Explaining Transitions from Neopatrimonial Dictatorships," *Comparative Politics* 24–4: 379–99
   1998. "Paths out of Sultanistic Regimes: Combining Structural and Voluntarist Perspectives," in Chehabi, Houchang E. and Linz, Juan (eds.), pp. 49–81
   2006a. "Does Lootable Wealth Breed Disorder? A Political Economy of Extraction Framework," *Comparative Political Studies* 39: 943–68

2006b. "Beyond Electoral Authoritarianism: the Spectrum of Non-Democratic Regimes," in Schedler, Andreas (ed.), pp. 219–32

Soesastro, M. Hadi 1989. "The Political Economy of Deregulation in Indonesia," *A Monthly Review of Contemporary Asian Affairs* **29**: 853–69

Souaidia, Habib 2001. *La Sale Guerre*. Paris: La Découverte

Spagnolo, John (ed.) 1992. *The Modern Middle East in Historical Perspective: Essays in Honour of Albert Hourani*. Ithaca, NY: Ithaca Press

Springborg, Robert and Henry, Clement M. 2001. *Globalization and the Politics of Development in the Middle East*. Cambridge, UK: Cambridge University Press

Steinberg, Guido 2005. "The Wahhabi Ulama and the Saudi State: 1745 to the Present," in Aarts, Paul and Nonneman, Gerd (eds.), pp. 11–34

Steinmo, Sven, Thelen, Kathleen and Longstreth, Frank (eds.) 1992. *Structuring Politics: Historical Institutionalism in Comparative Perspective*. Cambridge University Press

Stepan, Alfred 1978. "Political Leadership and Regime Breakdown: Brazil," in Linz, Juan and Stepan, Alfred (eds.), pp. 110–37

Stone, Martin 1997. *The Agony of Algeria*. New York: Columbia University Press

Stora, Benjamin 1982. *Messali Hadj, 1898–1974*. Paris: éditions Le Sycomore
    1992. *La Gangrène et l'Oubli: La mémoire de la guerre d'Algérie*. Paris: éditions La Découverte
    1995. "Algerie, absence et surabondandance de mémoire," *Esprit* [special issue: *Avec l'Algérie*] **208**: 62–7
    2006. *Les Trois Exils: Juifs d'Algérie*. Paris: Stock

Stork, Joe 1982. "State Power and Economic Structure: Class Determination and State Formation in Contemporary Iraq" in Niblock, Tim (ed.), pp. 27–46

Swearingen, Will 1992. "Agricultural Policies and the Growing Food Security Crisis," in Entelis, John P. and Naylor, Philip C. (eds.), pp. 117–50

Taguemout, Hanafi 1994. *L'Affaire Zeghar: Déliquescence d'un Etat, l'Algérie sous Chadli*. Paris: éditions Publisud

Talahite, Fatiha 1998. "La Corruption: Le Prix de la Contre-Réforme," *Libre Algérie* **5**: 9–22
    2000. "Economie Administrée, Corruption et Engrenage de la Violence en Algérie," *Revue du Tiers-Monde* **41**: 49–74

Talha, Larbi 1992. "Economie de Guerre en Algérie," *Le Monde Diplomatique* August

Tarrow, Sidney 1998. *Power in Movement: Social Movements and Contentious Politics*. Cambridge University Press

Taylor, John G. 1991. *Indonesia's Forgotten War: the Hidden History of East Timor*. London: Zed Books

Temple, Jonathan 2003. "Growing into Trouble: Indonesia after 1966," in Rodrik, Dani (ed.), pp. 152–83

Terki, Nour-Eddine 1987. "La Loi Algérienne de 1986 et l'Encouragement des Investissements Etrangers dans le Domaine des Hydrocarbures," *Revue Algérienne des Sciences Juridiques, Economiques et Politiques* **25**: 801–18

Testas, Abdelaziz 2002. "The Roots of Algeria's Religious and Ethnic Violence," *Studies in Conflict and Terrorism* **25**: 161–83

Tétreault, Mary Ann 2000. *Stories of Democracy: Politics and Society in Contemporary Kuwait*. New York: Columbia University Press

Thelen, Kathleen 1999. "Historical Institutionalism and Comparative Politics," *Annual Review of Political Science* 2: 369–404

2003. "How Institutions Evolve: Insights from Comparative Historical Analysis," in Mahoney, James and Rueschemeyer, Dietrich (eds.), pp. 208–40

Tigha, Abdelkader 2006. "L'indemnisation des patriotes, ou l'achat du silence des harkis du DRS," www.algeria-watch.de

Tilly, Charles (ed.) 1975. *The Formation of National States in Western Europe*. Princeton, NJ: Princeton University Press

1978. *From Mobilization to Revolution*. New York: McGraw-Hill

1985. "War-Making and State-Building as Organized Crime," in Evans *et al.*, (eds.), pp. 169–87

1990. *Coercion, Capital and European States A.D. 990–1990*. Oxford, UK: Basil Blackwell

2008. *Contentious Performances*, Cambridge, UK: Cambridge University Press

Tlemçani, Rachid 1986. *State and Revolution in Algeria*. Boulder, CO: Westview Press

1989. "Development and the State in Post-Colonial Algeria," *Journal of Asian and African Studies* 24 (1–2): 114–33

1990. "Chadli's Perestroika," *Middle East Report*, March–April: 14–18

Trimberger, Ellen Kay 1978. *Revolution from Above: Military Bureaucrats and Development in Japan, Turkey, Egypt, and Peru*. New Brunswick, NJ: Transaction Books

"Tripoli Program" 1962. *Annuaire de l'Afrique du Nord* 1: 683–704

Tripp, Charles 1996. "Symbol and Strategy: Iraq and the War for Kuwait" in Danspeckgruber, W. and Tripp, Charles (eds.), pp. 21–38

2007. A *History of Iraq*, 3rd edition. Cambridge, UK: Cambridge University Press

United Nations Development Program 1995. *Human Development Report*. New York: Oxford University Press

Vandewalle, Dirk 1988. *The Political Economy of Maghribi Oil: Change and Development in Algeria and Libya*. Ph.D. dissertation, Columbia University

1992. "Breaking with Socialism: Economic Liberalization and Privatization in Algeria," in Harik, Iliya and Sullivan, Denis J. (eds.), pp. 189–209

1998. *Libya since Independence: Oil and State-building*. Ithaca, NY: Cornell University Press

van de Walle, Nicolas 1994. "Neopatrimonialism and Democracy in Africa, with an Illustration from Cameroon," in Widner, Jennifer (ed.), pp. 129–57

2001. *African Economies and the Politics of Permanent Crisis, 1979–1999*. New York: Cambridge University Press

Vassiliev, Alexei 2000. *The History of Saudi Arabia*. London: Saqi Books

Vatikiotis, Michael 1997. *Indonesian Politics under Suharto: Order, Development and Pressure for Change*. New York: Routledge

Vatin, Jean-Claude 1974. *L'Algérie Politique: Histoire et Société*. Paris: Armand Colin

Vergès, Meriem 1995. "I Am Living in a Foreign Country Here: A Conversation with an Algerian Hittiste," *Middle East Report* 25: 14–17

Vitalis, Robert 2007. *America's Kingdom: Mythmaking on the Saudi Oil Frontier.* Stanford, CA: Stanford University Press

Waldner, David 1999. *State Building and Late Development.* Ithaca, NY: Cornell University Press

Wantchekon, Leonard 2002. "Why Do Resource Dependent Countries Have Authoritarian Governments?" *Journal of African Finance and Economic Development* 5 (2): 57–77

El Watan 2002. "L'Affaire Hadj Fergane fait encore des vagues," Algiers February 28

Waterbury, John 1973a. "Land, Man and Development in Algeria: Population, Employment and Emigration," *AUFS Field Staff Reports* 22: 1–21

1973b. "Land, Man and Development in Algeria: The Four Year Plan," *AUFS Field Staff Reports* 22: 1–19

1976. "Corruption, Political Stability and Development: Comparative Evidence from Egypt and Morocco," *Government and Opposition* 2: 426–45

El-Wattani, Idir 1949/1987. "L'Algérie Libre Vivra," reprinted in *Sou'al* [revue quadrimestrielle, Paris] 6: 129–94

Watts, Michael J. (ed.) 1987. *State, Oil, and Agriculture in Nigeria.* Berkeley, CA: Institute of International Studies

Weber, Max 1968. *Economy and Society.* New York: Bedminster Press

Werenfels, Isabelle 2003. "Obstacles to Privatization of State-Owned Industries in Algeria: the Political Economy of a Distributive Conflict," *Journal of North African Studies* 7: 1–28

2005. "Between Integration and Repression: Government Responses to Islamism in the Maghreb," SWP Research Paper [Stiftung Wissenschaft und Politik; German Institute for International and Security Affairs]

2007. *Managing Instability in Algeria: Elites and Political Change since 1995.* New York: Routledge

Wickham-Crowley, Timothy P. 1990. "Terror and Guerrilla Warfare in Latin America, 1956–1970," *Comparative Studies in Society and History* 32: 201–37

Widner, Jennifer (ed.) 1994. *Economic Change and Political Liberalization in Sub-Saharan Africa.* Baltimore, MD: Johns Hopkins University Press

Wieviorka, Michel 1997. "Le nouveau paradigme de la violence", *Cultures et Conflits* 27–28: 9–57

Willis, Michael 1996a. *The Islamist Challenge in Algeria: a Political History.* New York: New York University Press

1996b. "Algeria's Troubled Road Toward Political and Economic Liberalization, 1988–1995," in Nonneman, Gerd (ed.), pp. 199–225

Winters, Jeffrey A. 1996. *Power in Motion: Capital Mobility and the Indonesian State.* Ithaca, NY: Cornell University Press

World Bank 1960–2000. *Data Base: Algeria.* Washington, DC: World Bank

2001. *World Development Indicators.* Washington, DC: World Bank

Yacine, Tassadit 2001. "La Juste Révolte des Algériens." *Libération* June 27

Yates, Douglas A. 1996. *The Rentier State in Africa: Oil Rent Dependency and Neocolonialism in the Republic of Gabon.* Trenton, NJ: Africa World Press

Yefsah, Abdelkader 1990. *La Question du Pouvoir en Algérie*. Algiers: Editions ENAP
   1995. "Armée et Politique Depuis les Evénements d'Octobre 88," *Les Temps Modernes* **50**: 154–76
Yergin, Daniel 1991. *The Prize: The Epic Quest for Oil, Money, and Power*. New York: Touchstone
Young, Crawford 1988. "The African Colonial State and its Political Legacy," in Rothchild, Donald and Chazan, Naomi (eds.), pp. 25–66
   1994. *The African Colonial State in Comparative Perspective*. New Haven, CT: Yale University Press
   1999. "Resurrecting Sultanism," *Journal of Democracy* **10**: 165–8
Yous, Nesroulah 2000. *Qui a Tué à Bentalha?* Paris: La Découverte
Zartman, William (ed.) 1983. *Political Elites in North Africa: Morocco, Algeria, Tunisia, Libya and Egypt*. London: Longman
   1995. "What's Next for Algeria?" *Christian Science Monitor* **88**: 20
Zerouk (Lt.-Colonel) 2002. "Le Terrorisme: Le Précédent Algérien," paper presented at the International Symposium on Terrorism, Algiers, October 26–8
Zonis, Marvin 1971. *The Political Elite of Iran*. Princeton, NJ: Princeton University Press

Index

CAMBRIDGE MIDDLE EAST STUDIES 32

CPSIA information can be obtained at www.ICGtesting.com
Printed in the USA
LVOW080825040112

262318LV00001B/74/P